Interest Rates on Savings Deposits

Interest Rates on Savings Deposits

Theory, Estimation, and Policy

Myron B. Slovin
Marie Elizabeth Sushka
Board of Governors of the
   Federal Reserve System

Lexington Books
D.C. Heath and Company
Lexington, Massachusetts
Toronto   London

Library of Congress Cataloging in Publication Data

Slovin, Myron B
    Interest rates on savings deposits.

    Bibliography: p.
    Includes index.
    1. Saving and thrift. 2. Interest and usury—Mathematical models. 3. Monetary policy—United States. I. Sushka, Marie Elizabeth, joint author. II. Title.
HG1621.S55   332.8'2   74-16931
ISBN 0-669-96453-0

Copyright © 1975 by D.C. Heath and Company

All rights reserved. No part of this publication may be reproduced or transmitted in any form or by any means, electronic or mechanical, including photocopy, recording, or any information storage or retrieval system, without permission in writing from the publisher.

Published simultaneously in Canada

Printed in the United States of America

International Standard Book Number: 0-669-96453-0

Library of Congress Catalog Card Number: 74-16931

To Marie P. Sushka and Peter Sushka

Contents

	List of Figures	ix
	List of Tables	xi
	Preface	xiii
Chapter 1	Introduction	1
Chapter 2	A Profit Maximization Model of Savings Deposit Rate Setting	5
Chapter 3	A Deposit Maximization Model of Savings Deposit Rate Setting	17
Chapter 4	A Utility Maximization Model of Savings Deposit Rate Setting	27
Chapter 5	A Cross Section Analysis of Savings Deposit Rates at Savings and Loan Associations	37
	Specification and Description of the Variables	40
	Analysis of the Full Sample Results	43
	Disaggregation by Chartering Status: Stock versus Mutual	52
	Conclusions	54
Chapter 6	A Time Series Analysis of Savings Deposit Rates at Financial Intermediaries	59
	Savings and Loan Associations and Mutual Savings Banks	61
	Commercial Banks	68
	Conclusions	76
Chapter 7	An Economic Model of the Market for Negotiable Certificates of Deposit	79
	The Demand for Certificates of Deposit	80
	Interest Rates on Certificates of Deposit	85
	Conclusions	89

Chapter 8	**Regulation Q, The Credit Crunch of 1966, and the Structural Instability of the Demand for Money**	91
	A Velocity Specification	94
	Savings Deposit Rates and the Income Elasticity of Money Demand	99
	Conclusions	102
Chapter 9	**Monetary Policy, Economic Activity, and Interest Rates on Savings Deposits: A Theoretical Analysis**	105
	Case A: Regulation Q Ceilings Are Binding	107
	Case B: Regulation Q Ceilings Are Not Effective	116
	Case C: Regulation Q Ceilings Are Changed	124
	Conclusions	133
Chapter 10	**Monetary Policy, Economic Activity, and Interest Rates on Savings Deposits: An Empirical Analysis with the FMP Model**	135
	Case A: Regulation Q Ceilings Are Binding	137
	Case B: Regulation Q Ceilings Are Not Effective	142
	Case C: Regulation Q Ceilings Are Changed	147
	Conclusions	157
	Glossary	161
	Bibliography	165
	Index	169
	About the Authors	175

List of Figures

6-1	Differential between the Savings and Loan Deposit Rate and the Commercial Bank Time Deposit Rate	63
6-2	Commercial Loans, Mortgages, and Municipal Securities Held by Commercial Banks	71
6-3	Ratio of Commercial Bank Liquid Assets to Total Deposits	77
10-1	Effect of a $3 Billion Decrease in the Money Supply—Case A: Regulation Q Ceilings Are Binding	139
10-2	Effect of a 50 Basis Point Increase in Open Market Rates—Case A: Regulation Q Ceilings Are Binding	140
10-3	Effect of a $1 Billion Decrease in High Powered Money—Case A: Regulation Q Ceilings Are Binding	141
10-4	Effect of a $3 Billion Decrease in the Money Supply—Case B: Regulation Q Ceilings Are Not Effective; Case A: Regulation Q Ceilings Are Binding	144
10-5	Effect of a 50 Basis Point Increase in Open Market Rates—Case B: Regulation Q Ceilings Are Not Effective; Case A: Regulation Q Ceilings Are Binding	146
10-6	Effect of a $1 Billion Decrease in High Powered Money—Case B: Regulation Q Ceilings Are Not Effective; Case A: Regulation Q Ceilings Are Binding	148
10-7	Effect of a 100 Basis Point Increase in Regulation Q Ceilings—Money Supply Maintained at Historical Values	150
10-8	Effect of a 100 Basis Point Increase in Regulation Q Ceilings—Open Market Interest Rates Maintained at Historical Values	154
10-9	Effect of a 100 Basis Point Increase in Regulation Q Ceilings—High Powered Money Maintained at Historical Values	158

List of Tables

5-1	Summary of Signs for Variables Implied by the Theoretical Models	43
5-2	Full Sample Results for Specification I	44
5-3	Full Sample Results for Specification II	46
5-4	Summary of Interest Rate Coefficients for Specification I and Specification II	49
5-5	Stock-Mutual Dummy Coefficients for Full Sample Regressions	50
5-6	Mutual Association Results for Specification I	51
5-7	Mutual Association Results for Specification II	52
5-8	Stock Association Results for Specification I	55
5-9	Stock Association Results for Specification II	56
5-10	Chow Test Results for Stock and Mutual Association Regressions	58
6-1	Savings Deposit Rate Equation for Savings and Loan Associations	66
6-2	Savings Deposit Rate Equation for Mutual Savings Banks	67
6-3	Alternate Specification of Savings Deposit Rate Equation for Savings and Loan Associations	69
6-4	Savings Deposit Rate Equation for Commercial Banks	74
7-1	Equations for the Demand for Certificates of Deposit	83
7-2	Equations for the Interest Rate on Certificates of Deposit	88
8-1	Equations for the Velocity Specification of Money Demand—Dependent Variable MD/GNP—Double Logarithmic Form	96
8-2	Equations for Unconstrained Specification of Money Demand—Dependent Variable MD—Double Logarithmic Form	100
10-1	Equations for Demand Deposits and Currency Used in the Simulation Experiments	137

Preface

We express our appreciation to the Federal Home Loan Bank Board for the use of unpublished, confidential data which are used as the basis for the research in chapter 5. The views expressed in this volume are those of the authors alone and should not be associated with either the Federal Home Loan Bank Board or the Board of Governors of the Federal Reserve System.

We are indebted to Marie P. Sushka, who typed endless drafts of the manuscript with speed and accuracy, and to Peter Sushka, who carefully and persistently edited the material. We dedicate this volume to these two wonderful people whose understanding and encouragement sustained our efforts and strengthened our spirits throughout this endeavor.

1 Introduction

A financial intermediary is an institution that obtains funds from the public in the form of deposits in order to maintain a portfolio of earning assets. These institutions perform an important function in the financial market since they transform the funds of relatively small depositors into the financing of real investment. These intermediaries are able to exploit economies of scale in both the borrowing and lending of financial assets. More specifically, because of their size and specialization, transactions costs are lowered, risk is minimized through portfolio diversification, and expertise is developed that assures the safety and profitability of various forms of investment. Financial intermediaries characterized by these economies of scale permit more efficient allocation of resources in the economy by lowering borrowing costs for owners of real capital and increasing interest rates on savings deposits available to the public while earning a profit sufficient to fulfill their own needs for capital.

Research into the behavior of financial intermediaries can be classified into three major categories: one, the analysis of the determinants of the public's demand for deposit liabilities; two, the examination of the intermediary's portfolio allocation decisions; and three, the evaluation of the willingness of the financial intermediary to supply liabilities through the interest rates it offers on savings deposits. Although the literature of monetary economics has grown considerably during the postwar period, almost all of the research on financial behavior has centered on the first two of these problems, the public's demand for liquid liabilities (for example, studies by Feige [19], Hamburger [30], Kardouche [36], and Modigliani [42]) and the portfolio behavior of financial institutions (such as studies by de Leeuw [12], Goldfeld [22], and Silber [45]), with very limited attention given to the behavior of savings deposit rates and the supply of savings deposits.[a] To some extent, this lack of research reflects an orientation of most monetary economists toward the analysis of commercial bank behavior, which usually assumes that interest rates on savings deposits are exogenous to the system.

The purpose of this study is to provide an explicit economic analysis of the deposit rate setting behavior of commercial banks, mutual savings

---
[a]The lack of research on this topic has continued in recent years despite the early work of Gurley and Shaw [29] and Tobin [48] on the general character of financial intermediation, which stressed the idea that an intermediary's willingness to supply deposits is an endogenously determined factor.

banks, and savings and loan associations and to evaluate the impact of savings deposit rates on the level of economic activity and on the effectiveness of monetary policy. The determination of savings deposit rates is viewed as an essential supply factor in the distribution of deposit liabilities within the economy. Several theoretical models of deposit rate setting behavior are developed. Based upon this theoretical analysis, savings deposit rate functions are specified and estimated for both cross section and time series data. The theoretical and empirical results provide a basis for the development of an economic model for the demand and supply of negotiable certificates of deposits. Within a macroeconomic framework, it is demonstrated that interest rates on savings deposits affect the behavior of the demand for money and have an important influence on both the level of economic activity and the effectiveness of monetary policy. The remainder of this chapter presents an outline of the topics included in this study.

Several theoretical models of savings deposit rate setting behavior are developed, each of which incorporates a different objective function. The implications of each hypothesis for the empirical specification of savings deposit rate functions are thoroughly analyzed. In chapter 2, the hypothesis of profit maximization is considered. In chapter 3, it is assumed that the intermediary desires to maximize its size, subject to the constraint that a minimum rate of return on net worth is earned. The comparative statics properties of such an objective function are explored and contrasted with those intrinsic to profit maximization. It is shown that the two models differ substantially in their empirical implications. In chapter 4, a model is developed in which the intermediary seeks to maximize a utility function where both profits and deposits enter as arguments. This model, which is a hybrid of profit and deposit maximization, displays comparative statics properties that are similar to those of the profit maximization model.

In chapter 5, savings deposit rate functions for savings and loan associations are estimated based upon cross section data for individual associations. These data were obtained from unpublished, confidential balance sheet and income statements submitted to the Federal Home Loan Bank Board by each institution. This cross section work has three purposes. One, several previous observers have reported that the deposit rate setting behavior of savings and loan associations varies in a manner that is not easily susceptible to economic analysis. In this study it is demonstrated that meaningful structural equations for such savings deposit rates can be estimated through specifications that are consistent with a systematic body of theory. Two, these cross section results are used in order to test the appropriateness of the theoretical models developed in chapters 2, 3, and 4. It is demonstrated that judgments about the relative usefulness of these theoretical models can be made based upon empirical evidence. Three, the cross section results are used to analyze whether or not mutual and stock associations display systematic differences in deposit rate setting. Although there is no a priori reason for differences in behavior given the same economic environment, a controversy has developed about the effect of chartering status on savings deposit rates. During the nineteen sixties, an increasing number of mutual associations sought to convert their status to stock companies until the Federal Home Loan Bank Board declared a moratorium on such conversions pending study of the behavioral differences between the two types of associations (see Brigham and Pettit [7]). Several conclusions on this question are provided in chapter 5.

In chapter 6, savings deposit rate equations are estimated on time series data for commercial banks, savings and loan associations, and mutual savings banks. The objective of this empirical work is to make effective use of the theoretical and cross section results of earlier chapters in developing aggregate specifications for savings deposit rate functions. These equations have an important role as part of a larger econometric model of the economy. The final regressions are consistent with the theoretical and cross section results and indicate that these financial institutions display similar economic characteristics with regard to their deposit rate setting behavior despite their historical and regulatory differences.

In chapter 7, an economic model is developed to explain the behavior of the market for negotiable certificates of deposit. Interest rates on such certificates of deposit are explained within the framework of a deposit rate setting approach to commercial bank behavior. In addition, empirical evidence that explains the public's demand for these liabilities is developed.

The relationship between interest rates on savings deposits and the demand for money is investigated in chapter 8. In particular, the stability of the demand for money is examined, and the pattern of substitution between money and various forms of savings deposits is analyzed. These issues are important because in Keynesian economics the character and the stability of the money demand function is vital to the determination of efficient stabilization policy and particularly of monetary policy.

The impact of savings deposit rates on the level of economic activity and on the effectiveness of monetary policy is analyzed in chapters 9 and 10. More specifically, two important questions are investigated. One, is the effectiveness of monetary policy enhanced or curtailed if savings deposit rates are determined by intermediary behavior rather than by the level of legal ceiling restrictions better known as Regulation Q? Two, what is the macroeconomic impact of changes in these legal ceilings on savings deposit rates? These policy questions have become particularly important in recent years since government proposals have been made for the elimination of these ceiling restrictions. The most extensive and well known set of such proposals was formulated by the Hunt Commission [50]. The analysis in chapter 9 is theoretical and consists of comparative statics results derived from Keynesian models of income determination that incorporate the influence of savings deposit rates. In chapter 10, empirical results are reported for simulation experiments with the Federal Reserve-MIT-Penn (FMP) econometric model in order to complement the theoretical conclusions.

2 A Profit Maximization Model of Savings Deposit Rate Setting

In attempting to model the behavior of a corporate enterprise, economists view a business as a technical unit that purchases various inputs and transforms them into outputs that are sold in the market place. It is assumed that the rational entrepreneur seeks to maximize profits, that is, to maximize the difference between the revenues obtained from the firm's outputs and the costs incurred in obtaining the inputs needed to produce those outputs. Within this framework, a financial intermediary can be viewed as an enterprise that issues liabilities in the market place by offering a yield on these funds and uses the proceeds to invest in various financial instruments. The reason for the existence of financial intermediaries, and the source of their ability to earn a profit, lies in the economies of scale intrinsic to risk pooling, the reduction in transactions costs, and the investment knowledge that develops as a result of specialization. In modeling financial behavior, economists generally employ the assumption that a rational intermediary seeks to maximize profits. In this chapter a deposit rate setting model is developed in which the optimal deposit rate is determined as an outgrowth of the profit maximization behavior of an intermediary. (Earlier works on profit maximization models of deposit rate setting are Weber [51], Meyer [41], and Goldfeld and Jaffee [25].) We examine the behavior of interest rates on savings deposits by building a model of profit maximization and deriving its comparative statics properties. The theoretical results are used to specify the determinants of deposit rates and to provide the basis for empirical tests.

Most financial intermediaries draw their liabilities from a relatively small geographical area because of historical restrictions on the chartering of these institutions. Consequently, it is assumed that the market for savings deposits is characterized by a degree of imperfect competition and that each institution faces a sloping demand curve for its deposits. However, the market for most portfolio assets, such as open market securities, is often national in scope, so that the open market purchases by an intermediary are generally quite small relative to the size of the market. Thus, it is assumed that each institution is a price taker in the asset market and that interest rates on the financial instruments suitable for its portfolio are exogenous to the institution's decisions. As a result, it is reasonable to assume that each institution earns the market rate of return on its portfolio, so that its portfolio behavior is exogenous to the determination of deposit rates.

In this model we assume that financial intermediaries determine interest rates on savings deposits given that the objective of the institution is to maximize profits, which are revenue minus costs. Revenue R is defined in this framework as the market rate of return i earned on the portfolio of interest earning assets P, so that

$$R = iP. \tag{2.1}$$

For simplicity we assume that the quantity of assets held by intermediaries P is a constant fraction k of deposits D, so that revenue becomes

$$R = ikD, \tag{2.2}$$

where k can be viewed as a liquidity constraint, and the market rate of return i is exogenous to the intermediary.[a] Costs C in this framework are defined as the interest r paid by the intermediary on its deposits D

$$C = rD. \tag{2.3}$$

In general, the financial intermediary seeks to maximize profits each period by determining its optimal deposit rate r.[b] The profit equation is written as

$$\pi = ikD - rD \tag{2.4}$$

where i is exogenous to the intermediary, k is a constant, and r is endogenously determined.[c] It is assumed that deposits D are demand determined by the public given the yield offered on these liabilities and the other parameters of the demand function. Thus, the quantity of deposits demanded by the public is determined within the model. In specifying the determinants of the demand for deposits, general portfolio considerations suggest that demand is a function of both the own rate and the yield on close substitutes.[d] Consequently, in this model we assume that the public's demand for the liabilities of financial institutions is positively related to the own rate r and negatively to market interest rates i, so that

$$D = D(i, r) \quad \partial D/\partial i < 0 \quad \partial D/\partial r > 0. \tag{2.5}$$

---

[a]The market rate of return can also be considered a vector of interest rates on both assets held in the institution's portfolio and financial instruments held by the public. For the profit maximization model this differentiation of market rates does not affect the qualitative results.

[b]It is assumed that there are no legal restrictions on the interest rates the intermediary can offer on its deposits.

[c]Corporate stock or net worth has not been explicitly included in this analysis. Alternatively, it could be assumed that the firm has some initial capital, which it invests in a manner similar to its deposits. However, this extension does not affect any of the comparative statics properties of the model.

[d]It is also assumed that in the demand function, the cross partial $\partial^2 D/\partial i \partial r$ is either zero or is very small compared to the parameters of the demand function.

Substitution of expression (2.5) into equation (2.4) yields the profit function

$$\pi = ikD(i, r) - rD(i, r). \qquad (2.6)$$

The first order condition for a maximum is that

$$\partial\pi/\partial r = (ik - r)(\partial D/\partial r) - D(i, r) = 0. \qquad (2.7)$$

The importance of equation (2.7) is that the theoretical model of profit maximization indicates that the optimal interest rate on savings deposits r is primarily a function of market interest rates i and the parameters of the demand function. This result provides the basis for the empirical analysis of rate setting behavior contained in later chapters. Differentiating expression (2.7) gives the second order condition for a profit maximum

$$\frac{\partial^2\pi}{\partial r^2} = (ik - r)\frac{\partial^2 D}{\partial r^2} - 2\frac{\partial D}{\partial r} < 0, \qquad (2.8)$$

which must be negative in the neighborhood of equilibrium if profits are to be maximized. The character of the relationship between market interest rates and savings deposit rates, that is, the sign of the comparative statics effect dr/di, is determined by implicit differentiation of expression (2.7), which yields

$$\frac{dr}{di} = \frac{-k\dfrac{\partial D}{\partial r} + \dfrac{\partial D}{\partial i}}{(ik - r)\dfrac{\partial^2 D}{\partial r^2} - 2\dfrac{\partial D}{\partial r}} > 0. \qquad (2.9)$$

Expression (2.9) is positive, since each term in the numerator is negative using the signs of the partial derivatives in equation (2.5), and the denominator must be negative by the second order conditions for a profit maximum. Thus, the interest rate on savings deposits is a positive function of open market interest rates, so that if market rates increase, financial intermediaries will increase the rates offered on their liabilities. Moreover, this result also implies that if one intermediary operates in an environment characterized by higher market rates, such an institution will offer higher deposit rates than an intermediary operating in an environment of lower market rates. This result has particular relevance for savings and loan associations and mutual savings banks because mortgage rates have tended to display marked geographical variation over the postwar period, and the portfolios of these institutions are usually limited by law to mortgages originating in the local area. (For an analysis of the extent to which mortgage rates vary geographically, see Frederickson [20].)

Thus the theory of profit maximization suggests that the optimal deposit rate of an intermediary varies directly with movements in market yields. This result is relevant for a one-period case, which implicitly assumes that the intermediary has been established in the current period. However, it can be shown that this result is also applicable in a two-period analysis in which it is assumed that the intermediary has inherited a portfolio of assets from the previous period. That is, deposit rate setting in a given period is a function of open market rates in the same period regardless of the yields on previously acquired assets. Equation (2.6) is taken as the profit function for the previous period where the subscripts denote the time period

$$\pi_{-1} = i_{-1}kD_{-1} - r_{-1}D_{-1}. \tag{2.10}$$

In the current period, however, the description of revenues is more complicated, since revenues are composed of the return on the inherited assets, $i_{-1}kD_{-1}$, plus the rate of return in the current period obtained by investing newly acquired deposits at the current rate of interest, $i_0k(D_0 - D_{-1})$.[e] The current period profit function is written as

$$\pi_0 = i_{-1}kD_{-1} + i_0k(D_0 - D_{-1}) - r_0D_0, \tag{2.11}$$

and it is assumed that all deposits are paid the current deposit rate, r_0. If the public's demand for deposits in each period is taken as a function of the deposit rate and the relevant market yields in each period, then equation (2.11) can be rewritten as

$$\pi_0 = i_{-1}kD_{-1}(i_{-1}, r_{-1}) + i_0k[D_0(i_0, r_0) - D_{-1}(i_{-1}, r_{-1})] \\ - r_0D_0(i_0, r_0). \tag{2.12}$$

Differentiating with respect to r_0 gives the first order condition for a profit maximum in the present period

$$\frac{\partial \pi_0}{\partial r_0} = i_0k\frac{\partial D_0}{\partial r_0} - r_0\frac{\partial D_0}{\partial r_0} - D_0(i_0, r_0) \tag{2.13}$$

or

$$(i_0k - r_0)(\partial D_0/\partial r_0) - D_0(i_0, r_0) = 0. \tag{2.14}$$

This profit maximization condition is identical to the result developed earlier, expression (2.7). Thus, the optimal deposit rate set by a financial intermediary in a given period is a function of market rates in the same period i_0 and is not affected by the rate of return earned on the portion of the portfolio retained from earlier periods or by variation in earlier market rates

---

[e]For simplicity, it is assumed that all profits derived from the firm's operations in the first period are paid out to stockholders in the form of dividends at the end of that period. However, the character of the comparative statics results remain the same if instead it is assumed that such profits are reinvested at the current rate of return.

i_{-1}. This result has particular importance for the savings and loan industry. It is often suggested that these nonbank institutions do not pay a rate of return on their liabilities that is consistent with current asset yields because of the stock of low interest bearing mortgages they have accumulated from previous years (see for example, Fand [16]). However, it is clear that such an interpretation is not consistent with this model of profit maximization. In fact, the model implies that the adoption of a scheme of varying the yield on older mortgages to make their rate of return consistent with current market yields would have no direct impact on nonbank deposit rates and deposit flows if these institutions are profit maximizers. Instead, the only effect of such "variable rate mortgage" proposals would be to alter the level of intermediary profits.[f]

So far, we have considered two cases of rate setting behavior by a profit maximizing intermediary with a single-period planning horizon, that is, the intermediary sets the current optimal deposit rate based only upon current conditions. In one case, we assumed that the intermediary is established in the current period with the result that it sets its current optimal deposit rate in accordance with movements in current market rates. In the second case, we assumed that the operations of the intermediary are ongoing and that it has an inherited portfolio, but again has only a one-period planning horizon. The theoretical model indicates that under these circumstances the profit maximizing intermediary still uses only current market rates in setting the current optimal deposit rate. Thus, the inherited portfolio is of no concern to the intermediary's current rate setting problem.

We next consider another case of rate setting behavior. It is now assumed that the profit maximizing intermediary has a multiperiod planning horizon, that is, the intermediary seeks to set optimal deposit rates for more than one period. Although it is clear that past asset rates do not influence current rate setting decisions, such decisions may be affected by expectations about movements in future asset rates. The theoretical model for a two-period planning horizon is developed as follows. The objective of the intermediary is to set optimal deposit rates, r_0 in the current period and r_1 in the future period, given that it maximizes profits over the two-period horizon. Total profits are

$$\pi = \pi_0 + \pi_1, \qquad (2.15)$$

where the subscripts indicate the relevant time periods. The expressions for profit in each period are

$$\pi_0 = i_0 k D_0(i_0, r_0) - r_0 D_0(i_0, r_0) \qquad (2.16)$$

and

---

[f]This result holds unless the initiation of variable rate mortgages also has a direct impact on the current mortgage rate.

$$\pi_1 = i_0 k D_0(i_0, r_0) + i_1 k [D_1(i_1, r_1) - D_0(i_0, r_0)]$$
$$- r_1 D_1(i_1, r_1). \qquad (2.17)$$

Public demand in each period is assumed to be a function of current deposit and market rates in each period, that is,

$$D_0 = D_0(i_0, r_0) \qquad \partial D_0/\partial i_0 < 0 \qquad \partial D_0/\partial r_0 > 0 \qquad (2.18)$$

and

$$D_1 = D_1(i_1, r_1) \qquad \partial D_1/\partial i_1 < 0 \qquad \partial D_1/\partial r_1 > 0. \qquad (2.19)$$

Except for a change in the subscripts, expressions (2.16) and (2.17) are identical to expressions (2.10) and (2.12), which describe profit maximization in the single-period planning horizon case. However, the objective of the intermediary is to maximize total profit

$$\pi = 2 i_0 k D_0(i_0, r_0) - r_0 D_0(i_0, r_0) - r_1 D_1(i_1, r_1)$$
$$+ i_1 k [D_1(i_1, r_1) - D_0(i_0, r_0)] \qquad (2.20)$$

by choosing the optimal deposit rate for both the current and future periods, r_0 and r_1. The first order conditions for a profit maximum require that

$$\frac{\partial \pi}{\partial r_0} = 2 i_0 k \frac{\partial D_0}{\partial r_0} - r_0 \frac{\partial D_0}{\partial r_0} - D_0(i_0, r_0) - i_1 k \frac{\partial D_0}{\partial r_0} = 0 \qquad (2.21)$$

and

$$\frac{\partial \pi}{\partial r_1} = i_1 k \frac{\partial D_1}{\partial r_1} - r_1 \frac{\partial D_1}{\partial r_1} - D_1(i_1, r_1) = 0. \qquad (2.22)$$

We assume that $di_0 = 0$, that is, the level of current market rates is fixed. Taking the total differential of each equation and rewriting in matrix form yields

$$\begin{bmatrix} V_{r_0} & 0 \\ 0 & W_{r_1} \end{bmatrix} \begin{bmatrix} dr_0 \\ dr_1 \end{bmatrix} = \begin{bmatrix} Z_0 \\ Z_1 \end{bmatrix} di_1, \qquad (2.23)$$

where

$$V_{r_0} = (2 i_0 - i_1) k \frac{\partial^2 D_0}{\partial r_0^2} - r_0 \frac{\partial^2 D_0}{\partial r_0^2} - 2 \frac{\partial D_0}{\partial r_0}$$

$$W_{r_1} = (i_1 k - r_1)(\partial^2 D_1/\partial r_1^2) - 2(\partial D_1/\partial r_1)$$

$$Z_0 = k(\partial D_0/\partial r_0)$$

$$Z_1 = \partial D_1/\partial i_1 - k(\partial D_1/\partial r_1).$$

By employing Cramer's rule, we can solve for the comparative statics effect of a change in future market rates on the current optimal deposit rate:

$$\frac{dr_0}{di_1} = \frac{Z_0 W_{r_1}}{V_{r_0} W_{r_1}} < 0. \qquad (2.24)$$

This comparative statics result is negative, given that the second order conditions for an unconstrained profit maximum require that the upper left hand term be negative, $V_{r_0} < 0$, and that the determinant be positive, $V_{r_0} W_{r_1} > 0$ (see Henderson and Quandt, [32], p. 272). Consequently, W_{r_1} must be negative; and Z_0 is positive, given the sign of the partial derivative $\partial D_0 / \partial r_0$ from expression (2.18). Expression (2.24) implies that a change in expected future market rates i_1 inversely affects current deposit rates r_0. If, for example, there is a rise in expected market rates, a lower current deposit rate becomes optimal so that the intermediary can obtain more deposits in the next period to take advantage of the expected change in market rates. Since in empirical work expected interest rates are usually proxied by distributed lags on past rates, this theoretical result implies that lagged values of market interest rates should be specified in a regression that explains current deposit rates. If expectations are regressive, that is, the higher the level of past rates the lower the expectation for future rates, then lagged market rates should have a positive impact on current deposit rates. If expectations are extrapolative, then a negative result is expected. Overall, the model of profit maximization suggests that the yield on the portion of the portfolio inherited from previous periods does not affect current deposit rates, but that changes in expected market rates do have an impact.

Thus far, the profit maximization model has been used to demonstrate that the optimal deposit rate varies with movements in open market yields. Moreover, deposit rates in a given period are set in accordance with current and future expected market rates but are not affected by previous portfolio investment decisions. These comparative statics results are basic to the empirical work discussed in later chapters. However, additional information that has important implications for specifying empirical rate setting functions can be obtained from this model. With appropriate modifications, the profit maximization model can be used to determine the impact on the rate setting behavior of financial intermediaries caused by changes in the liquidity ratio of an intermediary's portfolio, shifts in the public's demand for liabilities, and the effect of allowing for the possibility of advertising expenditures.

In order to determine the effect of changes in the liquidity ratio k on the rate setting behavior of financial intermediaries, we again use the implicit differentiation rule on expression (2.7) to solve for the comparative statics result dr/dk. Thus

$$\frac{dr}{dk} = \frac{-i(\partial D/\partial r)}{(ik-r)\dfrac{\partial^2 D}{\partial r^2} - 2\dfrac{\partial D}{\partial r}} > 0, \tag{2.25}$$

which is positive, since the denominator is negative because it is the second order condition for a maximum, and the numerator is negative, given the sign of the partial derivatives in equation (2.5). Consequently, if there is a downward shift in liquidity because, for example, an intermediary invests a higher proportion of its deposits in earning assets, the profit maximizing intermediary will set a higher deposit rate.

To solve for the manner in which shifts in the public's demand for savings deposits affect deposit rate setting behavior, the demand function described by equation (2.5) is modified to include a shift variable s, so that

$$D = D(s, i, r) \qquad \partial D/\partial i < 0 \qquad \partial D/\partial r > 0. \tag{2.26}$$

In this relationship exogenous factors that affect demand are reflected through the influence of the variable s and may have either a positive or negative effect. An obvious source of such shifts in demand would be changes in income or population. Substituting equation (2.26) into (2.4), the profit function becomes

$$\pi = ikD(s, i, r) - rD(s, i, r), \tag{2.27}$$

where the first order condition for a maximum is again

$$\partial \pi/\partial r = (ik - r)(\partial D/\partial r) - D(s, i, r) = 0. \tag{2.28}$$

By the implicit function rule, the comparative statics result for the effect of a shift in public demand for deposits on the optimal deposit rate is

$$\frac{dr}{ds} = \frac{\partial D/\partial s}{(ik-r)\dfrac{\partial^2 D}{\partial r^2} - 2\dfrac{\partial D}{\partial r}} \gtreqless 0. \tag{2.29}$$

The sign of this expression is inversely related to the sign of the partial derivative $\partial D/\partial s$, since the denominator is negative by the second order conditions for a profit maximum. Thus, if there is an exogenous upward shift in the public's demand for savings deposits so that there is an increase in desired deposits, a profit maximizing intermediary lowers its optimal deposit rate. That is, for example, since income has a positive impact on the flow of deposits into an intermediary, $\partial D/\partial s > 0$, a rise in income induces a lower optimal deposit rate. Thus, exogenous economic factors that influence the public's demand for intermediary liabilities have an impact on the optimal deposit rate that is inversely related to the direction of the effect on demand.

Finally, the model of profit maximization is extended to include the effect of advertising. Presumably, the purpose of advertising by financial intermediaries is to influence favorably the public's demand function for liabilities. Given this purpose, an evaluation of the impact of advertising on rate setting behavior could be treated under the more general topic of factors that shift the public's demand function. The public's demand function can be written as

$$D = D(i, r, a) \qquad \partial D/\partial i < 0 \qquad \partial D/\partial r, \partial D/\partial a > 0, \qquad (2.30)$$

where a is the amount of advertising, and where it is assumed that an increase in advertising has a positive impact on the public's demand for liabilities. Although advertising is a factor that shifts public demand, it does, however, provide an additional cost to the firm that must be included in the profit function. There are two ways of evaluating the impact of advertising expenditures in the context of profit maximizing behavior. As one alternative, advertising can be taken as an endogenous variable determined simultaneously with deposit rates. Expenditures on advertising are then determined at the point where marginal cost equals marginal revenue for profits to be maximized. In such a case, the function for the total cost of advertising is expressed as

$$A = A(a), \qquad (2.31)$$

where the total cost of advertising A is a function of the amount a of advertising. The profit function becomes

$$\pi = ikD - rD - A(a). \qquad (2.32)$$

Substituting the demand function given in (2.30) into equation (2.32) and taking the partial derivatives with respect to the two endogenous variables, r and a, yields the first order conditions for profit maximization

$$\partial \pi/\partial r = ik(\partial D/\partial r) - r(\partial D/\partial r) - D(i, r, a) = 0 \qquad (2.33)$$

and

$$\partial \pi/\partial a = ik(\partial D/\partial a) - r(\partial D/\partial a) - \partial A/\partial a = 0. \qquad (2.34)$$

In equation (2.33), which is similar to equation (2.7), the first term $ik(\partial D/\partial r)$ represents marginal revenue, and the remaining terms indicate the marginal cost. The level of deposits enters as a variable since it is assumed that all liabilities are paid the same rate of return. Equation (2.34) is the similar condition for advertising, where the first term indicates marginal revenue, and the remaining terms measure marginal cost, which is composed of the direct marginal cost of advertising $\partial A/\partial a$, plus the additional expenditure incurred in paying the deposit rate on these funds $r(\partial D/\partial a)$. Such a result, however, provides little empirical information about the determinants of deposit rates.

An alternative treatment of the impact of advertising on deposit rate setting can be developed which has more definitive empirical implications. In this case, decisions about advertising expenditures are assumed to be exogenous to the setting of interest rates on savings deposits. There are several justifications for such an assumption. It is possible that advertising decisions are made at relatively infrequent intervals or according to a longer run horizon, so that the amount of advertising can be viewed as exogenous to the problem of deposit rate setting in a given period. It is also possible that the management of a financial intermediary sets the amount of advertising expenditures according to some rule such as a constant percentage or proportion of their liabilities. If advertising is taken as an exogenous variable on the basis of such assumptions, the profit function becomes

$$\pi = ikD - rD - A(a), \quad (2.35)$$

where $A(a)$ is advertising expenditures incurred for the exogenous quantity of advertising a. Substituting the demand function, equation (2.30), into equation (2.35), gives the first order condition for a profit maximum

$$\partial \pi / \partial r = (ik - r)(\partial D / \partial r) - D(i, r, a) = 0. \quad (2.36)$$

The second order condition is again

$$\partial^2 \pi / \partial r^2 = (ik - r)(\partial^2 D / \partial r^2) - 2(\partial D / \partial r) < 0, \quad (2.37)$$

which must be negative in the neighborhood of equilibrium if profits are to be maximized. Given that advertising is an exogenous variable that shifts public demand and adds a cost term to the profit function, the character of the relationship between advertising expenditures and savings deposit rates, that is, the comparative statics result dr/da, can be determined by implicit differentiation of expression (2.36)

$$\frac{dr}{da} = \frac{\partial D / \partial a}{(ik - r)\dfrac{\partial^2 D}{\partial r^2} - 2\dfrac{\partial D}{\partial r}} < 0. \quad (2.38)$$

Expression (2.38) is negative, given that the denominator is negative from the second order condition for a maximum, and the numerator is positive, given the sign of the partial derivative $\partial D / \partial a$ from expression (2.30). Therefore, the deposit rates of financial intermediaries are negatively related to the amount of advertising. In other words, advertising can be viewed as a substitute for changes in interest rates on savings deposits. As advertising expenditures are increased, the financial intermediary offers a lower optimal deposit rate, ceteris paribus.

In general, the profit maximization model of financial intermediary behavior provides useful theoretical insight for the empirical specification and testing of savings deposit rate equations. One, the optimal deposit rate is primarily a function of market interest rates and the parameters of the public's demand function. Two, the deposit rate is a positive function of current open market yields and a negative function of future expected yields. Three, the optimal deposit rate set by a financial intermediary in a given period is independent of past market rates. That is, past portfolio decisions do not affect current rate setting behavior. Four, as the proportion of deposits invested in earning assets is increased, that is, as the liquidity ratio declines, the corresponding savings deposit rate is higher. Five, exogenous economic factors, such as income or population, that influence the public's demand for savings deposits, have an impact on the optimal deposit rate that is inversely related to the direction of the effect on demand. Six, the amount of advertising expenditures incurred by an intermediary has an inverse impact on the level of savings deposit rates.

3 A Deposit Maximization Model of Savings Deposit Rate Setting

Although economists usually assume that the rational entrepreneur seeks to maximize profits, the economic implications of alternative motivations have also been explored as part of the development of the theory of the firm. The best known of these alternative hypotheses is based on the assumption that firms seek to maximize the scale of their operations, that is, the level of sales or revenues, rather than the level of profits. (This hypothesis is usually associated with the work of Baumol [3].) The rationale for such sales maximization models is that the modern corporation is characterized by a separation of interests between stockholders and managers. Within this framework stockholders are viewed as relatively passive investors who are either likely to be satisfied by less than the maximum level of profit or are unaware of the true profit potential of the firm. Consequently, the management of the firm is left relatively free to administer the activities of the corporation as long as a degree of profitability is maintained that is sufficient to prevent a takeover of the corporation by opposing interests. (This view of corporate behavior pervades much of the research of Galbraith [21].) Since the level of salaries and other forms of corporate remuneration are often a function of the size of the firm or its share of the industry, top management may derive substantial benefits from increasing the size of the corporation rather than the absolute level of profit.

The purpose of this chapter is to develop a model of financial intermediary behavior in which interest rates on savings deposits are determined as a result of the institution's desire to maximize deposits, subject to the constraint that a minimum amount of profit is earned. Deposits are taken as the quantity to be maximized, since the level of these liabilities is usually considered the relevant measure of an intermediary's scale of operations. The development of this type of model is particularly appropriate for financial intermediaries because these institutions are periodically ranked by size in both general and business publications for both the local and national markets. Consequently, changes in such rankings can draw considerable attention and prestige compared to variations in profitability. Furthermore, most nonbank institutions, that is, mutual savings banks and savings and loan associations are mutual institutions which have no stockholders. In such cooperative associations all depositors share theoretically in the ownership of the firm's net worth in proportion to their deposit holdings, where the net worth of such an institution consists of accumulated retained earnings and reserves. Nevertheless, it is reasonable to assume that in practice depositors are concerned only about the yield on their deposit holdings and have little or no interest in whether the earnings of the institution are being maximized. The validity of this assumption is reinforced by the fact that most deposits at such institutions are covered by federal insurance.[a] Consequently, management at mutual institutions is likely to be relatively unconstrained in its ability to pursue its own objectives. Since the concepts of profitability and responsibility to the owners of the firm are nebulous for these financial intermediaries, it is likely that the primary objectives of management may focus on improving the firm's scale of operation and pursuing the attendant rise in prestige associated with size. Consequently, the maximization of deposits, which are taken as the indicator of size, is an important alternative motive that may characterize the deposit rate behavior of financial intermediaries.

In this model we assume that the objective of the financial institution is to maximize deposits subject to the requirement that the intermediary earn some minimum level of profit. Many of the assumptions utilized in the profit maximization model of the previous chapter are retained. The public's demand for savings deposits is taken as

$$D = D(i, r) \quad \partial D/\partial i < 0 \quad \partial D/\partial r > 0 \quad (3.1)$$

where D is again the quantity of savings deposits, r the deposit rate, and i the market rate of return. Profits are revenue minus costs, where revenue R is the return i on the proportion k of deposits D held as earning assets by the intermediary. Costs C are the interest r paid on the intermediary's deposits D. The profit function is then written as

$$\pi = ikD - rD. \quad (3.2)$$

In this model the profit function is used to specify the constraint that limits the degree to which deposits can be maximized. In specifying the form of the constraint, the minimum profit level for efficient operation is proxied by a minimum rate of return to capital. This rate of return to capital is presumably the minimum amount implicitly required to satisfy stockholders or depositors and allow management to retain its authority. If there are stockholders, the return to capital is paid in the form of dividends or new investment from which stockholders benefit directly. If the institution is mutual in character, the earnings on capital provide indirect benefits as a source of new investment in offices and branches or as an addition to net worth, which serves to safeguard deposits in excess of the level protected by federal insurance. The minimum amount of profit that a deposit max-

---

[a]Deposits up to $40,000 are insured at most of these institutions by either the Federal Deposit Insurance Corporation or the Federal Savings and Loan Insurance Corporation.

imizing institution must earn can be defined in terms of a rate of return w required on capital K so that

$$\pi \geq wK \quad \text{where} \quad w > i > ik. \tag{3.3}$$

It is assumed that the required rate of return on capital exceeds the market return on assets, $w > i > ik$. If this inequality did not hold, then owners of net worth would invest their capital directly in earning assets rather than in the intermediary, a situation that would violate the basic reasons for the existence of financial institutions. The profit constraint can then be specified as

$$\pi = R - C \geq wK. \tag{3.4}$$

Since the objective of the intermediary is to maximize deposits subject to the constraint that it earn a minimum profit level, the model becomes the constrained maximization problem

$$\text{maximize } D \text{ subject to } \pi = R - C \geq wK \tag{3.5}$$

where the constraint is in the form of an inequality. Substituting expressions (3.1) through (3.4) into (3.5) and rewriting (3.5) in the formal terms of a constrained maximization problem causes the expression to be maximized to become

$$L = D(i, r) + \lambda[ikD(i, r) - rD(i, r) - wK] \tag{3.6}$$

where λ is a Lagrange multiplier.[b] Because the constraint is in the form of an inequality, however, it is necessary to utilize the Kuhn-Tucker conditions for constrained maximization rather than the calculus.[c] Using these conditions it can be shown that in equilibrium the minimum profit constraint always holds as an equality in this model and that as a consequence, the behavior of a deposit maximizing intermediary can be analyzed by differentiation of the profit constraint.

Applying the Kuhn-Tucker theorems gives the first order conditions for this maximization problem

$$\partial L/\partial r = (\partial D/\partial r) + \lambda(ik - r)(\partial D/\partial r) - \lambda D(i, r) \leq 0 \tag{3.7}$$

$$r(\partial L/\partial r) = 0 \tag{3.8}$$

$$\partial L/\partial \lambda = ikD(i, r) - rD(i, r) - wK \geq 0 \tag{3.9}$$

$$\lambda(\partial L/\partial \lambda) = 0 \tag{3.10}$$

---

[b]For simplicity it is assumed that net worth is not invested in funds that bear an explicit rate of return. However, none of the qualitative results derived from the model would be altered if it were assumed that net worth is invested in a manner similar to deposit liabilities.

[c]For an exposition of the Kuhn-Tucker conditions and their application to problems involving constrained maximization, see Baumol [4].

where

$$\lambda \geq 0 \quad r \geq 0$$

In order for the profit constraint (3.9) to hold as an inequality, that is, for the intermediary to earn greater than the minimum level of profit, λ must equal zero in order to insure that equality (3.10) is satisfied. However, if λ does equal zero, it is clear from expression (3.7) that $\partial D/\partial r \leq 0$. This result indicates that the only set of conditions under which a deposit maximizing intermediary would earn more profit than the required minimum is when a rise in deposit rates would either induce a decline in deposits or have no effect at all. However, as indicated in expression (3.1) it is assumed a priori that $\partial D/\partial r > 0$, so that it is clear that the minimum profit constraint, equation (3.9), must hold as an equality and that $\lambda > 0$. Furthermore, since the only interesting case is when there is a nontrivial deposit rate, that is when $r > 0$, it is clear from condition (3.8) that $\partial L/\partial r = 0$. Therefore, the condition that characterizes the equilibrium for deposit maximization is

$$\partial L/\partial r = (\partial D/\partial r) + \lambda(ik - r)(\partial D/\partial r) - \lambda D(i, r) = 0 . \quad (3.11)$$

In general, the analysis of deposit maximization behavior indicates that the profit constraint, equation (3.9), holds as an equality and that $\lambda \neq 0$; that is, the deposit maximizing intermediary always operates at a point where the profit constraint is effective and minimum profits are earned.[d]

Expression (3.11) can be used to illustrate the basic characteristic of a deposit maximizing intermediary. Rewriting expression (3.11), we see that

$$\lambda[(ik - r)(\partial D/\partial r) - D(i, r)] = -(\partial D/\partial r) \quad (3.12)$$

or

$$(ik - r)(\partial D/\partial r) - D(i, r) = -(\partial D/\partial r)(1/\lambda) < 0 , \quad (3.13)$$

since $\lambda > 0$. It is clear that the left hand side of equation (3.13) is the expression for marginal profit $\partial \pi/\partial r$, which in the profit maximization case is equal to zero. However, for the deposit maximization case, $\partial \pi/\partial r < 0$, that is, marginal profit must be negative. Consequently, the deposit maximizing intermediary operates at a point beyond that of a profit maximizer and in a region characterized by negative marginal profits. Thus, ceteris paribus, an intermediary that seeks to maximize deposits offers a higher deposit rate than an intermediary that maximizes profits.

Since the deposit rate setting behavior of a deposit maximizing intermediary is determined at the point at which the minimum profit constraint becomes binding, it is possible to analyze the behavior of the optimal deposit rate by analyzing the comparative statics properties of the profit constraint

---

[d]For a general proof that only the equality form of the minimum profit constraint is applicable in equilibrium for a revenue maximizing firm, see Baumol [3].

$$ikD(i, r) - rD(i, r) - wK = 0, \quad (3.14)$$

given a change in one of the exogenous parameters i, k, w, or K. It is assumed that net worth K is fixed, so that the total differential of expression (3.14) is

$$[(ik - r)(\partial D/\partial r) - D(i, r)]dr + [ik(\partial D/\partial i) + kD(i, r) - r(\partial D/\partial i)]di$$
$$+ [iD(i, r)] dk - K dw = 0. \quad (3.15)$$

The comparative statics effect of a change in open market rates on the optimal deposit rate is derived from expression (3.15) as

$$\frac{dr}{di} = - \frac{kD(i, r) + (ik - r)(\partial D/\partial i)}{(ik - r)(\partial D/\partial r) - D(i, r)}. \quad (3.16)$$

Given the sign of expression (3.13), the denominator of (3.16) is negative. Nevertheless, the sign of dr/di is unclear because the numerator consists of two terms with different signs. This result occurs because a rise in open market rates induces a positive effect on deposit rates through the impact on portfolio revenue $kD(i, r)$, but the substitution effect on the demand for savings deposits induces a decline in deposit rates through the term $(ik - r)$ $(\partial D/\partial i)$. The term $(ik - r)$ must be positive, since in order for expression (3.14) to hold

$$(ik - r) = \frac{wK}{D(i, r)} > 0. \quad (3.17)$$

These results can be clarified by assuming that the vector of open market rates i is dichotomized into a yield on portfolio assets i_a and a yield on instruments that are substitutes for deposits i_c. The division of market yields into separate asset and competing rates is particularly appropriate for nonbank intermediaries, since the portfolios of these institutions are usually restricted to mortgages, an asset that the public is unlikely to regard as a substitute for savings deposits. In such a case, the comparative statics results are

$$\frac{dr}{di_a} = - \frac{kD(i_c, r)}{(i_a k - r)(\partial D/\partial r) - D(i_c, r)} > 0 \quad (3.18)$$

and

$$\frac{dr}{di_c} = - \frac{(i_a k - r)(\partial D/\partial i_c)}{(i_a k - r)(\partial D/\partial r) - D(i_c, r)} < 0. \quad (3.19)$$

Expressions (3.18) and (3.19) indicate that a deposit maximizing intermediary raises its deposit rates if asset rates rise but lowers its deposit rates if competing rates rise. In contrast, a profit maximizing intermediary responds to a rise in open market rates by increasing its deposit rate, regardless of whether the rise in yields is specific to assets available for the portfolio of the institution or to the instruments that are close substitutes for its deposits. More intuitively, a deposit maximizer uses any potential profits above its minimum requirement as a pool to be sacrificed in order to offer higher deposit yields and obtain a larger amount of deposits. A rise in asset rates increases this potential profit and thus induces higher deposit rates. A rise in competing rates, however, lowers the size of this potential pool, ceteris paribus, and induces a decline in the optimal deposit rate. Consequently, the response of deposit rates to changes in competing yields differs between the models of deposit maximization and of profit maximization. Thus, the applicability of these contrasting hypotheses can be empirically tested by examining the character of the coefficients obtained when competing rate variables are specified in a deposit rate regression.

In the previous chapter it was demonstrated that if it is assumed that an intermediary maximizes profit, the rate of return on a portfolio of assets inherited from an earlier period has no impact on the determination of an optimal deposit rate for the current period. This property can also be analyzed within the framework of the hypothesis of deposit maximization. As in the case of the profit maximization model, revenues are composed of the rate of return on the assets inherited from the previous period, $i_{-1}kD_{-1}$, plus the return obtained by investing newly acquired deposits at the current rate of return, $i_0k(D_0 - D_{-1})$.[e] The relevant profit constraint, which holds as an inequality, is

$$i_{-1}kD_{-1}(i_{-1}, r_{-1}) + i_0k[D_0(i_0, r_0) - D_{-1}(i_{-1}, r_{-1})]$$
$$- r_0D_0(i_0, r_0) \geq wK. \quad (3.20)$$

Since the deposit maximizing intermediary is always induced to reach the minimum profit level, this constraint, (3.20), holds as an equality in equilibrium, so that the total differential is

$$[(i_0k - r_0)(\partial D_0/\partial r_0) - D_0(i_0, r_0)] dr_0 + [kD_{-1}(i_{-1}, r_{-1})$$
$$+ i_{-1}k(\partial D_{-1}/\partial i_{-1}) - i_0k(\partial D_{-1}/\partial i_{-1})] di_{-1} = 0 \quad (3.21)$$

where it is assumed that current market yields are given, $di_0 = 0$. The effect of a change in the yield of the inherited portfolio i_{-i} on the current deposit rate r_0 is

$$\frac{dr_0}{di_{-1}} = -\frac{kD_{-1}(i_{-1}, r_{-1}) + (i_{-1} - i_0)k(\partial D_{-1}/\partial i_{-1})}{(i_0k - r_0)(\partial D_0/\partial r_0) - D_0(i_0, r_0)}. \quad (3.22)$$

---

[e]As in the profit maximization model developed in chapter 2, it is again assumed for simplicity that the profits earned in the previous period are paid out to stockholders in the form of dividends or accumulated as noninterest bearing reserves rather than reinvested by the intermediary.

The sign of this comparative statics result is ambiguous, but the likely effect is positive. This is because the denominator is the expression for marginal profit, which has been shown to be negative for a deposit maximizer in expression (3.13). The first term in the numerator is clearly positive. Although the sign of the second term in the numerator is ambiguous, it will also be positive if the return on the inherited portfolio is larger than the current market rate of return $i_{-1} > i_0$. Even if $i_0 > i_{-1}$, the second term is likely to be smaller in absolute value than kD_{-1}. Consequently, if the objective of the financial intermediary is to maximize deposits subject to a minimum profit constraint, the current deposit rate of the institution is directly affected by the rate of return earned on the portion of the portfolio retained from earlier periods. Thus, for a deposit maximizing intermediary, the lower the rate of return on the inherited portfolio of assets, the lower the interest rate on savings deposits offered in the current period.

The reason for this result is intuitive. Since a deposit maximizer uses potential profits above the minimum as a pool with which to attract more deposits through a higher deposit rate, the higher the return it earns on its older assets, the larger this pool of potential profits and the higher its current deposit rate. This result has particular importance for the question of variable rate mortgages, which would allow for the adjustment of yields on older mortgages to reflect current levels of market interest rates. This proposal is especially relevant for nonbank intermediaries, since the portfolios of these institutions are dominated by mortgage holdings. Consequently, if the behavior of these institutions is characterized by deposit maximization, the introduction of variable rate mortgages would in fact influence the level of current deposit rates. If yields on older mortgages are adjusted upward, such a model predicts an increase in deposit rates, which would induce an increase in deposit flows, while the level of intermediary profits would remain at the constrained level.

Overall, in a deposit maximization model the optimal deposit rate is primarily a function of open market interest rates. However, such a financial intermediary behaves differently towards changes in asset and competing market yields. A rise in asset yields induces a rise in deposit rates, but a rise in competing yields induces deposit rates to fall. This behavior differs from the profit maximization model in which the optimal deposit rate varies directly with movements in all open market yields. Furthermore, current deposit rate setting decisions of a deposit maximizing intermediary are directly affected by past portfolio investment decisions. In contrast, past portfolio decisions do not affect current deposit rates if a profit maximization model is appropriate.[f]

---

[f] The behavior of a deposit maximizing intermediary with a multiperiod planning horizon is not developed here since a variety of alternative assumptions can be made about the specification of both the objective function and the relevant constraints. For example, it is not clear whether such an intermediary seeks to maximize final period deposits or a combination of interim and final period deposits.

As in the previous chapter, the deposit maximization model can be extended to obtain additional information about the determinants of deposit rates. We now investigate the impact on the determination of deposit rates induced by changes in the liquidity ratio of an intermediary's portfolio, shifts in the public's demand for liabilities, and the effect of allowing for advertising expenditures. We obtain comparative statics results which in some cases differ from the results obtained in the profit maximization model and thus complete the framework necessary to test empirically the validity of these two alternative hypotheses of financial behavior.

The effect of a change in the liquidity ratio k on the deposit rate setting behavior of financial institutions can be determined by assuming that $di = 0$ and $dw = 0$ and by solving expression (3.15), which describes the profit constraint. The comparative statics result is

$$\frac{dr}{dk} = - \frac{iD(i, r)}{(ik - r)(\partial D/\partial r) - D(i, r)} > 0. \tag{3.23}$$

As in the case of profit maximization, the higher the proportion of deposits that is invested in earning assets, the higher the optimal deposit rate for a deposit maximizing intermediary.

To solve for the effect on deposit rates of shifts in the public's demand for savings deposits, we modify the demand function to include a shift variable, s

$$D = D(s, i, r) \quad \partial D/\partial i < 0 \quad \partial D/\partial r > 0, \tag{3.24}$$

where the effect of the shift variable on demand can be either positive or negative. Substituting this modified demand function into the profit constraint, equation (3.15), the comparative statics result is

$$\frac{dr}{ds} = - \frac{(ik - r)(\partial D/\partial s)}{(ik - r)(\partial D/\partial r) - D(s, i, r)} \gtreqless 0. \tag{3.25}$$

It is clear that the denominator is negative from expression (3.13). Furthermore, $(ik - r)$, which appears in the numerator, is positive from expression (3.17). Therefore, the sign of dr/ds varies directly with the sign of $\partial D/\partial s$. In the profit maximizing model, the sign of dr/ds varies inversely with the sign of $\partial D/\partial s$. Consequently, favorable shifts in such variables as income or population induce deposit maximizing intermediaries to raise deposit rates. A profit maximizing intermediary in contrast responds to favorable shifts in demand in an opposite manner, by lowering its deposit rate. Thus, the two hypotheses yield opposite conclusions as to the impact of shifts in demand on deposit rates. The intuitive reason for the behavior that results from the model of deposit maximization is that a favorable shift in demand increases the pool of potential profit, which allows the intermediary to offer a higher deposit rate.

As in the case of profit maximization, the model of deposit maximization can also be extended to include the impact of advertising. In such a case, the public's demand function can be written as

$$D = D(i, r, a) \quad \partial D/\partial i < 0 \quad \partial D/\partial r > 0 \quad \partial D/\partial a > 0, \quad (3.26)$$

where it is assumed that advertising has a positive effect on demand. The goal of the intermediary is to maximize deposits subject to the constraint

$$ikD - rD - A(a) \geq wK \quad (3.27)$$

where advertising is an additional cost $A(a)$ to the intermediary that must be included in the determination of profit. The objective function, modified to include advertising, is

$$L = D(i, r, a) + \lambda[ikD(i, r, a) - rD(i, r, a) - A(a) - wK]. \quad (3.28)$$

If it is assumed that advertising policy is endogenous and determined simultaneously with deposit rate policy, the first order conditions for a maximum are

$$\frac{\partial L}{\partial r} = \frac{\partial D}{\partial r} + \lambda ik \frac{\partial D}{\partial r} - \lambda r \frac{\partial D}{\partial r} - \lambda D(i, r, a) \leq 0 \quad (3.29)$$

$$r(\partial L/\partial r) = 0 \quad (3.30)$$

$$\frac{\partial L}{\partial a} = \frac{\partial D}{\partial a} + \lambda ik \frac{\partial D}{\partial a} - \lambda r \frac{\partial D}{\partial a} - \lambda \frac{\partial A}{\partial a} \leq 0 \quad (3.31)$$

$$a(\partial L/\partial a) = 0 \quad (3.32)$$

$$\partial L/\partial \lambda = ikD(i, r, a) - rD(i, r, a) - A(a) - wK \geq 0 \quad (3.33)$$

$$\lambda(\partial L/\partial \lambda) = 0. \quad (3.34)$$

Once again it is clear that the profit constraint, equation (3.33), must hold as an equality since $\partial D/\partial r$ and $\partial D/\partial a$ are assumed to be greater than zero. Since λ must be positive, expression (3.31) can be rewritten as

$$(ik - r)(\partial D/\partial a) - (\partial A/\partial a) = -(\partial D/\partial a)/\lambda < 0. \quad (3.35)$$

This implies that in equilibrium the marginal cost of advertising exceeds marginal revenue,

$$(ik - r)(\partial D/\partial a) < \partial A/\partial a, \quad (3.36)$$

a result that contrasts with the profit maximizing model, where an intermediary sets marginal revenue equal to marginal cost. The deposit maximizing institution that advertises carries advertising to a point where marginal profit is negative and thus advertises more than a similar profit maximizing institution.

In an alternate view of advertising policy, it is assumed that decisions about advertising are exogenous to the setting of deposit rates. In this case, the comparative statics impact of changes in advertising on deposit rates can be derived from the profit constraint, equation (3.33), which holds as an equality. Differentiating equation (3.33) and assuming that open market interest rates are given ($di = 0$) yields

$$[(ik - r)(\partial D/\partial r) - D(i, r, a)]dr$$
$$+ [(ik - r)(\partial D/\partial a) - (\partial A/\partial a)]da = 0. \quad (3.37)$$

The comparative statics effect of a change in advertising on the deposit rate is

$$\frac{dr}{da} = -\frac{(ik - r)(\partial D/\partial a) - (\partial A/\partial a)}{(ik - r)(\partial D/\partial r) - D(i, r, a)} < 0, \quad (3.38)$$

which is clearly negative, since the numerator is negative from expression (3.35) and the denominator is negative from expression (3.13). Consequently, if the advertising decisions of a deposit maximizing intermediary are exogenous to deposit rate determination, the level of deposit rates varies inversely with the amount of advertising. Therefore, advertising can be viewed as a substitute for deposit rate changes, whether an institution maximizes profits or deposits.

Overall, a model in which deposits are maximized subject to a minimum profit constraint has many important analytical implications for the deposit rate setting behavior of financial intermediaries. One, such an institution always operates at the point where it earns its minimum profit and is bound by its profit constraint. Two, in these circumstances the intermediary always operates where marginal profit is negative and therefore offers a higher deposit rate than a profit maximizing intermediary in the same economic environment. Three, the optimal deposit rate is a positive function of current asset yields but is negatively related to yields on financial instruments that the public considers to be substitutes for the intermediary's liabilities. Four, the current deposit rate is directly related to the yield the institution earns on its inherited portfolio. Five, as the proportion of deposits invested in earning assets increases, that is, as the liquidity ratio declines, the optimal deposit rate rises. Six, movements in economic factors that exogenously affect the public's demand for savings deposits induce a change in the deposit rate in the same direction as the impact on demand. That is, changes that affect demand favorably induce higher deposit rates. Finally, if advertising decisions are assumed to be exogenous to the setting of deposit rates, the quantity of advertising has an inverse impact on the deposit rate. Therefore, changes in advertising can be viewed as a substitute for changes in interest rates on savings deposits.

4 A Utility Maximization Model of Savings Deposit Rate Setting

In the preceding chapters it has been assumed that the behavior of an intermediary is determined as a result of management's desire to pursue a single objective. Since economists usually assume that the behavior of a firm can be explained by management's attempt to maximize profits, we analyzed in chapter 2 the implication of a model of profit maximization for the determination of interest rates on savings deposits by a financial intermediary. Alternatively, some economists hypothesize that the separation of management and ownership that characterizes the modern corporation has resulted in a pattern of corporate behavior that can be explained by management's desire to maximize revenue or sales rather than profits. Consequently, in chapter 3 we analyzed the properties of a model in which an intermediary maximizes deposits subject to a minimum profit constraint, and we derived comparative statics results relevant to the determination of deposit rates. However, it is possible that corporate management may desire to maximize simultaneously both the level of the firm's profits and the scale of its operations.[a] Since there is an economic tradeoff between these goals, management may implicitly attempt to maximize some combination of both of these aims. More specifically, decision makers may make choices about the allocation of resources in order to maximize some objective function in which increments in either profits or size are considered beneficial. This is similar to an analysis in which economic policy makers are assumed to maximize some objective function in which increases in either unemployment or inflation are considered undesirable. The purpose of this chapter is to explore the implications for the deposit rate setting behavior of financial institutions given that the institution desires to maximize some combination of both profits and deposits. We develop a model of financial behavior in which an intermediary determines deposit rates in order to maximize a utility function in which both profits and deposits enter as positive arguments. Two types of utility functions are considered. In the first, profits and deposits are assumed to enter linearly as arguments in the utility function. In the second, the form of the utility function is assumed to be quadratic in deposits. (The quadratic form of a utility function is often used in the analysis of portfolio selection. See, for example, Markowitz [40].)

---

[a]For example, although a firm's management might seek to maximize profits it may also be seriously concerned about maintaining the firm's competitive position in the market, which at least partially depends on the size of the enterprise.

If a linear utility function can be assumed to characterize the deposit rate setting behavior of the financial intermediary, profits π and deposits D are specified in the function as follows

$$U = \alpha D + \beta \pi, \qquad (4.1)$$

where α and β are arbitrary weights that reflect management's view of the relative desirability of increases in deposits and profits respectively. The equations for profits and the demand for savings deposits are retained from the models in the previous chapters[b]

$$\pi = ikD - rD \qquad (4.2)$$

and

$$D = D(i, r) \quad \partial D/\partial i < 0 \quad \partial D/\partial r > 0. \qquad (4.3)$$

Substituting equations (4.2) and (4.3) into (4.1) yields the objective function

$$U = \alpha D(i, r) + \beta[ikD(i, r) - rD(i, r)]. \qquad (4.4)$$

The first order condition for utility maximization is

$$\partial U/\partial r = \alpha(\partial D/\partial r) + \beta[(ik - r)(\partial D/\partial r) - D(i, r)] = 0, \qquad (4.5)$$

and the second order condition is

$$\frac{\partial^2 U}{\partial r^2} = \alpha \frac{\partial^2 D}{\partial r^2} + \beta\left[(ik - r)\frac{\partial^2 D}{\partial r^2} - 2\frac{\partial D}{\partial r}\right] < 0, \qquad (4.6)$$

which must be negative in the neighborhood of equilibrium if utility is to be maximized. Rearranging the terms of expression (4.5), we obtain the relationship

$$(ik - r)(\partial D/\partial r) - D(i, r) = -(\alpha/\beta)(\partial D/\partial r) < 0. \qquad (4.7)$$

The left term of equation (4.7) is the familiar expression for marginal profit $\partial \pi/\partial r$, which in the profit maximizing model is equal to zero. Since α and β are assumed to be positive, and $\partial D/\partial r$ is positive from expression (4.3), it is clear that marginal profit $\partial \pi/\partial r$ must be negative for a utility maximizer. Consequently, in equilibrium a financial intermediary that attempts to maximize this utility function operates in a neighborhood characterized by negative marginal profits and offers a deposit rate higher than a profit maximizing intermediary but lower than a deposit maximizing intermediary. Furthermore, the greater the utility an intermediary derives from deposits relative to the weighting given to profits, the more negative is marginal profit and the higher is the optimal deposit rate in equilibrium

---

[b]It is also assumed that the cross partial derivative $\partial^2 D/\partial i \partial r$ of the demand function is either zero or is very small compared to the other parameters of the demand function.

compared to another utility maximizing intermediary that derives less utility from deposits relative to profits. This result can be demonstrated by implicit differentiation of equation (4.5), which yields

$$\frac{dr}{d\alpha} = \frac{-\partial D/\partial r}{\alpha \frac{\partial^2 D}{\partial r^2} + \beta \left[(ik - r)\frac{\partial^2 D}{\partial r^2} - 2\frac{\partial D}{\partial r} \right]} > 0. \quad (4.8)$$

This expression is positive, given that $\partial D/\partial r$ is positive from equation (4.3) and that the denominator must be negative, since it is the second order condition for a maximum. Similarly, the greater the utility that an intermediary gains from profits relative to deposits, the lower is the optimal deposit rate. The comparative statics result is

$$\frac{dr}{d\beta} = \frac{-[(ik - r)(\partial D/\partial r) - D(i, r)]}{\alpha \frac{\partial^2 D}{\partial r^2} + \beta \left[(ik - r)\frac{\partial^2 D}{\partial r^2} - 2\frac{\partial D}{\partial r} \right]} < 0, \quad (4.9)$$

which is negative, since marginal profits $[(ik - r)(\partial D/\partial r) - D(i, r)]$ are negative from expression (4.7), and the denominator is again negative because of the second order conditions for a maximum. Finally, as α approaches zero, so that less weight is attached to increases in deposits, the model gradually reduces to the case of profit maximization.

An important implication of expression (4.5) is that the level of deposit rates offered by intermediaries that maximize utility is primarily a function of movements in open market yields. The direction of this functional relationship can be determined by evaluating the comparative statics result dr/di, which indicates the effect of a change in open market rates on savings deposit rates. By implicit differentiation of expression (4.5) we obtain

$$\frac{dr}{di} = \frac{-\beta[k(\partial D/\partial r) - (\partial D/\partial i)]}{\alpha \frac{\partial^2 D}{\partial r^2} + \beta \left[(ik - r)\frac{\partial^2 D}{\partial r^2} - 2\frac{\partial D}{\partial r} \right]} > 0, \quad (4.10)$$

which is positive according to the signs of the partial derivative from equation (4.3) and given that the denominator must be negative since it is the second order condition for a utility maximum. As in the models of profit or deposit maximizing intermediaries, this result indicates that for a utility maximizing financial institution, deposit rates are a positive function of movements in open market yields.

This result applies for a one-period analysis in which it is implicitly assumed that the intermediary is established in the current period. We can show, however, that this result also holds in a two-period model in which the intermediary inherits a portfolio of assets from a previous period. In this situation current deposit rates of utility maximizing intermediaries are determined in accordance with current market yields and are not affected by past portfolio decisions. Using subscripts to denote the appropriate time period, profits in the current period are

$$\pi_0 = i_{-1}kD_{-1}(i_{-1}, r_{-1}) + i_0k[D_0(i_0, r_0) - D_{-1}(i_{-1}, r_{-1})] \\ - r_0D_0(i_0, r_0), \quad (4.11)$$

where the first term is the revenue obtained from the assets inherited from the past period, the second term is the revenue generated by investing the additional deposits acquired in the current period at the current market rate, and the third term is the cost incurred in the current period.[c] The public's demand for savings deposits in each period is taken as a function of the interest rate applicable for that period. Therefore, the institution's utility function for the current period is

$$U_0 = \alpha D_0(i_0, r_0) + \beta\{i_{-1}kD_{-1}(i_{-1}, r_{-1}) - r_0D_0(i_0, r_0) \\ + i_0k[D_0(i_0, r_0) - D_{-1}(i_{-1}, r_{-1})]\}. \quad (4.12)$$

The first order condition for a utility maximum in the current period requires that

$$\frac{\partial U_0}{\partial r_0} = \alpha \frac{\partial D_0}{\partial r_0} + \beta\left[(i_0k - r_0)\frac{\partial D_0}{\partial r_0} - D_0(i_0, r_0)\right] = 0. \quad (4.13)$$

Except for the subscripts, expression (4.13) is identical to expression (4.5), the first order condition for a maximum in a model in which the intermediary has no inherited portfolio. This result indicates that a financial intermediary that maximizes its utility derived from both profits and deposits determines interest rates on savings deposits for a given period in accordance with the level of open market yields in the same period and is not affected by its past investment choices. In this respect, the behavior of a utility maximizing institution is similar to the behavior of a profit maximizer because the determination of the optimal deposit rate for the current period is not influenced by past portfolio decisions, that is, $dr_0/di_{-1} = 0$, in contrast to an intermediary that maximizes deposits subject to a minimum profit constraint, where $dr_0/di_{-1} > 0$.

We can also use this utility maximization model to analyze the deposit rate setting behavior of an intermediary that has a multiperiod planning horizon in order to determine whether expectations held about future market interest rates affect current deposit rate decisions. In this case the intermediary seeks to set optimal deposit rates for more than one period; that is, the rate for the current period r_0 as well as the rate for the future

---

[c] As in the models developed in the previous chapters, it is again assumed that any profits earned in the past period are paid out to the stockholders in the form of dividends and are not retained for corporate investment.

period r_1, given that the institution attempts to maximize total utility for both periods. The utility function to be maximized is written as

$$U = \alpha[D_0(i_0, r_0) + D_1(i_1, r_1)] + \beta\{2i_0kD_0(i_0, r_0) - r_0D_0(i_0, r_0) \\ + i_1k[D_1(i_1, r_1) - D_0(i_0, r_0)] - r_1D_1(i_1, r_1)\}, \quad (4.14)$$

where the public's demand for savings deposits in each period is a function of the interest rates applicable in that period. The first order conditions for a utility maximum require that

$$\frac{\partial U_0}{\partial r_0} = \alpha\frac{\partial D_0}{\partial r_0} \\ + \beta\left[(2i_0k - r_0)\frac{\partial D_0}{\partial r_0} - D_0(i_0, r_0) - i_1k\frac{\partial D_0}{\partial r_0}\right] \quad (4.15)$$

and

$$\frac{\partial U_1}{\partial r_1} = \alpha\frac{\partial D_1}{\partial r_1} + \beta\left[(i_1k - r_1)\frac{\partial D_1}{\partial r_1} - D_1(i_1, r_1)\right]. \quad (4.16)$$

We assume that $di_0 = 0$, that is the current level of market rates is fixed, so that taking the total differential of each equation and rewriting in matrix form, the following expressions are obtained

$$\begin{bmatrix} V_{r_0} & 0 \\ 0 & W_{r_1} \end{bmatrix} \begin{bmatrix} dr_0 \\ dr_1 \end{bmatrix} = \begin{bmatrix} Z_0 \\ Z_1 \end{bmatrix} di_1 \quad (4.17)$$

where

$$V_{r_0} = \alpha\frac{\partial^2 D_0}{\partial r_0^2} + \beta\left[(2i_0 - i_1)k\frac{\partial^2 D_0}{\partial r_0^2} - r_0\frac{\partial^2 D_0}{\partial r_0^2} - 2\frac{\partial D_0}{\partial r_0}\right]$$

$$W_{r_1} = \alpha\frac{\partial^2 D_1}{\partial r_1^2} + \beta\left[(i_1k - r_1)\frac{\partial^2 D_1}{\partial r_1^2} - 2\frac{\partial D_1}{\partial r_1}\right]$$

$$Z_0 = \beta k\frac{\partial D_0}{\partial r_0}$$

$$Z_1 = \beta\left[\frac{\partial D_1}{\partial i_1} - k\frac{\partial D_1}{\partial r_1}\right].$$

Employing Cramer's rule gives the comparative statics effect of a change in the future market rate i_1 on the current deposit rate r_0

$$\frac{dr_0}{di_1} = \frac{Z_0 W_{r_1}}{V_{r_0} W_{r_1}} < 0. \quad (4.18)$$

Since the second order conditions for a utility maximum require that $V_{r_0} < 0$ and that $V_{r_0} W_{r_1} > 0$, it is clear that $W_{r_1} < 0$. (See Henderson and Quandt [32] for the second order conditions for a constrained maximization problem.) Furthermore, Z_0 is positive, given the sign of the partial derivative $\partial D_0/\partial r_0$ from expression (4.3). Thus, the comparative statics impact of future market rates on current deposit rates is negative. This result is identical in sign to that derived earlier for the profit maximization model. Since in empirical work expected future interest rates are proxied by past yields, this result implies that lagged values of open market rates should be specified in a deposit rate regression. If expectations are regressive, such variables should have a positive sign, while negative coefficients would indicate the presence of extrapolative expectations.

The utility maximization model can be used to derive results that have implications for the specification of empirical deposit rate functions. Specifically, we can evaluate the effects on deposit rate setting of changes in the liquidity ratio k and of exogenous shifts in public demand for deposits. By implicit differentiation of equation (4.5), the comparative statics result can be obtained for the effect of changes in the liquidity ratio on deposit rates, that is,

$$\frac{dr}{dk} = \frac{-\beta i(\partial D/\partial r)}{\alpha \dfrac{\partial^2 D}{\partial r^2} + \beta \left[(ik - r)\dfrac{\partial^2 D}{\partial r^2} - 2\dfrac{\partial D}{\partial r} \right]} > 0. \qquad (4.19)$$

Expression (4.19) is positive, given the sign of $\partial D/\partial r$ from expression (4.3) and the fact that the denominator must be negative since it is the second order condition for a maximum. This implies that a utility maximizing intermediary offers higher deposit rates as the proportion of deposits it holds as earning assets rises. This result is also the same as that obtained in the profit maximizing model.

Furthermore, if we specify the demand function for savings deposits to include an exogenous shift variable, we obtain

$$D = D(s, i, r) \qquad \partial D/\partial i < 0 \qquad \partial D/\partial r > 0, \qquad (4.20)$$

where the impact of changes in the shift variable s can be assumed to be either positive or negative. Substituting equation (4.20) into the utility function, equation (4.4), we can derive the comparative statics effect for the impact on deposit rates that results from an exogenous shift in public demand:

$$\frac{dr}{ds} = \frac{\beta(\partial D/\partial s)}{\alpha \dfrac{\partial^2 D}{\partial r^2} + \beta \left[(ik - r)\dfrac{\partial^2 D}{\partial r^2} - 2\dfrac{\partial D}{\partial r} \right]} \gtreqless 0. \qquad (4.21)$$

As in the profit maximizing model, the sign of this comparative statics result varies inversely with the sign of the partial derivative $\partial D/\partial s$. Therefore, an increase in an exogenous factor such as income or population that has a positive effect on the public's demand for deposits ($\partial D/\partial s > 0$) induces a decline in the optimal deposit rate ($dr/ds < 0$).[d]

Overall, the theoretical model describing the behavior of a financial intermediary that maximizes a linear utility function yields comparative statics results that are similar to those obtained for the profit maximization model.

Next, an alternative specification of an intermediary's utility function is examined. It is assumed that profits affect utility in a linear manner but deposits enter the function in quadratic form. The reason for using this type of objective function is that as an intermediary grows larger in size, it may derive less additional utility from a given increase in its scale of operations. In particular, as a financial institution becomes more dominant in its market, further increases in size may gradually expose the intermediary to antitrust action or to unfavorable treatment from the government, since the regulatory authorities desire to maintain effective competition in the market.[e] A utility function in which deposits enter in quadratic form can capture the behavioral response of financial intermediaries to this situation, since such a function implies that there exists diminishing marginal utility to increases in deposits.

The quadratic form of the utility function is written as

$$U = \gamma\pi + \theta D + \sigma D^2 \quad \gamma, \theta > 0 \quad \sigma < 0. \quad (4.22)$$

The parameters γ, θ, and σ, of this function must be restricted in order to assure that the intermediary operates in a region where the marginal utility of deposits is positive. This is the only neighborhood of serious interest, since it is assumed that, holding the level of profits constant, an institution would prefer to be larger rather than smaller in size. The expression for the marginal utility of deposits is

$$\partial U/\partial D = \theta + 2\sigma D. \quad (4.23)$$

Consequently, equation (4.23) must be restricted to the range where $\theta + 2\sigma D > 0$. It is clear that such a quadratic function provides for diminishing marginal utility from increases in deposits since

$$\partial^2 U/\partial D^2 = 2\sigma < 0. \quad (4.24)$$

---

[d]In a similar manner it can be demonstrated that the comparative statics response of a utility maximizing intermediary to changes in advertising is negative in sign, as was the case with the profit and deposit maximization models.

[e]For example, in ruling upon petitions for bank mergers, the Federal Reserve Board evaluates the likely effect of the bank acquisition on the competitive character of the local market [6].

As in the linear utility case, the objective of the institution is to choose a deposit rate that maximizes utility. The equations for both profits and deposits are retained from earlier models so that

$$\pi = ikD - rD \qquad (4.25)$$

and

$$D = D(i, r) \qquad \partial D/\partial i < 0 \qquad \partial D/\partial r > 0. \qquad (4.26)$$

Thus the utility function can be rewritten as

$$U = \gamma[ikD(i, r) - rD(i, r)] + \theta D(i, r) + \sigma[D(i, r)]^2. \qquad (4.27)$$

The first order condition for utility maximization requires that

$$\partial U/\partial r = \gamma[(ik - r)(\partial D/\partial r) - D(i, r)] + \theta(\partial D/\partial r) + 2\sigma(\partial D/\partial r)$$
$$= 0, \qquad (4.28)$$

and the second order condition requires that

$$\frac{\partial^2 U}{\partial r^2} = \gamma \left[(ik - r)\frac{\partial^2 D}{\partial r^2} - 2\frac{\partial D}{\partial r} \right] + (\theta + 2\sigma)\frac{\partial^2 D}{\partial r^2} < 0. \qquad (4.29)$$

Since by definition marginal profit is

$$\partial \pi/\partial r = (ik - r)(\partial D/\partial r) - D(i, r), \qquad (4.30)$$

the first order condition, equation (4.28), can be rewritten as

$$\frac{\partial \pi}{\partial r} = -\frac{(\theta + 2\sigma)}{\gamma}\frac{\partial D}{\partial r} < 0, \qquad (4.31)$$

which is negative given equations (4.23) and (4.26). This implies that in equilibrium the intermediary operates in a neighborhood characterized by negative marginal profits and offers a higher deposit rate than an intermediary that maximizes profits. Furthermore, as the weight assigned to profits γ is increased relative to the weight on deposits $(\theta + 2\sigma)$ the deposit rate of a utility maximizer decreases and approaches that of a profit maximizer. We can show this formally by deriving the comparative statics result for the effect of a change in γ, the weight attached to profits, on the deposit rate r. By implicit differentiation of equation (4.28) we obtain the result

$$\frac{dr}{d\gamma} = \frac{-[(ik - r)(\partial D/\partial r) - D(i, r)]}{\gamma \left[(ik - r)\frac{\partial^2 D}{\partial r^2} - 2\frac{\partial D}{\partial r} \right] + (\theta + 2\sigma)\frac{\partial^2 D}{\partial r^2}} < 0. \qquad (4.32)$$

Since the numerator must be negative from expression (4.31), and the denominator must be negative from the second order condition for a maximum, expression (4.32) must be negative. Therefore, the greater the weight assigned to profits, the lower the optimal deposit rate.

Again, the optimal deposit rate emerges as primarily a function of movements in open market interest rates. The direction of the impact of a change in open market rates on deposit rates dr/di is the same as in the linear case. This can be demonstrated by implicit differentiation of expression (4.28), which yields

$$\frac{dr}{di} = \frac{-[\gamma(k(\partial D/\partial r) - \partial D/\partial i)]}{\gamma\left[(ik - r)\frac{\partial^2 D}{\partial r^2} - 2\frac{\partial D}{\partial r}\right] + (\theta + 2\sigma)\frac{\partial^2 D}{\partial r^2}} > 0. \qquad (4.33)$$

This must be positive, given the signs of the partial derivatives from equation (4.26) and the fact that the denominator must be negative from the second order condition for a maximum. This result is essentially identical to the linear case, equation (4.10), and differs only in its inclusion of the final term in the denominator.

Since the properties of the quadratic case are similar to the properties of the linear case, several additional results are not derived explicitly but merely stated here. In each case the direction of these comparative statics results is identical to that of the profit maximization model. More specifically, changes in the past market interest rate i_{-1} do not affect the current deposit rate r_0 of an intermediary with a quadratic utility function, that is,

$$dr_0/di_{-1} = 0. \qquad (4.34)$$

Changes in the expected future market rate i_1, however, have an inverse impact on the current optimal deposit rate r_0, that is,

$$dr_0/di_1 < 0. \qquad (4.35)$$

Furthermore, the comparative statics effect on deposit rates that results from a change in the liquidity ratio is

$$\frac{dr}{dk} = \frac{-\gamma i(\partial D/\partial r)}{\gamma\left[(ik - r)\frac{\partial^2 D}{\partial r^2} - 2\frac{\partial D}{\partial r}\right] + (\theta + 2\sigma)\frac{\partial^2 D}{\partial r^2}} > 0. \qquad (4.36)$$

This expression is positive, which implies that the lower the liquidity ratio, that is, the higher k, the higher the optimal deposit rate. Finally, if a shift variable s is included in the demand function for savings deposits, shifts in demand have an inverse impact on deposit rates, that is,

$$\frac{dr}{ds} = \frac{\gamma(\partial D/\partial s)}{\gamma\left[(ik - r)\frac{\partial^2 D}{\partial r^2} - 2\frac{\partial D}{\partial r}\right] + (\theta + 2\sigma)\frac{\partial^2 D}{\partial r^2}} \gtreqless 0. \qquad (4.37)$$

Thus, increases in factors that favorably influence demand ($\partial D/\partial s > 0$) lower deposit rates, while increases in unfavorable factors raise deposit rates.[f]

Overall, if it is assumed that financial intermediaries maximize utility where both profits and deposits are positive linear arguments of the utility function, the comparative statics properties are quite similar to those derived from a model of profit maximization. If the assumptions are altered so that deposits enter the utility function in quadratic form, the character of the comparative statics results is not affected.

---

[f] The comparative statics result for the effect of advertising has the same negative sign as in the linear utility function case.

5 A Cross Section Analysis of Savings Deposit Rates at Savings and Loan Associations

The theoretical models developed in the previous chapters provide substantial information about the deposit rate setting behavior of financial intermediaries. These theoretical results provide the framework for empirical specification and testing of deposit rate functions, which is the focus of this chapter. In the three previous chapters we have analyzed the implications of alternative motives for the behavior of financial intermediaries. We have hypothesized that these institutions may seek to maximize profit, maximize deposits, or maximize the utility derived from some combination of both profits and deposits. For each theoretical model we have obtained comparative statics results that provide considerable insight for the empirical testing of deposit rate equations. All three models imply that deposit rate setting behavior can be viewed as basically a function of three categories of variables: market interest rates, factors that alter the public's demand for savings deposits, and variables that reflect the operating efficiency of an intermediary. In general, the models of profit and utility maximization yield identical comparative statics results for the determinants of deposit rates. In both of these models, the level of deposit rates is a positive function of current market rates, a category that includes both interest rates on assets available for the intermediary's portfolio and yields on instruments that the public regards as substitutes for the intermediary's liabilities. Past portfolio investment decisions do not affect current deposit rate setting behavior. Economic factors, such as income or population, that shift the public's demand for savings deposits have an inverse effect on the optimal deposit rate. The level of advertising by the intermediary also has a negative influence on deposit rates. Finally, the theoretical results indicate that the higher the reserve ratio and the degree of liquidity of an institution, the lower its revenues from portfolio holdings and thus the lower its deposit rate. It is also possible that intermediaries with little liquidity may be viewed as risky by depositors, and as a result the public might require a risk premium in order to hold the liabilities of such an institution. In either case, the indicated impact of liquidity on the pattern of deposit rates is negative.

The theoretical results derived for a model of deposit maximization are similar to the profit maximization case, but there are several important differences. The optimal deposit rate of an intermediary that maximizes deposits directly follows movements in asset rates but is inversely related to movements in yields on instruments that are close substitutes for its deposits. In addition, past portfolio decisions do have an important role in this model, since current deposit rates are a positive function of the yields on the institution's inherited portfolio. Finally, economic factors, such as income or population, that shift the public's demand for savings deposits have a positive effect on the optimal deposit rate. In this model the institution responds to favorable shifts in demand by raising its deposit rate, whereas a profit maximizing institution responds by lowering its deposit rate.

Since several important differences emerge in the empirical implications of the theoretical models developed in chapters 2 through 4, it is possible to test empirically these alternate hypotheses in order to determine which type of behavior characterizes financial intermediaries. The purpose of this chapter is to undertake a quantitative investigation of the deposit rate setting behavior of financial institutions and to test empirically which model can explain the behavior of financial intermediaries. The empirical results for specifications derived from these theoretical models are evaluated by using the hypothesized signs of the comparative statics results.

The three theoretical models describe the microeconomic behavior of the individual intermediary. Consequently, the empirical investigation of deposit rate setting begins with an analysis using cross section data. The magnitude of the requirements for data collection and processing preclude the use of samples of all of the major types of financial intermediaries, that is, commercial banks, savings and loan associations, and mutual savings banks. As a result, the cross section analysis is confined to a sample of savings and loan associations for the period 1961-1967. There are several reasons for this decision. First, there has been a considerable amount of research that has successfully used profit maximization models to explain commercial bank behavior. A well known empirical study of commercial bank behavior is Goldfeld [22]. In the case of the savings and loan industry, however, economists have not reached a consensus on the behavioral motivation of savings and loan associations and have generally concluded that the industry appears to act without well defined goals. Hester [34] and Goldfeld [24], for example, each concluded that savings and loan deposit rates could not be explained on the basis of any consistent behavioral hypothesis. Using a cross section analysis of the savings and loan industry, we can establish whether this type of financial intermediary behaves rationally, and we can evaluate what type of model is most applicable. Second, during most of the sample period there were ceiling restrictions on deposit rates at commercial banks but not on savings and loan deposit rates. Therefore, the estimation of savings and loan deposit rate equations for most of these years is not biased by rate ceilings. Third, savings and loan associations comprise the only important form of financial intermediaries that includes both stock and mutual types of ownership. This cross section analysis includes both types of savings and loan associations in the sample in order to evaluate whether chartering status affects the deposit rate behavior of financial intermediaries. Fourth, the deposit rate behavior of savings and loan associations has been characterized by substantial geographical variation, which previous researchers have had little success in explaining. This makes a cross section analysis of these institutions particularly appropriate. Fifth, given the developed character of the savings market in the United States, it seems reasonable to assume that the response of savings and loan associations to their economic environment is a good proxy for the behavior of savings institutions in general.

The cross section analysis is carried out for a sample of 544 savings and loan associations located in six major areas of the United States. The six areas comprise the following metropolitan centers: Cleveland, Chicago, Houston, Dallas, Los Angeles, and San Francisco. These areas are chosen because they include not only highly urban as well as less developed economic areas but also substantial numbers of both stock and mutual associations.[a] The six areas comprise a total of 25 Standard Metropolitan Statistical Areas (SMSAs) and seven additional counties. The cross section analysis is yearly over the period 1961-1967.[b]

The previous empirical literature on the deposit rate setting behavior of savings and loan associations is limited. A 1968 study by Hester [34] based on a large sample of savings and loan associations for the years 1961-1964 concluded that deposit rate setting is characterized by sharp regional disparities, which he presumed were due to disequilibrium phenomena. Furthermore, Hester found that stock associations typically pay higher deposit rates and apparently absorb more risk in their portfolios than mutual associations. In a 1969 cross section study covering the years 1961-1964, Goldfeld [24] confirmed Hester's findings and further established that geographical variation in deposit rates is also substantial within states and even individual SMSAs. Goldfeld had little success explaining this phenomena but again confirmed that stock associations pay significantly higher deposit rates than mutual associations. In another 1969 study, Dhrymes and Taubman [15] estimated time series of cross section deposit rate equations for about 100 SMSAs. Their final equations have little structure, however, and are essentially limited to lagged dependent variables. To a large extent these studies relied primarily on the use of dummy

---

[a]The sample does not include associations from the eastern portions of the United States because the institutions in this area are predominantly mutual in chartering status.

[b]The sample consists of annual observations for individual savings and loan associations. The data were obtained from unpublished confidential balance sheet and income reports filed with the Federal Home Loan Bank Board. The associations included in the sample were in operation for all seven years and did not change chartering status during the period. No data were available for years prior to 1961.

variables in order to hold constant the serious geographical variation in savings and loan deposit rates. Nevertheless, the conclusions of each study were quite pessimistic about the degree to which the variation in deposit rates can be explained even with the inclusion of such dummies. In fact in both Hester's and Goldfeld's studies, the percentage of variation in deposit rates explained by their regressions seldom exceeds 30-40 per cent.

In this study, the specification of the independent variables for the deposit rate equations is derived from the comparative statics results obtained from the theoretical models. Our objective is to explain the behavior of savings and loan deposit rates based on the variables suggested by these theoretical models without recourse to the use of geographical dummy variables. Our purpose is to make more positive economic statements about the variation of deposit rates than can be obtained by means of dummies, which are presumably just proxies for unspecified economic variables.

Specification and Description of the Variables

The independent variables used in the regression analysis can be grouped into several categories, which directly follow from the theoretical results. (All variable symbols are defined in the glossary.) First, the comparative statics results indicated that movements in market rates have an important impact on deposit rates. Consequently, one category of independent variable is market yields, that is, both asset and competing interest rates. Specifically, we test four interest rate series. Current asset rates are proxied by the current mortgage rates i_1 and a mortgage fees variable i_2.[c] The average yield on an institution's mortgage portfolio i_3 is also included as a variable that can be regarded as either a reflection of past portfolio decisions, or a measure of lagged mortgage rates which serve as a proxy for future expected market rates. The commercial bank time deposit rate i_4 is taken as a measure of competing rates available to depositors at savings and loan associations.[d]

Second, the comparative statics results indicated that changes in the liquidity ratio affect the pattern of deposit rates. In the empirical analysis the concept of the liquidity ratio is generalized to include a measure of the

---

[c]Regional data for mortgage rates and mortgage fees were obtained from periodic releases of the Federal Home Loan Bank Board, which were issued beginning in 1963. Consequently, these variables are omitted in regressions for 1961 and 1962. Mortgage fees are quoted as a percentage rate.

[d]This variable is the effective time deposit rate at Federal Reserve System member banks in the central cities of the major geographical areas included in the sample. The data were obtained from balance sheet and income reports for individual banks, which are submitted to the Board of Governors on an annual basis.

riskiness of the institution's interest earning assets. Two variables are tested in this category: the ratio of reserves and surplus to the level of deposits k_1 and the ratio of scheduled items, that is, mortgages in default or foreclosure, to the quantity of mortgages k_2.

The third category of independent variables is derived from the comparative statics result that the level of deposit rates is affected by factors that shift the public's demand for savings deposits. Three variables are included in this category. One variable is per capita income s_1, while the other two are measures of the degree of competition in the local financial market, namely, savings and loan offices per capita s_2 and the number of commercial bank employees per capita s_3.[e]

The fourth category of independent variables reflect alternative methods of obtaining deposits that are substitutes for deposit rate changes. More specifically, the theoretical analysis indicated that the level of deposit rates is inversely related to the degree of advertising carried out by the institution. Thus, the ratio of advertising expenditures to deposits a_1 is specified in the deposit rate equations. Similarly, the number of branches maintained by a savings and loan association a_2 is included in this category, since it is possible that the opening of branches may serve as a substitute for changes in deposit rates.[f]

The final category of variables consists of miscellaneous factors not directly derived from the theoretical models but instead drawn from general financial considerations. There are three variables in this category. First, it is assumed that in the short run a substantial proportion of new mortgage holdings are demand determined. Therefore, the change in mortgages scaled by deposits x_1 is used as a variable to test whether sudden changes in the public's demand for mortgages have a temporary impact on deposit rates. Second, the ratio of fee income to total income x_2 is used to measure the importance of a variety of fees, such as prepayment penalties and fees required for a mortgage assumption, that are closely associated with the presence of rapid turnover in mortgages and thus reflect the mobility of the population. Such a variable tests whether the rapid turnover of mortgages, hence higher fees, raises effective mortgage rates, which might influence deposit rates. A third variable included in this category is a measure of economies of scale x_3, which is taken as the logarithm of total assets. A positive sign is indicative of economies of scale.

---

[e]Population data for these variables were obtained by interpolation of SMSA figures for the 1960 and 1970 census [9] using the assumption that there was a constant rate of population growth over the decade. Data for taxable payroll income and the number of commercial bank employees on a regional basis were obtained from surveys by the Census Bureau [8]. Since data for the year 1961 are unavailable, variables s_1 and s_3, are omitted from the regressions for that year.

[f]Data on the number of branches were not collected after 1963; consequently this variable is only included in regressions for the years 1961, 1962, and 1963.

The dependent variable in the regression analysis is the effective rate of interest offered by each individual savings and loan association on its savings deposits.[g]

Table 5-1 provides a summary of the expected signs of the regression coefficients predicted a priori on the basis of the theoretical results reported in chapters 2 through 4 and general financial considerations. This table constitutes a framework for evaluating the empirical results and drawing conclusions as to whether the behavior of financial intermediaries can be best characterized by a model of profit, deposit, or utility maximization.

Deposit rate equations are estimated on a cross section basis for the years 1961 through 1967 using combinations of the 14 independent variables. Separate regressions are estimated for each year. The equations are first estimated for all 544 savings and loan associations in the sample. The sample is then disaggregated on the basis of chartering status, and regressions are estimated separately for stock and mutual associations in order to determine if these types of associations are characterized by different deposit rate setting behavior.

Because of the multicollinearity intrinsic to the independent variables, it was impossible to obtain effective estimation results for equations that contained all 14 independent variables in the specification. Since collinearity was most severe between the series for market interest rates, which vary regionally, and the variables that reflect shift factors in the public's demand for savings deposits, the following estimation procedure was adopted. The deposit rate regressions are first estimated for each year with all of the interest rate variables included in the specification but with the shift variables, per capita income s_1, commercial bank employment s_3, and savings and loan offices s_2 excluded from the equation. The results for this specification are reported in Table 5-2. Next, these equations are reestimated with the shift variables included in the regressions but with interest rate variables omitted. In most cases the omitted interest rate variables are the current mortgage rate i_1 and the mortgage fee variable i_2, with the commercial bank time deposit rate i_4 retained in the specification. This choice seems preferable since the bank deposit rate is available for all years in the sample, but mortgage rates are not available for 1961 and 1962. The estimation results for this specification are reported in Table 5-3. Because of further multicollinearity problems for 1964, an additional equation is reported in Table 5-3 in which the commercial bank time deposit rate is omitted and the mortgage rate variables are included. In each table the estimated coefficients are reported with the relevant t statistics found in parentheses below the coefficients. The multiple correlation coefficient R

---

[g]This variable is obtained by dividing the dividends paid out to depositors by the average quantity of deposits during the year.

Table 5-1
Summary of Signs for Variables Implied by the Theoretical Models

	Profit	Deposit	Utility
i_1	+	+	+
i_2	+	+	+
i_3	+	+	+
i_4	+	−	+
k_1	−	−	−
k_2	+	+	+
s_1	−	+	−
s_2	−	+	−
s_3	+	−	+
a_1	−	−	−
a_2	−	−	−
x_1	+	+	+
x_2	+	+	+
x_3	+	+	+

and the Durbin-Watson statistic are also reported. The equations are listed in chronological order. First, the results for the full sample of associations are examined followed by an analysis of the results obtained when the sample is disaggregated by organizational form.

Analysis of the Full Sample Results

The equations for the pooled sample are examined first for Specification I, in which the shift variables are omitted but all of the interest rate series are included (Table 5-2) and second for Specification II, which includes the shift variables along with a selection of the available asset or competing interest rates (Table 5-3). Overall, the empirical results are quite good in both the degree of explanatory power and the significance of the independent variables, particularly since we are dealing with cross section variation.[h] Previous researchers concluded that the substantial variation in deposit rates at savings and loan associations could not be satisfactorily resolved by the techniques of economic analysis. For example, the regressions in Hester [34], Goldfeld [24], and Dhrymes and Taubman [15] generally explain only 30 to 40 per cent of the variation in deposit rates. The character of the results reported in Tables 5-2 and 5-3, however, clearly indicates that the behavior of the interest rates on savings deposits is susceptible to theoretical modeling and can be substantiated by empirical testing. In general, the estimated coefficients exhibit a clear behavioral

---
[h]In this volume, coefficients are considered to be significant if they are statistically different from zero at the 95 per cent level of significance.

Table 5-2
Full Sample Results for Specification I

	i_1	i_2	i_3	i_4	k_1	k_2	a_1	a_2	x_1	x_2	x_3	C	R/DW
1961			0.3536 (13.53)	0.2722 (2.93)	0.0037 (1.23)	0.0011 (0.90)	−0.0817 (−1.41)	−0.0004 (−4.27)	0.0000 (3.10)	−0.0002 (−0.08)	0.0010 (7.29)	−0.0044 (−1.60)	0.67 1.76
1962			0.3112 (10.66)	−0.1878 (−2.16)	0.0058 (1.34)	0.0268 (2.73)	−0.3423 (−3.71)	−0.0002 (−2.63)	0.0045 (8.73)	0.0062 (2.17)	0.0014 (12.71)	0.0050 (1.14)	0.72 1.47
1963	0.6717 (2.00)	0.4643 (4.88)	0.2576 (8.65)	−1.143 (−5.26)	0.0071 (1.77)	−0.0054 (−1.02)	−0.1952 (−2.48)	−0.0000 (−1.58)	0.0025 (5.07)	0.0104 (3.84)	0.0008 (7.95)	0.0115 (0.44)	0.79 1.80
1963a	2.129 (11.00)	0.6833 (7.79)	0.2500 (8.20)		0.0065 (1.59)	−0.0059 (−0.91)	−0.2229 (−2.77)	−0.0000 (−1.56)	0.0028 (5.81)	0.0109 (3.93)	0.0007 (7.26)	−0.1146 (−10.21)	0.78 1.77
1964	0.0089 (0.11)	0.2545 (3.77)	0.1801 (4.14)	−2.247 (−7.66)	0.0015 (0.28)	0.0020 (0.25)	−0.2500 (−1.65)		0.0074 (6.78)	0.0031 (0.61)	0.0004 (3.05)	0.1044 (8.00)	0.71 1.66
1964a	0.1239 (1.55)	0.1391 (2.01)	0.2669 (6.05)		0.0010 (1.80)	0.0047 (0.55)	−0.2974 (−1.86)		0.0053 (4.81)	0.0228 (5.01)	0.0005 (4.05)	0.0076 (2.20)	0.67 1.60
1965	0.4338 (8.06)	−0.0438 (−0.73)	0.3055 (12.46)	0.7320 (9.94)	0.0061 (1.69)	0.0033 (0.86)	−0.3076 (−3.03)		0.0005 (1.16)	0.0211 (5.87)	0.0007 (8.96)	−0.0418 (−10.47)	0.86 1.76
1966	0.5516 (4.74)	−0.0654 (−1.39)	0.4105 (13.78)	0.2198 (4.89)	0.0186 (4.05)	0.0048 (1.02)	0.0834 (0.57)		−0.0025 (−1.57)	0.0360 (6.78)	0.0012 (13.31)	−0.0049 (−6.67)	0.81 1.61
1967	0.9470 (7.59)	0.1237 (2.59)	0.3161 (9.10)	0.1916 (4.73)	0.0123 (2.51)	0.0050 (0.98)	0.2603 (1.55)		−0.0005 (−0.67)	0.0003 (1.64)	0.0012 (11.44)	−0.0530 (−8.38)	0.81 1.71

Symbol definitions: i_1, current mortgage rate; i_2, mortgage fees; i_3, average mortgage rate; i_4, commercial bank time deposit rate; k_1, ratio of reserves and surplus to deposits; k_2, ratio of scheduled items to total mortgages; a_1, ratio of advertising expenditures to deposits; a_2, number of branches; x_1, change in mortgages scaled by deposits; x_2, ratio of fee income to total income; x_3, logarithm of total assets; C, constant.

pattern, and the *t* statistics are quite good despite the problems of multicollinearity. Moreover, depending upon the year and the specification chosen, the regressions explain from 50 per cent to 80 per cent of the variation in deposit rates. Overall, the pattern of estimated coefficients suggests that the deposit rate setting behavior of financial intermediaries is in accordance with the results suggested by the profit or utility maximization models and does not support the hypothesis of deposit maximization.

More specifically, in Table 5-2, results are reported for the full sample of savings and loan associations including all of the independent variables except the variables that reflect shifts in demand. Almost all of the asset rate coefficients are positive, which is consistent with the theoretical expectations for both the profit and deposit maximization models. Most of the coefficients are significant at the 5 per cent level. The current mortgage rate and the mortgage fees variables i_1 and i_2 behave particularly well over the period. The average mortgage yield i_3 is also strongly significant in each year, with the coefficients ranging in size from about 0.2 to 0.4, which indicates that a 100 basis point rise in the yield on the mortgage portfolio would induce a 20 to 40 basis point rise in deposit rates. (In Hester's results [34], this variable has a coefficient of only 0.086.) There is some variation in the sign of the competing rate coefficients i_4 in 1963 and 1964, which is probably due to the presence of multicollinearity. Consequently, for these two years regression results that exclude this rate are also reported. Nevertheless, the positive sign of most of the coefficients for the competing rate variable i_4 provides some evidence supporting the applicability of the profit maximization model. For most years in the sample the sum of all the interest rate coefficients is quite large. This result, which is in contrast to earlier studies, provides substantial evidence that deposit rates do respond significantly in movements in market rates.

Both the advertising and branch-office variables a_1 and a_2 respectively, generally have a negative sign and are often statistically significant. This indicates that changes in advertising policy and the opening of new branches can serve as substitutes for changes in deposit rates at savings and loan associations. Nevertheless, the coefficients are small in absolute size, which indicates that normal variation in these variables can serve as only a limited substitute for deposit rate changes.[i]

The coefficients of the two variables that are proxies for the degree of risk that characterizes the association's portfolio generally fail to be statistically significant. The ratio of reserves to deposits k_1 is uniformly positive, which is contrary to the result predicted by the theoretical models. How-

---

[i]The advertising variable fails to obtain the correct sign in 1966 and 1967 although it is not statistically different from zero. This may be due to the presence of ceiling restrictions on deposit rates, which were instituted during these years. Since deposit rates for some of the institutions in the sample were at or near the legal ceiling, deposit rate increases could no longer be effectively used as substitutes for advertising during these years.

Table 5-3
Full Sample Results for Specification II

	i_1	i_2	i_3	i_4	s_1	s_2	s_3
1961			0.3602 (13.57)	0.4220 (2.66)		25.76 (0.64)	
1962			0.2435 (7.22)	1.025 (3.71)	−0.0001 (−4.66)	−376.2 (0.00)	2.084 (5.77)
1963			0.2718 (9.31)	0.7487 (2.06)	−0.0000 (−2.64)	−231.7 (−5.94)	2.907 (5.99)
1964			0.1895 (4.62)	−1.784 (−6.13)	−0.0000 (−3.61)		1.427 (4.98)
1964a	0.4728 (4.33)	0.0228 (0.31)	0.2071 (4.80)		0.0000 (0.93)		2.035 (6.64)
1965			0.3232 (13.72)	0.8935 (6.52)	−0.0000 (−7.92)		0.1228 (0.45)
1966			0.2562 (8.37)	0.0722 (1.37)	−0.0000 (−11.91)		1.255 (5.90)
1967			0.2736 (8.00)	0.1298 (2.31)	−0.0000 (−13.20)		1.299 (5.08)

ever, the coefficients are seldom significant. The ratio of scheduled items to total assets k_2 is sometimes positive, which would be consistent with the view that depositors require a risk premium from institutions with risky portfolios, but the variable is usually insignificant and is actually negative in several cases. Thus, the evidence suggests that depositors do not require any risk premium to compensate for the character of the loans of an intermediary. Although these results contrast with the conclusions of previous researchers (both Hester [34] and Goldfeld [24] found several risk variables to be quite significant), it does seem logical that in most cases depositors have little awareness of the character of an institution's portfolio, especially since all of the institutions in the sample have insurance provisions for their deposits.

The remaining variables, x_1, x_2, and x_3, generally obtain the expected sign and are usually significant. The mortgage flow variable x_1 has positive and significant coefficients in all years except 1966 and 1967. It is likely that the initiation of ceiling restrictions on savings deposit rates during these years may have prevented associations from adjusting their deposit rates upward in response to sudden increases in mortgage demand. Nevertheless, it appears that these institutions generally alter deposit rates in order to balance short run asset and liability flows. The pattern of the coefficients for the fee income variable x_2 is strongly positive throughout the period. This probably indicates that institutions in areas characterized by rapid turnover in mortgages offer higher deposit rates than those in areas where

k_1	k_2	a_1	a_2	x_1	x_2	x_3	C	R/DW
0.0033	0.0078	−0.0827	−0.0004	0.0000	−0.0015	0.0009	−0.0080	0.69
(1.14)	(0.64)	(−1.43)	(−4.01)	(3.05)	(−0.54)	(6.66)	(−1.32)	1.78
0.0030	0.0187	−0.3169	−0.0002	0.0041	0.0058	0.0013	−0.0068	0.74
(0.71)	(1.93)	(−3.48)	(−2.58)	(7.85)	(1.97)	(11.49)	(−0.00)	1.53
0.0039	−0.0107	−0.2063	−0.0000	0.0026	0.0069	0.0007	−0.0020	0.81
(0.98)	(−1.70)	(−2.69)	(−1.56)	(5.45)	(2.54)	(7.61)	(−0.11)	1.89
0.0012	0.0019	−0.1949		0.0070	0.0020	0.0004	0.0876	0.71
(0.22)	(0.23)	(−1.30)		(6.57)	(0.40)	(3.57)	(6.64)	1.67
0.0005	0.0040	−0.3154		0.0064	0.0124	0.0004	−0.0158	0.70
(0.10)	(0.49)	(−2.05)		(5.94)	(2.70)	(3.10)	(−2.22)	1.65
0.0105	0.0030	−0.2437		0.0001	0.0203	0.0008	−0.0200	0.86
(2.94)	(0.78)	(−2.39)		(3.45)	(5.54)	(10.92)	(−4.29)	1.71
0.0180	0.0036	0.0698		−0.0016	0.0292	0.0010	0.0128	0.85
(4.32)	(0.86)	(0.52)		(−1.10)	(6.00)	(10.67)	(2.97)	1.62
0.0128	0.0037	0.2388		−0.0004	0.0003	0.0011	0.0137	0.82
(2.68)	(0.74)	(1.47)		(−0.54)	(1.55)	(10.81)	(3.01)	1.77

Symbol definitions: i_1, current mortgage rate; i_2, mortgage fees; i_3, average mortgage rate; i_4, commercial bank time deposit rate; s_1, income per capita; s_2, savings and loan offices per capita; s_3, commercial bank employment per capita; k_1, ratio of reserves and surplus to deposits; k_2, ratio of scheduled items to total mortgages; a_1, ratio of advertising expenditures to deposits; a_2, number of branches; x_1, change in mortgages scaled by deposits; x_2, ratio of fee income to total income; x_3, logarithm of total assets; C, constant.

fees associated with mortgage services represent a smaller proportion of total income. The results for the logarithm of total assets x_3 are always positive and generally highly significant. Although the size of the coefficients is small, it seems clear that the savings and loan industry is characterized to some degree by the presence of economies of scale.

As previously explained, severe problems of multicollinearity necessitate the omission of some independent variables in the estimation procedure. In Table 5-2 we reported equations for all associations in the sample for the years 1961-1967, which included all of the interest rate variables but omitted the variables that reflect shifts in the public's demand for deposits. Next we undertake the reestimation of these equations based upon specifications that include the three shift variables and omit the current mortgage rate and mortgage fees variables. In these regressions the commercial bank time deposit rate i_4 serves as a general proxy for the regional variation in current market rates.

The full sample regression results are reported in Table 5-3. Overall, these results represent considerable improvement over the results for the previous specification. In every case the goodness of fit is substantially increased and the number of incorrect signs is reduced, particularly for the interest rate variables. The statistical significance of most of the coefficients is also enhanced. Since the coefficients of the variables included in both specifications generally display similar properties in the two sets of estimation results, only the results for the added shift variables are discussed here. These variables are of particular importance because the comparative statics properties developed in the previous chapters demonstrated that the impact of these shift variables on deposit rates is different for a profit maximizer compared to a deposit maximizer. It was demonstrated that a profit maximizing intermediary responds to favorable changes in these shift variables by lowering its deposit rate, but a deposit maximizing intermediary responds by increasing its deposit rate. Thus, the estimation results for these shift variables provide a clear indication of the relative usefulness of the two models.

The results for the income per capita variable s_1 are quite good. Although the coefficients appear small in absolute size, they are consistently negative as predicted by the profit maximization model and are strongly significant in each year. Consequently, savings and loan deposit rates do reflect regional difference in per capita income. Most of the coefficients of s_1 are approximately -0.00002, which indicates that an increase of $50 in per capita income induces savings and loan associations to lower deposit rates by ten basis points. The shift variable s_3 is the number of commercial bank employees in the area, which is specified in order to reflect the degree of competition from commercial banks. The results for this variable are also consistent with the model of profit maximization. The coefficients are positive for every year and are almost uniformly statistically significant. This suggests that in areas characterized by the extensive presence of commercial banking facilities, savings and loan associations offer higher deposit rates. Because of data limitations, the variable for the number of savings and loan offices in the area s_2 can be calculated only for the years 1961, 1962, and 1963. The estimated coefficients for these three years do not, however, indicate any clear pattern. Moreover, it is not clear a priori whether an increase in the number of offices would necessarily represent a favorable shift in demand for an individual association. Although an increase in offices would tend to make the industry more well known to the public relative to commercial banks which would be a favorable factor, it would also heighten the degree of competition for the individual association, which would cause an unfavorable shift in the demand function. As a result, the lack of an unambiguous sign in the estimation results for this variable is not surprising. Nevertheless, the overall empirical results for the variables s_1 and s_3 clearly indicate that regional variations in the economic environment in which savings and loan associations operate have a significant effect on deposit rates and that the direction of this impact is

Table 5-4
Summary of Interest Rate Coefficients for Specification I and Specification II

	Specification I						Specification II				
	i_1	i_2	i_3	i_4	Σi_t	i_1	i_2	i_3	i_4	Σi_{tt}
1961			0.35 (13.55)	0.27 (2.93)	0.62			0.36 (13.57)	0.42 (2.66)	0.78
1962			0.31 (10.66)	−0.19 (−2.16)	0.12			0.24 (7.22)	1.02 (3.71)	1.26
1963	0.67 (2.00)	0.46 (4.88)	0.26 (8.65)	−1.14 (−5.26)	0.25			0.27 (9.31)	0.75 (2.06)	1.02
1963a	2.13 (11.00)	0.68 (7.79)	0.25 (8.20)		3.06					
1964	0.01 (0.11)	0.25 (3.77)	0.18 (4.14)	−2.25 (−7.66)	−1.81			0.19 (4.62)	−1.78 (−6.13)	−1.59
1964a	0.12 (1.55)	0.14 (2.01)	0.27 (6.05)		0.53	0.47 (4.33)	0.02 (0.31)	0.21 (4.80)		0.70
1965	0.43 (8.06)	−0.04 (−0.73)	0.31 (12.46)	0.73 (9.94)	1.43			0.32 (13.72)	0.89 (6.52)	1.21
1966	0.55 (4.74)	−0.07 (−1.39)	0.41 (13.78)	0.22 (0.489)	1.11			0.26 (8.37)	0.07 (1.37)	0.33
1967	0.95 (7.59)	0.12 (2.59)	0.32 (9.10)	0.19 (4.73)	1.58			0.27 (8.00)	0.13 (2.31)	0.40

Table 5-5
Stock-Mutual Dummy Coefficients for Full Sample Regressions

	Specification I	Specification II
1961	−0.0010	−0.0010
	(−3.04)	(−2.83)
1962	−0.0005	−0.0004
	(−1.75)	(−1.24)
1963	−0.0003	0.0001
	(−1.23)	(0.31)
1963a	−0.0004	
	(−1.54)	
1964	−0.0003	−0.0004
	(−0.87)	(−1.04)
1964a	−0.0008	−0.0004
	(−2.21)	(−1.04)
1965	0.0002	0.0000
	(1.07)	(0.07)
1966	−0.0003	0.0000
	(−1.01)	(0.82)
1967	−0.0003	−0.0004
	(−1.14)	(−1.39)

consistent with the theory of profit maximization and contrary to the hypothesis of deposit maximization.

Furthermore, the strong significance of these shift variables suggests that in the estimation results for the equations without these variables, reported earlier in Table 5-2, the pattern of interest rate coefficients, especially the mortgage rate and mortgage fees variables, probably reflected the influence of these shift factors as well as the behavior of interest rates. The explicit inclusion of these shift factors enhances the estimation results for the remaining interest rate variables. Table 5-4 is a summary of the interest rate results for the two specifications estimated over the full sample. The values for the sum of the interest rate coefficients for the second specification Σi_{II} are more reasonable than the values for the initial specification Σi_I. For 1961 through 1963 and 1965 the sums for Specification II are close to unity, which implies that the savings and loan industry transmitted to depositors approximately the full amount of an increase in open market yields. The rate coefficients for 1964 sum to an unreasonable negative figure because of the coefficient of the commercial bank time deposit rate. There is, however, a substantial improvement in the sum when the equation for 1964 is estimated using the current mortgage rate variables i_1 and i_2 and omitting the commercial bank time deposit rate i_4. The coefficients in this case sum to 0.70, which indicates that at least until 1966, savings and loan associations passed on to depositors almost the full amount of market rate increases. Only the summed values for 1966 and

Table 5-6
Mutual Association Results for Specification I

	i_1	i_2	i_3	i_4	k_1	k_2	a_1	a_2	x_1	x_2	x_3	C	R/DW
1961			0.2456	0.4348	0.0269	0.0506	−0.3914	−0.0003	0.0088	0.0058	0.0008	−0.0028	0.76
			(6.47)	(4.58)	(4.64)	(3.33)	(−3.70)	(−2.61)	(6.42)	(1.59)	(7.08)	(−0.99)	1.56
1962			0.3297	−0.1604	0.0257	0.0360	−0.4362	−0.0003	0.0079	0.0035	0.0011	0.0074	0.72
			(9.03)	(−1.41)	(4.60)	(2.26)	(−3.34)	(−2.52)	(7.04)	(0.90)	(9.16)	(1.34)	1.73
1963	1.112	0.5734	0.1936	−0.8926	0.0201	0.0085	−0.3044	−0.0000	0.0064	0.0078	0.0007	−0.0214	0.81
	(2.18)	(4.17)	(4.60)	(−2.85)	(4.17)	(1.02)	(−2.32)	(−3.35)	(6.40)	(2.00)	(6.82)	(−0.53)	1.70
1963a	2.383	0.8158	0.1857		0.0198	0.0094	−0.3352	−0.0000	0.0066	0.0077	0.0007	−0.1282	0.80
	(9.35)	(7.13)	(4.37)		(4.07)	(1.12)	(−2.53)	(−2.71)	(6.55)	(1.96)	(6.56)	(−8.64)	1.71
1964	0.0669	0.1907	0.1808	−0.2339	0.0177	0.0084	−0.1400		0.0108	0.0063	0.0003	0.1057	0.65
	(0.63)	(1.86)	(2.75)	(−4.78)	(2.34)	(0.77)	(−0.57)		(4.21)	(0.67)	(1.49)	(4.88)	1.58
1964a	0.2087	0.1891	0.2657		0.0192	0.0074	−0.2359		0.0084	0.0279	0.0003	0.0044	0.62
	(1.99)	(1.79)	(4.06)		(2.45)	(0.65)	(−0.93)		(3.22)	(3.29)	(1.83)	(0.97)	1.56
1965	0.3991	−0.1980	0.3286	0.8282	0.0144	−0.0036	−0.6283		−0.0010	0.0398	0.0009	−0.0474	0.77
	(1.73)	(−1.36)	(9.72)	(3.11)	(3.11)	(−0.69)	(−3.50)		(−1.70)	(6.64)	(8.79)	(−2.16)	1.74
1966	0.4582	−0.2723	0.4627	0.3556	0.0174	−0.0180	−0.5886		−0.0027	0.0298	0.0013	−0.0494	0.78
	(2.82)	(−4.21)	(14.25)	(4.60)	(3.45)	(−2.60)	(−3.03)		(−1.36)	(4.36)	(12.10)	(−4.18)	1.88
1967	0.6383	−0.1915	0.5641	0.2320	0.0122	−0.0169	−0.3609		−0.0006	0.0204	0.0013	−0.0624	0.76
	(3.05)	(−2.88)	(13.04)	(3.09)	(2.05)	(−1.79)	(−1.66)		(−0.62)	(2.45)	(11.00)	(−4.21)	1.81

Symbol definitions: i_1, current mortgage rate; i_2, mortgage fees; i_3, average mortgage rate; i_4, commercial bank time deposit rate; k_1, ratio of reserves and surplus to deposits; k_2, ratio of scheduled items to total mortgages; a_1, ratio of advertising expenditures to deposits; a_2, number of branches; x_1, change in mortgages scaled by deposits; x_2, ratio of fee income to total income; x_3, logarithm of total assets; C, constant.

Table 5-7
Mutual Association Results for Specification II

	i_1	i_2	i_3	i_4	s_1	s_2	s_3
1961			0.2399	0.3994		−11.76	
			(6.24)	(2.24)		(−0.26)	
1962			0.2452	1.506	−0.0001	−3750.	2.909
			(5.50)	(3.52)	(−3.97)	(−0.00)	(5.65)
1963			0.1832	0.8014	−0.0000	−253.5	2.795
			(4.43)	(1.55)	(−1.60)	(−4.40)	(4.49)
1964			0.2055	−2.023	−0.0000		1.541
			(3.27)	(−4.19)	(−2.21)		(3.46)
1964a	0.6200	−0.0808	0.2122		0.0000		2.542
	(3.89)	(−0.66)	(3.31)		(0.90)		(4.98)
1965			0.2123	0.5974	−0.0000		0.5376
			(5.92)	(2.66)	(−6.78)		(1.13)
1966			0.2450	0.1116	−0.0000		1.335
			(6.67)	(1.58)	(−12.39)		(4.19)
1967			0.2922	0.0670	−0.0000		1.373
			(5.18)	(0.79)	(−8.82)		(3.30)

1967 are substantially less than unity. The results for these years probably reflect the effectiveness of the ceiling rate restrictions established during this time by the Federal Home Loan Bank Board.

Overall, the cross section results for the full sample of savings and loan associations indicate that the deposit rate setting behavior of financial intermediaries is susceptible to theoretical modeling and economic analysis. The empirical specifications drawn from the theoretical models yield many coefficients with strong t statistics and explain from 50 to 80 per cent of the cross section variation in deposit rates. Furthermore, the pattern of the coefficients supports the hypothesis that intermediary behavior is characterized by profit, not deposit, maximization. In general, the use of specifications that include variables that reflect shifts in the public's demand for savings deposits substantially improves the significance of the coefficients and the overall fit of the regressions. Also, the estimation results for Specification II indicate that the sum of the interest rate coefficients is close to unity, at least until 1966. This implies that increases in open market yields were almost fully passed on to depositors through changes in deposit rates.

Disaggregation by Chartering Status: Stock versus Mutual

The savings and loan industry is comprised of both mutual and stock associations. Consequently, an important policy question for the govern-

k_1	k_2	a_1	a_2	x_1	x_2	x_3	C	R/DW
0.0259	0.0487	−0.4162	−0.0003	0.0088	0.0044	0.0008	−0.0007	0.76
(4.50)	(3.21)	(−3.92)	(−2.57)	(6.38)	(1.15)	(7.04)	(−0.10)	1.61
0.0240	0.0330	−0.3693	−0.0003	0.0067	0.0030	0.0010	0.1013	0.75
(4.45)	(2.15)	(−2.94)	(−2.39)	(5.82)	(0.72)	(8.75)	(0.00)	1.98
0.0188	0.0058	−0.2809	−0.0000	0.0064	0.0051	0.0007	−0.0088	0.82
(3.97)	(0.71)	(−2.18)	(−3.05)	(6.59)	(1.31)	(6.65)	(−0.52)	1.76
0.0178	0.0054	−0.0627		0.0100	0.0034	0.0003	0.0951	0.67
(2.39)	(0.51)	(−0.26)		(3.96)	(0.36)	(1.94)	(4.48)	1.57
0.0167	0.0069	−0.0809		0.0096	0.0120	0.0002	−0.0264	0.66
(2.22)	(0.63)	(−0.33)		(3.82)	(1.38)	(1.38)	(−2.33)	1.58
0.0134	−0.0008	−0.5304		−0.0014	0.0260	0.0007	0.0023	0.81
(3.15)	(−0.17)	(−3.22)		(−2.65)	(4.54)	(6.85)	(0.03)	1.86
0.0166	−0.0125	−0.3185		−0.0033	0.0216	0.0008	0.0183	0.85
(3.79)	(−2.14)	(−1.92)		(−1.94)	(3.71)	(7.92)	(3.65)	1.65
0.0127	−0.0142	−0.1052		−0.0012	0.0132	0.0009	0.0180	0.80
(2.34)	(−1.66)	(−0.53)		(−1.33)	(1.76)	(7.39)	(2.73)	1.85

Symbol definitions: i_1, current mortgage rate; i_2, mortgage fees; i_3, average mortgage rate; i_4, commercial bank time deposit rate; s_1, income per capita; s_2, savings and loan offices per capita: s_3, commercial bank employment per capita; k_1, ratio of reserves and surplus to deposits; k_2, ratio of scheduled items to total mortgages; a_1, ratio of advertising expenditures to deposits; a_2, number of branches; x_1, change in mortgages scaled by deposits; x_2, ratio of fee income to total income; x_3, logarithm of total assets; C, constant.

mental authorities that regulate the industry is whether deposit rate setting behavior differs with respect to chartering status. Evidence presented by earlier researchers indicated that there are important differences in the rate setting behavior of mutual and stock savings and loan associations. Specifically, as a result of introducing a stock-mutual dummy into deposit rate regressions, conclusions were drawn in previous studies that stock associations offer higher deposit rates than mutual associations. (See Hester [34] and Goldfeld [24].) In order to test whether such a difference in deposit rates is associated with the type of chartering status, a similar procedure is followed in this analysis. A stock-mutual dummy variable that takes on the value of unity for stock associations and zero for mutual associations is added to each of the estimated equations in Tables 5-2 and 5-3. The coefficients for the dummy variable are reported in Table 5-5. The coefficients for all of the other variables are essentially unaffected by the inclusion of the stock-mutual dummy and therefore are not reported. In contrast to the findings of previous researchers, the signs of thirteen of the seventeen coefficients are negative, which indicates that stock associations apparently offer lower yields on their liabilities than mutual associations. However, the variables are statistically significant in only three cases.

More importantly, the absolute value of the coefficients is insignificant, since the largest value is only −0.001. This implies that mutual and stock association deposit rates differ by less than ten basis points, ceteris paribus. Consequently, we can conclude that, given the same economic environment, both types of organizations offer the same level of deposit rates. Previous findings evidently captured differences in the economic environments within which stock and mutual associations operate rather than any differences in behavior.

In order to test further whether there are any important differences in the behavior of stock and mutual associations, the deposit rate equations are reestimated separately for the two types of associations. The results for the sample of mutual associations are reported in Tables 5-6 and 5-7 and the results for the sample of stock association are reported in Tables 5-8 and 5-9. Overall, there seem to be very few systematic differences between the pattern of the coefficients for the two sets of equations.

The question of whether to accept or reject the hypothesis that these two sets of coefficients are equal, is more formally examined by using the Chow test [10]. The results are reported in Table 5-10. Since the appropriate F statistic at the 5 per cent confidence level is 1.57, the Chow test results generally indicate rejection of the hypothesis that the two sets of coefficients are equal when the shift variables are omitted (Specification I). However, when the additional shift variables are included (Specification II), the Chow test results are fairly weak. Given these results and the fact that no systematic differences emerge in the empirical results when equations for stock and mutual associations are estimated separately, we can conclude that there are no substantial differences in the deposit rate setting behavior of the two types of associations. In the case of both stock and mutual associations, the behavior of deposit rates is fully consistent with the results for the theory of profit maximization and opposite to that of deposit maximization. Furthermore, the evidence clearly indicates that, given the same economic environment, both types of savings and loan associations offer the same level of deposit rates.

Conclusions

The empirical evidence about the pattern of deposit rates at a cross section of savings and loan associations provides substantial information about the deposit rate setting behavior of financial intermediaries. Several important conclusions about the determination of interest rates on savings deposits can be drawn from these empirical results. The first and most important conclusion is that deposit rates at savings and loan associations can be explained quite effectively on the basis of specifications derived from a

Table 5-8
Stock Association Results for Specification I

	i_1	i_2	i_3	i_4	k_1	k_2	a_1	a_2	x_1	x_2	x_3	C	R/DW
1961			0.3661 (9.13)	0.2962 (1.42)	0.0014 (0.28)	0.0040 (0.20)	0.0743 (0.84)	−0.0004 (−2.93)	0.0000 (2.47)	−0.0049 (−1.23)	0.0012 (3.55)	−0.0100 (−1.77)	0.67 1.71
1962			0.3211 (6.54)	−0.3270 (−2.36)	−0.0058 (−0.77)	0.0248 (1.78)	−0.1150 (−0.85)	−0.0003 (−2.40)	0.0045 (6.30)	0.0068 (1.60)	0.0021 (9.37)	−0.0024 (−0.34)	0.71 1.46
1963	0.5463 (1.10)	0.3036 (2.20)	0.2673 (5.89)	−1.3310 (−4.09)	−0.0087 (−1.17)	−0.0096 (−0.92)	−0.0667 (−0.61)	−0.0000 (−0.33)	0.0014 (2.14)	0.0117 (2.70)	0.0007 (3.52)	0.0286 (0.75)	0.77 1.77
1963a	2.1903 (7.18)	0.4537 (3.30)	0.2556 (5.44)		−0.0121 (−1.59)	−0.0100 (−0.93)	−0.1141 (−1.02)	−0.0000 (−0.33)	0.0019 (2.95)	0.0144 (3.25)	0.0005 (2.64)	−0.1123 (−6.57)	0.74 1.72
1964	−0.1342 (−0.94)	0.3051 (2.89)	0.1841 (3.01)	−0.2065 (−5.22)	−0.0139 (−1.54)	−0.0015 (−1.18)	−0.1651 (−0.84)		0.0063 (5.20)	0.0071 (1.09)	0.0007 (3.15)	0.1014 (5.23)	0.74 1.95
1964a	−0.1944 (−0.14)	0.0885 (0.85)	0.2933 (4.83)		−0.0212 (−2.25)	0.0096 (0.71)	−0.1422 (−0.68)		0.0047 (3.79)	0.0252 (4.37)	0.0009 (4.09)	0.0059 (0.88)	0.67 1.89
1965	−0.1890 (−1.60)	0.1884 (1.64)	0.4388 (13.26)	0.5347 (2.25)	−0.0013 (−0.18)	0.0078 (1.14)	−0.0993 (−0.70)		0.0014 (1.54)	0.0196 (3.79)	0.0011 (8.49)	−0.0088 (−0.49)	0.87 1.62
1966	−0.0305 (−0.22)	−0.0996 (−1.80)	0.3859 (8.81)	0.4619 (5.66)	0.0067 (0.78)	0.0047 (0.75)	0.4669 (2.21)		0.0013 (0.54)	0.0216 (2.60)	0.0012 (8.32)	−0.0195 (−1.85)	0.83 1.65
1967	0.4044 (2.19)	−0.1214 (−0.19)	0.3966 (9.32)	0.4920 (6.19)	0.0021 (0.21)	0.0046 (0.64)	0.7754 (2.59)		0.0016 (1.14)	0.0002 (0.74)	0.0015 (8.28)	−0.0533 (−3.86)	0.78 1.70

Symbol definitions: i_1, current mortgage rate; i_2, mortgage fees; i_3, average mortgage rate; i_4, commercial bank time deposit rate; k_1, ratio of reserves and surplus to deposits; k_2, ratio of scheduled items to total mortgages; a_1, ratio of advertising expenditures to deposits; a_2, number of branches; x_1, change in mortgages scaled by deposits; x_2, ratio of fee income to total income; x_3, logarithm of total assets; C, constant.

Table 5-9
Stock Association Results for Specification II

	i_1	i_2	i_3	i_4	s_1	s_2	s_3
1961			0.3670 (9.01)	0.2769 (0.97)		−0.3092 (−0.37)	
1962			0.2580 (4.96)	0.9600 (2.30)	−0.0001 (−3.26)	−3350. (−0.00)	1.507 (2.72)
1963			0.2911 (6.52)	0.2758 (0.43)	−0.0000 (−1.23)	−205.5 (−3.41)	2.599 (2.80)
1964			0.1875 (3.21)	−1.483 (−4.00)	−0.0000 (−2.08)		1.150 (2.98)
1964a	0.2739 (1.62)	0.0621 (0.58)	0.2230 (3.61)		0.0000 (0.32)		1.532 (3.76)
1965			0.3300 (9.16)	1.117 (6.28)	−0.0000 (−5.05)		0.0010 (0.01)
1966			0.2858 (5.33)	0.1026 (1.07)	−0.0000 (−4.91)		0.9138 (3.04)
1967			0.2542 (5.54)	0.1770 (1.89)	−0.0000 (−8.49)		1.230 (3.62)

straightforward theoretical model of profit or utility maximization. Despite the sharp geographical variations in deposit rates that characterize the savings and loan industry, the equations derived from the theoretical models successfully explain the pattern of deposit rates. This demonstrates that a rigorous analytical approach to the determination of deposit rates provides the basis for obtaining useful empirical results.

Two, the behavior of deposit rates at savings and loan associations indicates that these institutions act in a manner consistent with profit maximization and that a model of deposit maximization is not applicable. This conclusion is based on the fact that independent variables specified in the deposit rate equations to reflect the impact of exogenous shifts in the demand for savings deposits, universally obtain the sign consistent with profit maximization and opposite to that of deposit maximization.[j] These results contradict the belief held by many observers that the savings and loan industry is basically composed of associations that act without well defined goals. Instead, we can conclude that deposit rate setting behavior by financial intermediaries is fully consistent with profit maximization behavior.

Three, there are no substantive differences between the deposit rate setting behavior of mutual and stock associations, since the empirical

---

[j]The empirical results are also consistent with the utility maximization hypothesis since the comparative statics properties are identical to the profit maximization case. Throughout the remainder of this volume, we use the term profit maximization to encompass both profit and utility maximization hypotheses.

k_1	k_2	a_1	a_2	x_1	x_2	x_3	C	R/DW
0.0003	0.0003	0.0590	−0.0004	0.0000	−0.0050	0.0010	−0.0049	0.68
(0.05)	(0.02)	(0.67)	(−2.61)	(2.31)	(−1.19)	(2.89)	(−0.42)	1.74
−0.0112	0.0158	−0.0611	−0.0002	0.0040	0.0092	0.0019	0.0949	0.73
(−1.48)	(1.12)	(−0.44)	(−2.10)	(5.58)	(2.03)	(8.05)	(0.00)	1.45
−0.0119	−0.0176	−0.1010	−0.0000	0.0014	0.0071	0.0006	0.0063	0.78
(−1.63)	(−1.70)	(−0.96)	(−0.55)	(2.21)	(1.60)	(3.32)	(2.6)	1.83
−0.0172	0.0018	−0.1513		0.0062	0.0078	0.0007	0.0739	0.74
(−1.93)	(0.14)	(−0.78)		(5.16)	(1.21)	(3.39)	(4.26)	1.95
−0.0175	0.0059	−0.2621		0.0055	0.0181	0.0007	−0.0075	0.72
(−1.89)	(0.44)	(−1.26)		(4.46)	(3.06)	(3.30)	(−0.78)	1.88
0.0084	0.0107	−0.0925		0.0030	0.0124	0.0011	−0.0342	0.89
(1.29)	(1.67)	(−0.70)		(3.36)	(2.52)	(8.70)	(−5.54)	1.63
0.0133	0.0130	0.4775		−0.0004	0.0304	0.0012	0.0033	0.83
(1.45)	(2.03)	(2.23)		(−0.16)	(3.69)	(7.46)	(0.43)	1.52
0.0090	0.0124	0.7998		0.0009	0.0002	0.0014	0.0067	0.82
(0.94)	(1.88)	(2.90)		(0.73)	(1.03)	(7.97)	(0.90)	1.82

Symbol definitions: i_1, current mortgage rate; i_2, mortgage fees; i_3, average mortgage rate; i_4, commercial bank time deposit rate; s_1, income per capita; s_2, savings and loan offices per capita; s_3, commercial bank employment per capita; k_1, ratio of reserves and surplus to deposits; k_2, ratio of scheduled items to total mortgages; a_1, ratio of advertising expenditures to deposits; a_2, number of branches; x_1, change in mortgages scaled by deposits; x_2, ratio of fee income to total income; x_3, logarithm of total assets; C, constant.

evidence indicates that both types of associations offer the same level of deposit rates. Consequently, the differences that were observed in earlier studies apparently reflected differences in environment rather than in structural behavior patterns.

Four, the cross section analysis of savings and loan associations is a clear example of the applicability of the theory of financial intermediation which explains how savings institutions operate. In this study, the intermediary emerges as a service institution that offers liabilities to the public and in return purchases a portfolio of assets that the individuals themselves could not easily obtain. Furthermore, the rationale for the usefulness of financial intermediaries lies in the economies of scale in risk pooling and transaction costs as well as in the specialization of labor, all of which are intrinsic to their operation. Thus, the intermediary permits small depositors to gain access to the breadth of the financial market. In general, the interest rate coefficients in the estimated equations sum to values that are close to unity, which indicates that variations in market interest rates are fully reflected in the pattern of interest rates on savings deposits.

Five, the empirical results indicate that there is an active market for savings that has the characteristics that economists recognize as consistent

Table 5-10
Chow Test Results for Stock and Mutual Association Regressions

	Specification I	*Specification II*
1961	6.02	4.78
1962	5.29	2.04
1963	3.28	1.51
1963a	3.52	
1964	1.53	0.75
1964a	2.46	0.81
1965	4.63	1.85
1966	5.94	1.89
1967	2.66	1.30

with the efficient allocation of scarce resources. Consequently, this counters the basic justification for the establishment of ceiling restrictions on savings and loan deposit rates in 1966 and suggests that deposit rates at savings and loan associations responded to market forces in a manner consistent with the economics of intermediation during the period previous to the initiation of ceiling restrictions.

Finally, despite the fact that savings and loan associations are institutions characterized by relatively little portfolio flexibility as a result of a variety of legal regulations and traditions, the empirical evidence indicates that the savings and loan industry determines deposit rates in a rational and systematic manner that is susceptible to economic analysis.

6 A Time Series Analysis of Savings Deposit Rates at Financial Intermediaries

The theoretical models developed in chapters 2, 3, and 4 and the cross section empirical work reported in chapter 5 provide considerable insight into the determinants of the deposit rate setting behavior of financial intermediaries and demonstrate that the determination of interest rates paid on savings deposits is fully susceptible to economic modeling. Three theoretical models were developed based upon the alternate assumptions of profit maximization, deposit maximization, and utility maximization; and implications were drawn for the empirical specification of deposit rate functions. Based upon these specifications, the estimation results for deposit rates at a cross section of savings and loan associations support several conclusions about the behavior of deposit rate setting. One, the deposit rate setting behavior of savings and loan associations is consistent with the comparative statics results implied by a model of profit maximization or utility maximization where both profits and deposits yield positive utility. The empirical evidence clearly indicates that a model of deposit maximization is inappropriate. Two, deposit rate setting behavior is apparently not affected by the organizational form of the financial institution, since mutual and stock associations set similar deposit rates if they operate in similar economic environments. Three, a large percentage of the cross section variation in deposit rates, about 50 to 80 per cent, can be explained by the structural variables derived from these theoretical models. Overall, this provides strong evidence that financial intermediaries in general, and specifically savings and loan associations, set deposit rates in a rational and systematic manner that is thoroughly susceptible to the power of economic analysis.

In the previous chapter, the empirical investigation of deposit rates focused on the microeconomic level. More specifically, deposit rate equations were tested for cross section data using a sample of institutions from the savings and loan industry as a proxy for financial intermediaries in general. The cross section results demonstrate the applicability of the theoretical model of profit maximization to a microeconomic analysis of deposit rate behavior. The purpose of this chapter is to investigate the behavior of deposit rates on a time series basis by applying empirical specifications derived from our previous theoretical and cross section results. Savings deposit rate equations on a time series basis are estimated not only for savings and loan associations but also for commercial banks and mutual savings banks. The time series estimation of these deposit rate equations has an important role in determining and evaluating the overall behavior of the macroeconomic system in addition to providing definitive evidence about the behavior of financial intermediaries. The development of these equations describes the degree to which deposit rates respond to changes in financial conditions. This provides a basis for a more sophisticated analysis of the response of financial markets to changes in monetary policy or other exogenous variables and the evaluation of the quantitative impact on the economy that results from changes in the ceilings on savings deposit rates.

Earlier research centered on the estimation of time series equations for savings deposit rates is limited. De Leeuw [12] and Hendershott [33] each estimated equations for only the commercial bank time deposit rate, while Gramlich and Hulett [27] attempted to explain the yields on the deposits of each of the three major types of financial institutions. In the works of de Leeuw and Hendershott, specifications for the commercial bank time deposit rate are estimated using annual data without providing any formal theoretical model for intermediary behavior. In Gramlich and Hulett's work, deposit rate specifications are drawn from a simple profit maximization model and are estimated on quarterly data. However, the character of the resulting equations is not satisfactory, since deposit rates are consistently found to be relatively insensitive to movements in market interest rates. This result is in marked contrast to both the predictions of the profit maximization model and the cross section estimation evidence presented in chapter 5.

In this chapter our objective is to estimate effective time series equations for deposit rates at savings and loan associations, mutual savings banks, and commercial banks by applying specifications drawn from the comparative statics properties of the theoretical model in which a financial intermediary seeks to maximize profits. Since the cross section estimation results provide considerable evidence that the profit or utility maximization models best describe the deposit rate setting behavior of savings and loan associations, we use the profit maximization model as the framework for the estimation of time series equations for deposit rates at the three major types of institutions. The theoretical results for the model of profit maximization developed in chapter 2 establish that the primary determinant of deposit rates is the level of open market interest yields, which includes interest rates on assets suitable for the institution's portfolio and yields on instruments that the public regards as substitutes for the intermediary's liabilities. More specifically, the comparative statics results demonstrate that current deposit rates are a positive function of current market interest rates and a negative function of expected future yields.

Although a substantial number of variables other than interest rates can be drawn from the theoretical models and were specified in the cross section work, most of these factors are appropriate only on the microeconomic level in order to capture regional variation. Consequently, for empirical analysis at the aggregate level, these variables are either not relevant or the required data are unavailable on a consistent national basis. The time series analysis of the deposit rate setting behavior is developed first for nonbank institutions, that is, savings and loan associations and mutual savings banks, to be followed by a similar analysis for the case of commercial banks.

Savings and Loan Associations and Mutual Savings Banks

The equations for the interest rates on savings deposits at savings and loan associations and mutual savings banks include three categories of variables in each specification: yields on assets held in the institution's portfolio, competing rates available in the open market and in the savings deposit market, and impact variables that reflect the importance of short term imbalances in asset and liability flows. The first category of variables is asset rates. Since mortgages dominate the asset portfolios of both savings and loan associations and mutual savings banks, the mortgage rate RM is the only asset rate variable entered in both deposit rate equations. The comparative statics results from the model of profit maximization suggest that deposit rates are a positive function of the level of current asset rates.

For the category of competing rates, however, the developed state of the financial market implies that there are numerous available financial instruments that depositors might regard as substitutes for nonbank deposits. Some of the major potential substitutes are Treasury bills, commercial bank time deposits, corporate bonds, and the deposits of the competing savings institution. Nevertheless, the severe multicollinearity that characterizes time series data for interest rates makes it impossible to obtain effective estimation results if all of these variables are specified as independent regressors in a deposit rate equation that also includes the mortgage rate. Consequently, the selection of which competing yields should be specified in each deposit rate equation becomes an important estimation problem. In order to alleviate this difficulty we develop a single composite competing rate variable for each institution by using, as a priori information, empirical results for the public's demand functions for savings deposits as estimated in Modigliani's [42] work. We construct the composite yield variable for each deposit rate equation by weighting each competing yield in the respective demand function by its relative impact on deposit flows to the institution in question, with the sum of the weights constrained to unity for scaling purposes.[a]

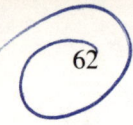

An additional problem arises in developing a composite competing rate variable because a change occurred during the early 1960s in the character of the competition in the savings deposit market between commercial banks and nonbank intermediaries. This change was probably due to the administration of Regulation Q, which is the legal ceiling on the level of interest rates that commercial banks may pay on time deposits.[b] Prior to 1962, the Regulation Q ceiling effectively restricted commercial bank time deposit rates to a level considerably below the interest rates offered by nonbank institutions. The differential between bank and nonbank deposit rates ranged from 120 to 160 basis points as shown in Figure 6-1.[c] Early in 1962 the Federal Reserve Board raised the Regulation Q ceiling by 100 basis points, and as a result the differential between bank and nonbank deposit rates decreased substantially to about 40 to 60 basis points. It therefore seems reasonable to hypothesize that the degree of commercial bank competition in the savings market became an important factor in the public's demand for savings deposits at nonbank institutions only after 1961, because prior to the rise in Regulation Q ceilings, nonbank intermediaries offered considerably higher deposit rates than commercial banks. The empirical evidence reported by Modigliani [42] in his work on the demand side of the savings market is consistent with this view. Consequently, we incorporate this shift in the structure of financial competition in specifying the composite competing rate variable. Prior to 1962, the composite variable relevant for both savings and loan associations and mutual savings banks consists of the following appropriately weighted competing rates: the Treasury bill rate RTB, the corporate bond rate RCB, and the competing nonbank rate, which is the mutual savings bank rate RMS in the savings and loan association equation and the savings and loan rate RSL in the mutual savings bank equation. After 1962 the composite variable consists of the Treasury bill rate RTB, the corporate bond rate RCB, and the commercial bank time deposit rate RTD. Based upon the comparative statics results for the theoretical model of profit maximization, we expect positive coefficients for the composite competing rate variable in each deposit rate equation.

In addition to the result that deposit rates are directly related to movements in the current level of open market yields, that is, both asset and

---

[a]The steady state effect on deposit flows induced by a change in a competing yield is first calculated. Then the ratios of these derivatives are used as the weights for the competing yields.

[b]Prior to 1966, legal ceilings on savings deposit rates were applicable only for commercial bank deposit rates. Nonbank deposit rates were unrestricted until 1966.

[c]The nonbank rate used in the figure is the savings and loan deposit rate. Movements in the mutual savings bank deposit rate are generally similar.

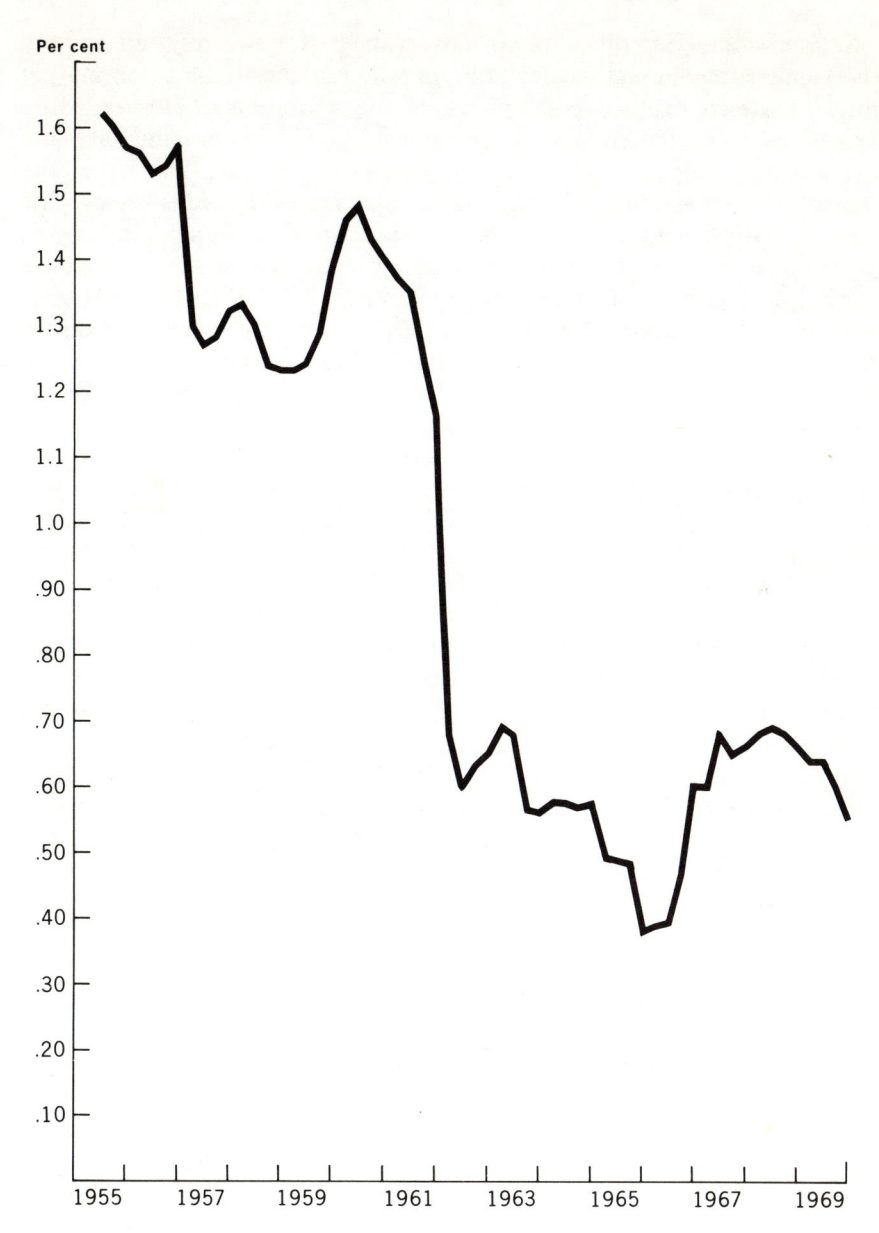

Figure 6-1. Differential between the Savings and Loan Deposit Rate and the Commercial Bank Time Deposit Rate.

competing rates, the theoretical model of profit maximization also indicates that deposit rates are a negative function of the level of expected future market yields. However, expectations held about the level of future asset and competing rates are not observable. Consequently, we employ the standard econometric technique of using distributed lags on market interest rates to proxy expectations held about future market rates. More specifically, distributed lags on the current asset and competing rates are estimated through the use of the Almon [1] technique. Therefore, the impact of current and expected interest rates are estimated together. The pattern of the lagged coefficients is constrained to lie along a second degree polynomial with the endpoint constrained to be zero. The comparative statics results for the profit maximization model indicate that deposit rates are inversely related to future market yields. Therefore in the empirical results, positive coefficients for the lagged interest rate variables would indicate that the expectations mechanism is regressive in character, that is, low values of current rates relative to past interest rates engender expectations of higher future rates. Negative coefficients would indicate the opposite result, that is, expectations are extrapolative in character, with low levels of current interest rates relative to past rates inducing an expectation of even lower rates in the future.

The final category of variables specified in the deposit rate regressions are impact variables incorporated in order to reflect the possible short term effects on deposit rates induced by temporary imbalances in asset and liability flows. In order to minimize the effect of multicollinearity only one impact variable is specified in the deposit rate equations for savings and loan associations and mutual savings banks. In each case the variable captures the effect of an imbalance in the flows of mortgages and deposits and consequently is defined as the difference between the percentage rate of growth of mortgages and deposits at the relevant type of institution. The expected sign of the coefficients is positive, so that if the rate of mortgage growth exceeds the inflow of deposits, the intermediary tends to increase deposit rates in the short run in order to attract more funds. Similarly there is a depressing effect on deposit rates if the growth in deposits temporarily exceeds the rate at which mortgages can be purchased.[d] Since the share of mortgages in the portfolios of savings and loan associations has been relatively stable in the past, this flow variable is entered in the savings and loan deposit rate equation for the full sample period. However, during the 1950s and early 1960s there was a gradual shift in the portfolio holdings of mutual savings banks from securities to mortgages. Consequently, the flow variable is entered in the mutual savings bank deposit rate equation only for the period after 1963.2, by which time the proportion of mortgages in the portfolios of these institutions had stabilized.

---

[d]This impact variable serves a useful role within the context of simulating a larger econometric model of the economy in which the demand for savings deposits is also determined. If, for example, the demand for savings deposits is oversimulated, deposit rates fall, which tends to bring the demand equation back on track.

The deposit rate equations estimated for savings and loan associations and mutual savings banks are reported in Tables 6-1 and 6-2. The equations are estimated on quarterly data by ordinary least squares using the Cochrane-Orcutt [11] autoregressive technique in order to correct for the presence of serial correlation in the residuals. The sample period is 1955.2-1968.4.[e] The t statistics appear in parenthesis below the estimated coefficients. The standard adjusted multiple correlation coefficients R^2 and the standard error statistics SE are reported along with similar statistics for the case in which the coefficients of the lagged error terms are set equal to zero.

Overall, both equations fit very well with low standard errors of about 2 to 3 basis points, or 5 to 6 basis points when the coefficients of the lagged errors are set equal to zero. In each equation the market interest rate variables, that is, the mortgage rate and the composite competing rate, perform strongly. In both equations the lag on the mortgage rate RM is estimated to be ten quarters in length and the coefficients for each lag are strongly positive and significant. The results for the competing rate variables indicate that deposit rates also respond strongly to movements in the yields on close substitutes. In each equation the lag on the composite variable specified for the early portion of the sample period is five quarters in length, while that for the competing rate variable included for the later portion of the sample period is four quarters in length. Again, the t statistics are quite large for each set of lag coefficients. Consequently, the empirical evidence indicates that the deposit rates at savings and loan associations and mutual savings banks are a function of current and past values of market interest rates. The signs of the coefficients on the asset and competing rates are positive, which is consistent with the comparative statics results from the model of profit maximization. The positive signs of the coefficients on the lagged interest rate variables indicate that the formation of expectations about future movements in interest rates is regressive in character, that is, if current interest rates are low relative to past rates, yields are expected to rise in the future. Furthermore, the sums of the coefficients on the asset and competing rate variables are close to unity for both types of nonbank institutions. For savings and loan associations the interest rate coefficients sum to 1.04 for the early period and to 0.94 for the later period. For mutual savings banks the sum is 0.90 in the early period and 1.13 in the later period. Consequently, we can conclude that the impact of a change in market rates is fully reflected, with a lag, in the behavior of interest rates on savings deposits at nonbank intermediaries.

The impact variable is also entered in the specifications with a distributed lag in order to allow the adjustment to changes in mortgage and deposit

---

[e]The sample ends in 1968.4 because after this period the level of savings deposit rates has been seriously restricted by legal ceilings.

Table 6-1
Savings Deposit Rate Equation for Savings and Loan Associations

$$RSL = -1.0886 + Q_1 \sum_{i=0}^{5} a_i(0.51RMS + 0.43RCB + 0.06RTB)_{-i}$$
$$(-3.91)$$

$$+ Q_2 \sum_{i=0}^{4} b_i(0.203RCB + 0.083RTB + 0.713RTD)_{-i}$$

$$+ \sum_{i=0}^{10} c_i RM_{-i} + \sum_{i=0}^{9} d_i \left[\frac{MKSL_{-1} - MKSL_{-2}}{MKSL_{-2}} - \frac{MSL_{-1} - MSL_{-2}}{MSL_{-2}} \right]_{-i}$$

$$+ 0.8232 Q_2 + 0.74 u_{-1}$$
$$(3.24)$$

$$Q_1 = \begin{cases} 1.00 & \text{if } TIME < 1962.1 \\ 0 & \text{if } TIME \geq 1962.1 \end{cases} \qquad Q_2 = \begin{cases} 0 & \text{if } TIME < 1962.1 \\ 1.00 & \text{if } TIME \geq 1962.1 \end{cases}$$

$a_0 = 0.1513$ (4.08)	$b_0 = 0.1684$ (3.32)
$a_1 = 0.1308$ (7.43)	$b_1 = 0.1261$ (7.52)
$a_2 = 0.1084$ (7.63)	$b_2 = 0.0881$ (6.82)
$a_3 = 0.0842$ (4.49)	$b_3 = 0.0545$ (2.66)
$a_4 = 0.0580$ (3.03)	$b_4 = 0.0251$ (1.51)
$a_5 = 0.0299$ (2.30)	
$\Sigma a_i = 0.5626$ (8.62)	$\Sigma b_i = 0.4622$ (10.62)
$c_0 = 0.0738$ (4.46)	$d_0 = -0.6422$ (-1.10)
$c_1 = 0.0686$ (5.68)	$d_1 = 0.0326$ (0.06)
$c_2 = 0.0630$ (6.92)	$d_2 = 0.5718$ (1.07)
$c_3 = 0.0572$ (7.29)	$d_3 = 0.9752$ (1.62)
$c_4 = 0.0511$ (6.48)	$d_4 = 1.2429$ (1.90)
$c_5 = 0.0447$ (5.33)	$d_5 = 1.3750$ (2.06)
$c_6 = 0.0380$ (4.39)	$d_6 = 1.3714$ (2.15)
$c_7 = 0.0310$ (3.68)	$d_7 = 1.2321$ (2.21)
$c_8 = 0.0237$ (3.17)	$d_8 = 0.9571$ (2.25)
$c_9 = 0.0161$ (2.78)	$d_9 = 0.5464$ (2.28)
$c_{10} = 0.0082$ (2.48)	
$\Sigma c_i = 0.4755$ (7.12)	$\Sigma d_i = 7.622$ (1.62)

$R_e^2 = 0.9984 \qquad R_u^2 = 0.9941 \qquad D.W. = 1.74$
$SE = 0.0242 \qquad SU = 0.0465 \qquad$ Sample Period: 1955.2-1968.4

flows to be distributed over time. Each lag is estimated to be nine quarters in length and the coefficients obtained for both intermediaries are positive as expected. The size of the coefficients implies that deposit rate setting at

Table 6-2
Savings Deposit Rate Equation for Mutual Savings Banks

$$RMS = -0.8252 + Q_1 \sum_{i=0}^{5} a_i(0.51RSL + 0.43RCB + 0.06RTB)_{-i}$$
$$(-1.46)$$

$$+ Q_2 \sum_{i=0}^{4} b_i(0.203\ RCB + 0.083\ RTB + 0.713\ RTD)_{-i}$$

$$+ \sum_{i=0}^{10} c_i RM_{-i} + Q_3 \sum_{i=0}^{9} d_i \left[\frac{MKMS_{-1} - MKMS_{-2}}{MKMS_{-2}} - \frac{MMS_{-1} - MMS_{-2}}{MMS_{-2}} \right]_{-i}$$

$$- 0.1938 Q_2 - 0.2646 Q_3 + 0.867 u_{-1}$$
$$(-0.35)\quad (-3.08)$$

$$Q_1 = \begin{cases} 1.00 & \text{if } TIME < 1962.1 \\ 0 & \text{if } TIME \geq 1962.1 \end{cases} \qquad Q_2 = \begin{cases} 0 & \text{if } TIME < 1962.1 \\ 1.00 & \text{if } TIME \geq 1962.1 \end{cases}$$

$$Q_3 = \begin{cases} 0 & \text{if } TIME < 1963.2 \\ 1.00 & \text{if } TIME \geq 1963.2 \end{cases}$$

$a_o = 0.1366\ (3.03)$	$b_o = 0.2834\ (4.93)$
$a_1 = 0.1142\ (4.12)$	$b_1 = 0.1989\ (8.60)$
$a_2 = 0.0917\ (3.47)$	$b_2 = 0.1284\ (6.79)$
$a_3 = 0.0691\ (2.36)$	$b_3 = 0.0717\ (2.92)$
$a_4 = 0.0462\ (1.70)$	$b_4 = 0.0289\ (1.51)$
$a_5 = 0.0232\ (1.31)$	
$\Sigma a_i = 0.4810\ (3.87)$	$\Sigma b_i = 0.7112\ (9.71)$
$c_o = 0.0580\ (2.32)$	$d_o = 0.9825\ (0.57)$
$c_1 = 0.0558\ (2.81)$	$d_1 = 2.7819\ (1.99)$
$c_2 = 0.0530\ (3.19)$	$d_2 = 4.1596\ (3.10)$
$c_3 = 0.0495\ (3.29)$	$d_3 = 5.1156\ (3.60)$
$c_4 = 0.0455\ (3.11)$	$d_4 = 5.6500\ (3.74)$
$c_5 = 0.0408\ (2.81)$	$d_5 = 5.7625\ (3.74)$
$c_6 = 0.0355\ (2.50)$	$d_6 = 5.4534\ (3.70)$
$c_7 = 0.0297\ (2.24)$	$d_7 = 4.7226\ (3.66)$
$c_8 = 0.0232\ (2.03)$	$d_8 = 3.5701\ (3.61)$
$c_9 = 0.0161\ (1.85)$	$d_9 = 1.9959\ (3.57)$
$c_{10} = 0.0083\ (1.71)$	
$\Sigma c_i = 0.4154\ (3.25)$	$\Sigma d_i = 40.1943\ (3.60)$

$R_e^2 = 0.9981$ $R_u^2 = 0.9923$ $D.W. = 1.58$

$SE = 0.0286$ $SU = 0.0575$ Sample Period: 1955.2-1968.4

mutual savings banks is highly sensitive to changes in mortgage and deposit flows especially in comparison to savings and loan association behavior. Furthermore, in the case of savings and loan associations no significant adjustment takes place until four quarters have passed, whereas the adjustment process begins immediately for mutual savings banks. There are several reasons why mutual savings banks should be more sensitive than savings and loan associations to short run changes in asset and liability flows. Savings and loan associations have access to advances through the Federal Home Loan Bank Board. Mutual savings banks, however, do not have access to a lender of last resort and must utilize deposit rate changes as their primary instrument for obtaining additional funds in the short run. In addition, since the ratio of mortgage commitments to deposits tends to be larger for mutual savings banks than for savings and loan associations, it is reasonable that mutual savings banks must be especially sensitive to changing deposit flows in order to be able to fulfill these mortgage commitments. (The series for mutual savings bank deposits and commitments are reported monthly in the Federal Reserve Bulletin [5].)

In order to test the robustness of the regression results for these equations, an alternate formulation of the composite competing rate variable for savings and loan associations is tested which utilizes a different set of weights for the composite competing yield. To derive this alternative composite variable, empirical results for the demand for savings deposits that differ substantially from Modigliani's reported research are used to calculate the relative impact of changes in competing rates on deposit flows into the appropriate institution. The demand equations used to derive this composite variable are reported in Gramlich and Hulett [27]. This variable is entered for the full period in the deposit rate equation for savings and loan associations, and the estimation results are reported in Table 6-3. The character of the results is very similar to that obtained for the initial specification. The sum of the coefficients for market interest rates is 0.90, which is again close to unity and approximately equal to the sum for the earlier results. In general, the specification for the deposit rate equations, as drawn from the theoretical work, is quite robust with respect to changes in the specific estimates used for the relative importance of various competing yields in the public's demand for savings deposits.

Commercial Banks

Commercial bank behavior is considerably more complex than the behavior of nonbank intermediaries for several reasons. One, nonbank institutions are generally smaller in size than commercial banks and conse-

Table 6-3
Alternate Specification of Savings Deposit Rate Equation for Savings and Loan Associations

$$RSL = \sum_{i=0}^{4} b_i \left[0.78RCB + 0.10RTD + 0.06RMS + 24.0 \left(\frac{PCON - PCON_{-1}}{PCON_{-1}} \right) \right]_{-i}$$

$$+ \sum_{i=0}^{9} c_i \left[\frac{MKSL_{-1} - MKSL_{-2}}{MKSL_{-2}} - \frac{MSL_{-1} - MSL_{-2}}{MSL_{-2}} \right]_{-i}$$

$$+ \sum_{i=0}^{9} d_i RM_{-i} + \underset{(2.03)}{3.6666} \left(\frac{ZAFH}{MSL} \right)_{-1} Q_1$$

$$+ \underset{(0.37)}{0.0291} Q_1 + 0.8000 u_{-1} - \underset{(-0.60)}{0.2986}$$

$$Q_1 = \begin{cases} 0 & \text{if } TIME < 1962.1 \\ 1.00 & \text{if } TIME \geq 1962.1 \end{cases}$$

$b_0 = 0.1223$ (5.12)
$b_1 = 0.1366$ (6.99)
$b_2 = 0.1315$ (5.20)
$b_3 = 0.1071$ (4.18)
$b_4 = 0.0632$ (3.63)
$\Sigma b_i = 0.5607$ (6.37)

$c_0 = -0.8719$ (−1.07)	$d_0 = -0.0230$ (−0.64)
$c_1 = 0.6832$ (0.91)	$d_1 = 0.0046$ (0.17)
$c_2 = 1.9121$ (2.49)	$d_2 = 0.0265$ (1.25)
$c_3 = 2.8148$ (3.45)	$d_3 = 0.0429$ (2.53)
$c_4 = 3.3913$ (4.00)	$d_4 = 0.0536$ (3.68)
$c_5 = 3.6416$ (4.33)	$d_5 = 0.0588$ (4.39)
$c_6 = 3.5657$ (4.53)	$d_6 = 0.0582$ (4.69)
$c_7 = 3.1636$ (4.66)	$d_7 = 0.0521$ (4.76)
$c_8 = 2.4353$ (4.75)	$d_8 = 0.0404$ (4.73)
$c_9 = 1.3807$ (4.81)	$d_9 = 0.0230$ (4.66)
$\Sigma c_i = 22.1165$ (3.45)	$\Sigma d_i = 0.3371$ (2.53)

$R_e^2 = 0.9974$ $R_u^2 = 0.9896$ D.W. = 1.37
$SE = 0.0307$ $SU = 0.0616$ Sample Period: 1954.1-1968.4

quently manage smaller portfolios. Two, as a result of legal requirements, the asset portfolios of nonbanks are restricted primarily to mortgages. The legal requirements on the types of assets that can be held by commercial banks are more flexible, and as a result commercial banks hold a larger variety of assets than nonbank institutions. Three, nonbank intermediaries are constrained by law to issue only savings deposits, which bear interest and have a maturity requirement. Nonbanks are prohibited from issuing demand deposits. However, commercial banks can issue both demand and time deposits. Four, since the Great Depression, commercial banks have been subject to a ceiling on the level of interest rates that can be paid on time deposits. Nonbank intermediaries in contrast were free of such restrictions until late in 1966. In order to reflect the complexities intrinsic to commercial bank behavior, the specification for the interest rate on savings deposits at commercial banks is more detailed compared to the case of nonbank intermediaries. There are basically four categories of variables included in the specification: yields on assets held in the portfolios of commercial banks, competing rates available to depositors in the open market and in the savings market, impact variables that capture the response of commercial banks to short term imbalances in asset and liability flows, and variables that reflect characteristics uniquely applicable to commercial banks.

Because of the diversified nature of commercial bank portfolio holdings, there are a variety of asset rate variables available for empirical testing, among which are the commercial loan rate *RCL,* the mortgage rate *RM,* and the municipal bond rate *RMUN.* These series, however, are characterized by severe multicollinearity, which prevents the effective estimation of separate coefficients for each of these asset rates. Nevertheless, since the relative amounts of municipal bonds, mortgages, and commercial loans held by commercial banks have been fairly stable over the sample period, as graphed in Figure 6-2, we utilize a composite asset rate variable composed of a weighted average of these three assets, with the weights based on their relative proportions in bank portfolios.[f]

Furthermore, there is a wide variety of financial instruments that the public might regard as substitutes for bank deposits. In order to alleviate multicollinearity problems in estimating the impact of movements in competing yields on time deposit rates, a composite competing rate variable is also incorporated in the specification. The empirical estimates found in Modigliani's work [42] on the public's demand for time deposits again provide the basis for specifying the components of the composite variable and their weights.[g] More specifically, the weights are determined by the relative impact of a change in each competing yield on the deposit flows to commercial banks. As explained earlier in this chapter, there is strong empirical evidence that the competitive structure of the savings market

---

[f]Data for each of these quantities are reported in the Federal Reserve Bulletin [5]. These three financial instruments have accounted for approximately 85 per cent of the interest bearing assets held in the portfolios of commercial banks.

[g]The choice of different weights has little effect on the estimation results obtained for the commercial bank time deposit rate equation.

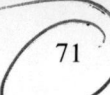

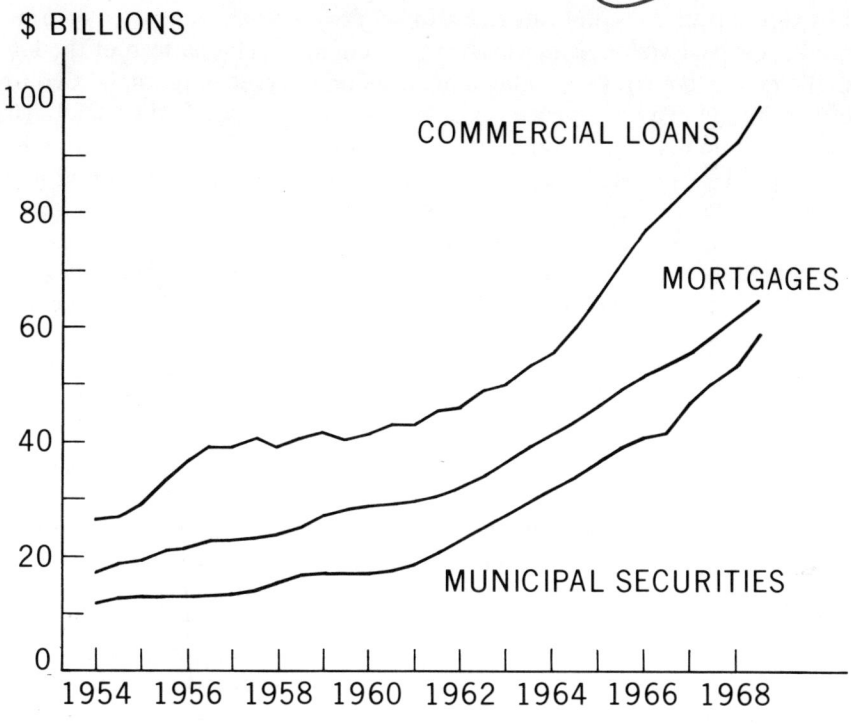

Figure 6-2. Commercial Loans, Mortgages, Municipal Securities Held by Commercial Banks.

shifted during the early 1960s due to the administration of Regulation Q ceilings on commercial bank time deposit rates. Prior to 1962, nonbank rates were considerably higher than commercial bank time deposit rates due to the restrictiveness of ceiling rates on bank time deposits, which may have prohibited commercial banks from competing for interest sensitive funds. After Regulation Q ceilings on commercial bank time deposit rates were raised by 100 basis points in 1962, the differential between deposit rates narrowed considerably so that banks became more competitive with nonbank institutions. The specification for the time deposit rate equation allows for this shift by specifying only the Treasury bill rate RTB for the sample period prior to 1962.1, but a combination of the Treasury bill rate and a nonbank rate for the post-1962.1 period. The nonbank rate is constructed as a weighted average of the yields on savings and loan shares RSL and mutual savings bank deposits RMS, with the weights determined by average deposit flows to these institutions for the previous year.

The model of profit maximization implies that deposit rates are a positive function of current asset and competing yields and an inverse function of expected future market rates. Again we proxy future rates by a distributed lag on past yields using the Almon technique. The pattern of the lag coefficients is constrained to lie along a second degree polynomial tied to zero at the tail. The asset rate variable, however, is specified with a third degree polynomial constrained to zero at both the tail and period $t + 1$.

In the deposit rate equations for savings and loan associations and mutual savings banks, impact variables are included in the specification in order to capture the effect of short run imbalances in the flow of mortgages and deposits. Since both the asset and liability portfolios of commercial banks are more diversified than for nonbank institutions, the construction of impact variables is somewhat more complicated. Over the sample period, commercial loans and mortgages were the two primary earning assets of commercial banks and thus are used to indicate the pattern of short term asset flows at commerical banks.[h] On the liability side, commercial banks offer more than one type of deposit. In order to allow for the possibility that commercial banks respond differently to changes in the flow of demand and time deposits, separate variables are specified for each type of deposit. Thus, each impact variable is defined as the difference between the rate of growth in either time or demand deposits and the growth in commercial loans plus mortgages. We expect a negative sign for the coefficients of these impact variables. Consequently, if the growth of deposits exceeds the rate at which commercial loans or mortgages can be disbursed, it is assumed that commercial banks respond by lowering deposit rates in the short run in order to rectify this imbalance in asset and liability flows.

Several additional variables are specified in the equation in order to reflect the unique complexities of commercial bank behavior and the more varied economic influences to which banks must react in comparison with nonbank behavior. First, the differential between the composite asset rate and the discount rate *RDIS* is entered in order to capture the fact that commercial banks may use the discount mechanism as a substitute for deposit rate changes in obtaining temporary funds. A negative sign is expected for this variable since a narrowing of this differential makes borrowing at the discount window less attractive and induces a rise in deposit rates. Second, the change in the ceiling rate on time deposits *QTD* is specified in order to reflect the possibility that changes in ceiling rates by the central bank may be a substitute for price leadership in the commercial banking industry or may create the expectation that competing rates are likely to rise. A positive sign is expected. The inclusion of such a change variable in the specification in effect allows for the possibility that ceiling rate changes serve as a trigger mechanism for movements in deposit rates.

---

[h]Only in recent years have municipal securities become a substantial proportion of the assets in commercial bank portfolios.

There is, however, no steady state effect, so that in the long run, if there are no changes in market interest rates, the deposit rate desired by commercial banks is not affected by ceiling rate changes.

The dependent variable is defined as the interest paid by commercial banks on time deposits. The series is quarterly and consists of a weighting of the yields offered on both passbook savings accounts and consumer savings certificates but excludes large denomination certificates of deposit. The Regulation Q ceiling on time deposit rates became seriously restrictive after 1968. Since the derivation of the specification for the deposit rate equation attempts to explain bank behavior in the absence of a binding ceiling, the sample period utilized for the regression is 1955.2 to 1968.4.[1] The equation is estimated by ordinary least squares since the Durbin-Watson statistic did not indicate the presence of any serial correlation in the residuals. The results are reported in Table 6-4.

Overall, the equation fits extremely well with a standard error of only 5 basis points. Most important, the interest rate variables perform very strongly. The results for the coefficients of the asset rates are particularly powerful and are larger in size than the coefficients on the asset rate variables in the nonbank rate equations. The eight quarter sum of the asset rate coefficients is almost 0.90 and strongly significant. The sums of the competing rate coefficients, in contrast, are much smaller. The sum is 0.17 for the pre-1962 composite competing rate variable, which has a four quarter lag, and 0.25 for the comparable post-1962 variable, which has a two quarter lag. Overall, however, it is the combined effect of both asset and competing rates that is of particular interest in assessing the character of the response of commercial banks to movements in market interest rates. In this regard, the sum of the asset and competing rate coefficients are close to unity. The figures are 1.07 for the pre-1962 period and 1.15 for the post-1962 period. Consequently, there is strong empirical evidence that movements in market yields are fully transmitted to the holders of commercial bank time deposits via the deposit rate setting mechanism. The signs of the current and lagged interest rate coefficients are positive, so that these results, as in the case of the nonbank deposit rate equations, are consistent with the model of profit maximization. The pattern of the lagged coefficients implies that expectations about future movements in market rates are regressive in character.

Preliminary estimation results indicated that the two impact variables in the specification were not significant when entered for the full sample period. Inspection of the historical data, however, reveals that prior to 1962 commercial banks maintained a large proportion of their portfolios in

---

[1] When these deposit rate equations are simulated, the ceiling rate is taken as the solution value for the deposit rate whenever the equations yield a desired deposit rate that exceeds the relevant legal ceiling.

Table 6-4
Savings Deposit Rate Equation for Commercial Banks

$$RTD = -2.0075 + Q_1 \sum_{i=0}^{4} a_i RTB_{-i}$$
$$(-15.92)$$

$$+ Q_2 \sum_{i=0}^{2} b_i \left[0.23 RTB + 0.77 \left(\frac{RSL(MSL_{-1} - MSL_{-5}) + RMS(MMS_{-1} - MMS_{-5})}{MSL_{-1} + MMS_{-1} - MSL_{-5} - MMS_{-5}} \right) \right]_{-i}$$

$$+ \sum_{i=0}^{8} c_i (0.45 RCL + 0.30 RM + 0.25 RMUN)_{-i}$$

$$- 0.0909[(0.45 RCL + 0.30 RM + 0.25 RMUN) - RDIS]_{-1}$$
$$(-1.80)$$

$$+ \sum_{i=0}^{9} d_i (QTD - QTD_{-1})_{-i}$$

$$+ Q_2 \sum_{i=0}^{6} e_i(100) \left[\frac{MT_{-1} - MT_{-2}}{MT_{-2}} - \frac{(MKCB_{-1} + MCL_{-1}) - (MKCB_{-2} + MCL_{-2})}{MKCB_{-2} + MCL_{-2}} \right]_{-i}$$

$$+ Q_2 \sum_{i=0}^{6} f_i(100) \left[\frac{MD_{-1} - MD_{-2}}{MD_{-2}} - \frac{(MKCB_{-1} + MCL_{-1}) - (MKCB_{-2} + MCL_{-2})}{MKCB_{-2} + MCL_{-2}} \right]_{-i}$$

$$+ 0.2194 Q_2$$
$$(0.59)$$

$$Q_1 = \begin{cases} 1.00 & \text{if } TIME < 1962.1 \\ 0 & \text{if } TIME \geq 1962.1 \end{cases} \qquad Q_2 = \begin{cases} 1.00 & \text{if } TIME \geq 1962.1 \\ 0 & \text{if } TIME < 1962.1 \end{cases}$$

$a_0 = 0.0615\ (5.06)$	$b_0 = 0.1832\ (1.88)$	$c_0 = -0.0313\ (-1.47)$	$d_0 = 0.3804\ (6.17)$
$a_1 = 0.0463\ (3.43)$	$b_1 = 0.0633\ (0.91)$	$c_1 = -0.0200\ (-0.67)$	$d_1 = 0.3537\ (6.60)$
$a_2 = 0.0325\ (2.02)$	$b_2 = 0.0022\ (0.02)$	$c_2 = 0.0206\ (0.74)$	$d_2 = 0.3244\ (6.16)$
$a_3 = 0.0202\ (1.32)$		$c_3 = 0.0770\ (3.91)$	$d_3 = 0.2926\ (5.25)$
$a_4 = 0.0094\ (0.94)$		$c_4 = 0.1358\ (15.54)$	$d_4 = 0.2583\ (4.41)$
$\Sigma a_i = 0.1699\ (2.85)$	$\Sigma b_i = 0.2488\ (2.21)$	$c_5 = 0.1838\ (21.92)$	$d_5 = 0.2215\ (3.76)$
		$c_6 = 0.2076\ (12.06)$	$d_6 = 0.1822\ (3.27)$
		$c_7 = 0.1938\ (9.10)$	$d_7 = 0.1404\ (2.90)$
		$c_8 = 0.1291\ (7.75)$	$d_8 = 0.0961\ (2.61)$
			$d_9 = 0.0493\ (2.38)$
		$\Sigma c_i = 0.8964\ (15.54)$	$\Sigma d_i = 2.2992\ (5.25)$

$e_0 = -0.0068\ (-0.74)$	$f_0 = -0.0270\ (-2.97)$
$e_1 = -0.0222\ (-3.28)$	$f_1 = -0.0273\ (-3.73)$
$e_2 = -0.0322\ (-4.32)$	$f_2 = -0.0262\ (-3.59)$
$e_3 = -0.0368\ (-4.33)$	$f_3 = -0.0237\ (-3.12)$
$e_4 = -0.0358\ (-4.19)$	$f_4 = -0.0199\ (-2.72)$
$e_5 = -0.0294\ (-4.06)$	$f_5 = -0.0146\ (-2.42)$
$e_6 = -0.0174\ (-3.96)$	$f_6 = -0.0080\ (-2.11)$
$\Sigma e_i = -0.1806\ (-4.32)$	$\Sigma f_i = -0.1467\ (-3.59)$

$R^2 = 0.9974$ $D.W. = 1.98$

$SE = 0.0492$ Sample Period: 1955.2–1968.4

Treasury bills and other short term liquid assets, as indicated in Figure 6-3. Consequently, banks may have actively adjusted their liquidity instead of altering time deposit rates in response to short term imbalances in asset and liability flows during the period prior to 1962. The lower liquidity ratios of the post-1962 period may reflect a greater reliance by commercial banks on the use of deposit rate changes in order to correct such imbalances. In order to test this hypothesis, the asset-liability flow variables are specified only for the post-1962 period. The estimation results are more satisfactory and indicative of the fact that commercial banks, at least in the more recent period, have actively managed deposit rates in order to stabilize short run asset and liability flows. Each impact variable is specified with a six quarter distributed lag and obtains strongly significant coefficients. Furthermore, the results indicate that the adjustment of deposit rates is somewhat more sensitive to changes in the flow of time deposits compared to demand deposits.

In order to allow for some lag in the response of deposit rates to changes in the discount rate, the variable that measures the differential between the level of asset rates and the discount rate is specified with a one quarter lag. The size of the coefficient is a fairly small -0.09 and is not significant at the 5 per cent confidence level. Nevertheless, it does have the correct sign and indicates that commercial banks apparently regard discount borrowing as a possible, although limited, substitute for deposit rate changes as a means for increasing the level of liabilities.

Finally, the variable that captures the effect of changes in the Regulation Q ceiling rate as a trigger mechanism for deposit rate changes is specified with a nine period distributed lag. The results for the variable $(QTD - QTD_{-1})$ indicate that such ceiling changes have a sharp and fairly long impact on the deposit rate. Nevertheless, there is no steady state effect, so that in the absence of changes in market rates, deposit rates return to their original level.

Conclusions

Overall, the empirical results in this chapter indicate that financial intermediaries determine interest rates on savings deposits in a rational and consistent manner that is susceptible to economic analysis. The deposit rate regressions detail the response of deposit rates to changes in financial conditions and provide a basis for more accurate analysis of the reaction of financial markets to changes in monetary policy or other economic instruments. These deposit rate functions are also essential in evaluating the quantitative macroeconomic impact of changes in the legal ceilings on deposit rates. The empirical evidence from the time series data is consistent

PERCENT

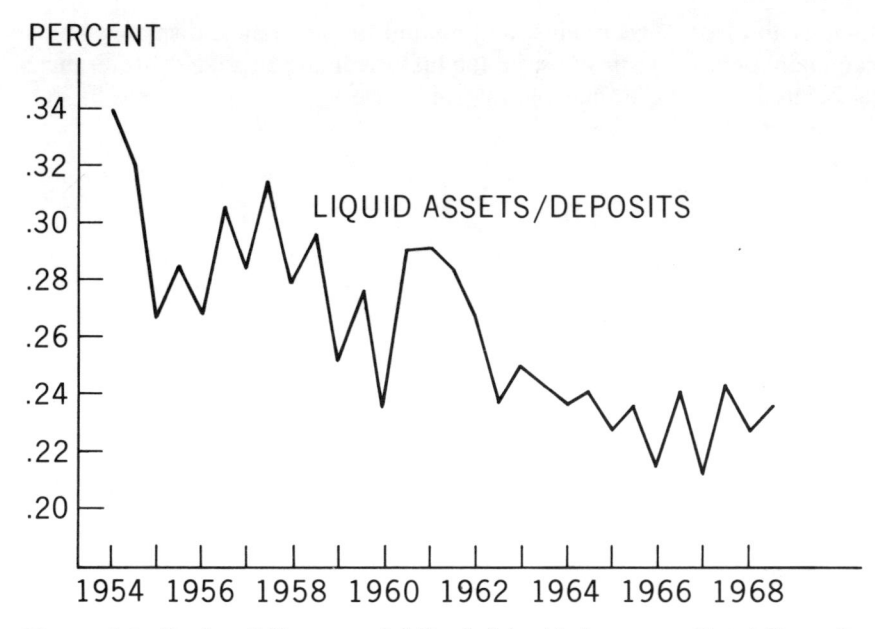

Figure 6-3. Ratio of Commercial Bank Liquid Assets to Total Deposits.

with the results obtained for a cross section of savings and loan associations and confirms that the deposit rate setting behavior of both commercial banks and nonbank intermediaries can be explained by the theory of profit maximization. Deposit rates at savings and loan associations, mutual savings banks, and commercial banks are primarily a function of movements in open market yields. The time series regression results indicate that deposit rates are a function of both current and expected future market yields, where distributed lags are used in order to proxy expectations held about future market rates. In each case the distributed lags prove to be rather lengthy, which implies that expectations at these institutions adjust fairly slowly to changes in market yields. Furthermore, there is substantial evidence that both bank and nonbank institutions utilize deposit rate changes in order to correct short run imbalances in asset and liability flows. On the aggregate level the deposit rate setting behavior of both bank and nonbank institutions is similar. The only differences that arise are due to the differing degree of complexity intrinsic to their operations, since commercial banks maintain a more varied portfolio of assets and liabilities than nonbank institutions. Nevertheless, the empirical evidence indicates that movements in open market rates were fully transmitted to depositors through the mechanism of deposit rates at least until 1969, when Regulation Q ceilings became severly restrictive on the deposit rates at all financial institutions. Thus, the deposit rate setting behavior of commercial banks, savings and loan associations, and mutual savings banks displays similar economic characteristics despite the historical and regulatory differences associated with these financial intermediaries.

7

An Economic Model of the Market for Negotiable Certificates of Deposit

The theoretical and empirical research developed in the earlier chapters has focused on the determination of interest rates on consumer savings deposits, which until recently have been the only form of interest bearing liabilities issued by financial intermediaries. Our objective has been to explore the supply relationships for these savings deposits by developing models of deposit rate setting behavior and estimating deposit rate equations. This problem has been neglected in monetary research especially in comparison to the analysis of the determinants of the public's demand for savings deposits, a subject that has been extensively investigated in several studies. Several of the best known are Modigliani [42], Feige [19], and Hamburger [30]. The purpose of this chapter is to apply this analysis of financial intermediary behavior in order to develop a theoretical model and to explain empirically the determinants of the behavior of the market for negotiable certificates of deposit (CDs). This demonstrates the general applicability of a deposit rate setting approach to the analysis of the supply of any liability issued by financial intermediaries. In addition, empirical evidence is reported that explains the behavior of the public's demand for CDs. This investigation of the supply and demand for certificates of deposit has become increasingly important since CDs are a relatively new money market instrument, which has grown in volume and significance at a rapid rate, particularly following the removal of the Regulation Q ceilings on most of these deposits in 1970.

A negotiable certificate of deposit is a large denomination commercial bank time deposit that has a specific date of maturity but may be freely bought or sold in the secondary market. These deposits were originated in February 1961 when the First National City Bank of New York issued large denomination CDs and a group of government securities dealers announced that they would make a resale market in these certificates. (For historical background on the organization of the certificate of deposit market, see Heebner [31].) The volume of negotiable CDs has since grown to about $90 billion; thus CDs have become a major money market instrument. The model developed in this chapter explains both the demand for CDs and the rate of interest on this instrument. In the process of modeling this market, it is necessary to recognize that the behavior of these functions is characterized by a dichotomy caused by the administration of Regulation Q by the Federal Reserve Board. During much of the period since 1961 the

Regulation Q ceiling had no impact on the behavior of the CD market. During such periods we hypothesize that the CD market reflected standard forces of demand and supply. However, during several time spans, the Regulation Q ceilings effectively bound offering rates on CDs. This restricted the quantity of new CD offerings and induced a runoff in the outstanding stock of CDs while the secondary CD rate was bid up above the ceiling rate to the level of open market interest rates. Consequently, we develop a model of the CD market in which the demand and supply equations each consist of different sets of variables for normal and runoff periods in order to explain this dichotomy.

The Demand for Certificates of Deposit

In explaining the demand side of the CD market, we begin by evaluating the public's demand behavior during periods when the Regulation Q ceilings are not binding and the quantity of CDs offered freely reflects the usual financial market forces. In specifying the determinants of the demand for CDs during normal periods, we use some standard portfolio considerations that are usually applied as a framework for analyzing the demand for liquid liabilities. This approach suggests that the quantity demanded is a function of both the own rate and the yield on close substitutes. Consequently, we specify the demand for CDs as

$$CD = CD(r_{CD}, i) \quad \partial CD/\partial r_{CD} > 0, \quad \partial CD/\partial i < 0 \qquad (7.1)$$

where r_{CD} represents the own rate and i represents competing rates. In an empirical formulation of the demand for CDs, the own rate is taken as the market yield on certificates of deposit *RCD*, and competing rates are proxied by the Treasury bill rate *RTB* and the commercial paper rate *RCP*, since these short term liquid assets are presumably close substitutes for CDs. We assume that during normal periods the demand for CDs is homogeneous with respect to income, so that the dependent variable is the ratio of CDs to current dollar Gross National Product *GNP*. (This development is similar to many empirical analyses of the demand for bank liabilities such as de Leeuw [12], Gramlich and Hullett [27], Goldfeld [22], and Silber [45].) The basic empirical specification becomes

$$CD/GNP = a_0 + a_1 RCD + a_2 RTB + a_3 RCP \qquad (7.2)$$

where a_1 is assumed positive and a_2 and a_3 negative, given the signs of the partial derivatives. We hypothesize that this function can effectively explain the demand for CDs during normal periods, that is, periods when the Regulation Q ceiling is not binding and the volume of CDs can freely reflect the public's preference for CDs relative to other short term liquid liabilities at the given level of market interest rates.

However during certain periods, Regulation Q ceilings have bound the offering rate on CDs to a level below that of market rates, and as a result new sales of CDs were less than the quantities maturing. Since these periods are characterized by a runoff in which the outstanding stock of CDs falls, equation (7.2) does not appropriately describe the behavior of the demand side of the market.[a] Instead, we hypothesize that during runoff periods the current quantity of CDs is primarily a function of the previously issued volume of CDs, since commercial banks cannot offer yields on new issues that are competitive with market rates. The functional relationship becomes

$$CD = CD(CD_{-1}) \qquad \partial CD/\partial CD_{-1} > 0. \qquad (7.3)$$

Furthermore, during normal periods the secondary rate on CDs closely approximates the offering rate on new issues. In contrast, when Regulation Q is binding, the secondary rate on CDs is bid above the ceiling rate on new offerings of CDs to a level competitive with market yields. As the spread widens between market interest rates and the ceiling rate QCD, we assume that the decline in the stock of CDs is intensified. We also hypothesize that the extent of this decline in the volume of CDs due to the differential between market and offering rates is dependent upon the previous stock of CDs outstanding. Rewriting equation (7.3) to reflect this assumption yields

$$CD = CD[CD_{-1}, (i - QCD)CD_{-1}] \qquad (7.4)$$
$$\partial CD/\partial CD_{-1} > 0, \quad \partial CD/\partial (i - QCD) < 0.$$

During normal periods we assumed that the demand for CDs is homogeneous with respect to income, but for runoff periods such an assumption may be inappropriate because of the ceiling rate constraint. Nevertheless, since movements in income may still have an independent effect on the public's willingness to hold the given volume of CDs, the level of income y is specified as an independent variable so that the runoff function becomes

$$CD = CD[CD_{-1}, (i - QCD)CD_{-1}, y] \qquad (7.5)$$
$$\partial CD/\partial CD_{-1}, \partial CD/\partial y > 0 \quad \partial CD/\partial (i - QCD) < 0.$$

For estimation purposes we specify equation (7.5) as follows

$$CD = a_0 + a_1 CD_{-1} + a_2(RCD - QCD)CD_{-1} + a_3 GNP, \qquad (7.6)$$

where RCD is the secondary CD rate, which is a measure of the level of market interest rates, and QCD is the Regulation Q ceiling rate, which is a

---
[a]The restrictiveness of Regulation Q ceilings induced a runoff in CDs during the following periods: 1966.3-1966.4, 1968.2 and 1968.4-1970.2

proxy for the level of offering rates on new CDs. Given the a priori signs of the partial derivatives in equation (7.5), the estimated coefficients a_1 and a_3 should obtain positive signs, and the coefficient a_2 should be negative, since a widening in the differential between market and offering rates should induce a further decline in the demand for CDs relative to the previous quarter.

Therefore, during normal periods when Regulation Q ceilings do not have a restrictive impact on the CD offering rate, the behavior of the demand for CDs is described by equation (7.2). If market interest rates and the secondary CD rate rise above the Regulation Q ceiling, a runoff in the stock of CDs occurs, so that equation (7.6) becomes the relevant description of demand behavior. We estimate these two specifications for the demand for CDs jointly using dummy variables to allow the proper set of variables to enter for the appropriate time spans in the sample. The function is estimated by means of ordinary least squares for the period 1962.1 to 1972.4 using quarterly data. The results are reported in Table 7-1. The figures in parenthesis below the coefficients are the relevant t statistics.

Equation (7.1.1) reports the estimation results for the normal period regression in which Regulation Q ceilings on CD rates are not binding. The own rate *RCD* is strongly positive and quite significant. The commercial paper rate *RCP* has a large negative coefficient, which indicates that short term commercial paper is apparently a strong substitute for negotiable CDs. The coefficient is approximately the same size as the own rate and has a t statistic in excess of five. Although the Treasury bill rate *RTB* also has a negative sign, the coefficient is much smaller than the coefficients of the other rates and is not significant. This result, however, may be due to the multicollinearity intrinsic to time series data for these rates rather than to a lack of substitution between Treasury bills and CDs.

In addition to interest rates, several other variables are specified in order to reflect the impact of corporate behavior on the demand for CDs since most negotiable certificates of deposit are held by corporations, who view them as a convenient means for holding short term inflows of cash instead of building up noninterest bearing demand deposit balances.[b] A major factor in corporate demand for CDs is assumed to be the level of after tax corporate profits. As profit flows to corporations increase, funds are invested in CDs in the short run, since profits are only gradually diverted into dividends to stockholders or future investment projects. Thus, ceteris paribus, a positive sign for this variable is expected, since it is assumed that a rise in profits increases the demand for CDs. The variable specified in the regression, *PROFIT,* is defined as corporate profits plus depreciation allowances. Depreciation is a deduction from profit but does not produce a

---

[b]A 1964 survey by the American Bankers Association [2] indicated that corporations held 46 per cent of CDs smaller than $500,000 in denomination and 70 per cent of CDs larger than $500,000 in denomination.

Table 7-1
Equations for the Demand for Certificates of Deposit

(7.1.1) Normal period: Regulation Q ceiling is not binding

$$\frac{CD}{GNP} = \underset{(4.68)}{0.0133 RCD} - \underset{(-1.17)}{0.0025 RTB}$$
$$- \underset{(-5.08)}{0.0155 RCP} + \underset{(13.77)}{0.0003 PROFIT}$$
$$- \underset{(-1.31)}{0.0009} (DIV_{-1} - DIV_{-2}) + .0027$$

$R^2 = 0.959 \quad SE = 0.0015 \quad D.W. = 1.46$

(7.1.2) Runoff period: Regulation Q ceiling is binding

$$CD = \underset{(13.83)}{0.7964 CD_{-1}} - \underset{(-2.92)}{0.0975} (RCD - QCD) CD_{-1}$$
$$+ \underset{(3.98)}{0.0042 GNP} - 0.0015$$

cash drain. Instead, these funds are retained for future investment in order to replace depreciating plant and equipment. Consequently, depreciation allowances as well as profits are a potential source of funds for investment in CDs. The estimated coefficient of the profit variable is positive with a t statistic in excess of 13.

Another variable is specified in the function in order to capture the possible impact of corporate dividend behavior on CD demand. Although corporations eventually disburse a portion of their profits as dividend payments to stockholders, dividends are changed only at infrequent intervals. Consequently, when dividend rates are increased, it is possible that in the short run a corporation might liquidate some CD holdings in order to fund the dividend payment. Consequently, the change in corporate dividends ($DIV_{-1} - DIV_{-2}$) is specified in the demand equation. Although the coefficient fails to be significant at the 90 per cent level, it does have the expected negative sign, which provides some evidence that a change in dividends may alter the quantity of CDs demanded in the short run.

Overall, when the Regulation Q ceiling is not binding, that is, when equation (7.1.1) pertains, we assume that the primary CD rate is set by the behavior of commercial banks, and the public demands a quantity of CDs that is appropriate given competing rates and other factors. However, when the Regulation Q ceiling is binding, we hypothesize that the normal demand specification is not appropriate. Commercial banks are restrained from offering CD yields higher than the ceiling rate and have difficulty in renewing maturing CDs with the result that a decline occurs in the outstanding stock of CDs. During these runoff periods when the secondary CD rate rises above the ceiling rate on new offerings, we hypothesize that the demand for CDs is described by equation (7.6).

In the regression results for the runoff function equation (7.1.2), the coefficient of the lagged stock is estimated to be 0.80 with a t statistic of almost 14. This indicates that if the secondary CD rate, which closely follows market yields, is equal to the ceiling rate on new CDs ($RCD = QCD$), there will be a 20 per cent per quarter decline in the stock of CDs. A coefficient of -0.10 is obtained for the variable that measures the difference between the secondary CD rate and the Regulation Q ceiling. This indicates that as market rates rise, there is an increase in the rate at which the stock of CDs runs off. For example, if there is a 100 basis point spread between market rates and the ceiling rate, the outstanding stock of CDs declines at the rate of 30 per cent per quarter. Furthermore, the GNP variable obtains a positive coefficient of 0.004 with a t statistic of almost four. This provides evidence that movements in *GNP* have a significant influence on the public's willingness to hold CDs even during periods when Regulation Q ceilings restrict the volume of new offerings.

Interest Rates on Certificates of Deposit

In explaining the supply side of the CD market we use a theoretical model of deposit rate setting as the framework for analyzing the yield on certificates of deposit. Again we hypothesize that the behavior of CD rates is contingent upon whether or not Regulation Q ceilings are binding. During periods when the Regulation Q ceiling is not a restrictive factor, the secondary rate on CDs is closely tied to the primary rate on new offerings. Consequently, we apply the theory of deposit rate setting in order to explain the rate at which commercial banks are willing to supply CDs. For periods when Regulation Q is binding on offering rates and the secondary rate is bid above the ceiling, we assume that a term structure relationship ties the market rate on CDs to yields on other short term financial instruments.

During normal periods when ceiling rates are not effective and supply behavior can freely reflect the usual market forces, we analyze CD rate behavior by using a model in which commercial banks are assumed to maximize profits in each period. We retain the assumption from the demand section of this chapter that the public's demand for CDs is positively related to the own rate and negatively related to market interest rates[c] so that

$$CD = CD(r_{CD}, i) \quad \partial CD/\partial r_{CD} > 0 \quad \partial CD/\partial i < 0. \tag{7.7}$$

Profits π are defined as revenue minus costs. It is hypothesized that commercial banks invest a given proportion of their deposits in assets that earn the market rate of return. Thus, revenues are the market rate of return i on the proportion k of liabilities held as earning assets. The total of commercial bank liabilities is defined as the sum of demand deposits, time deposits, and certificates of deposit. Costs are measured as the appropriate interest rate paid on the relevant type of bank liabilities. Therefore, profits can be written as

$$\pi = ik(MD + MT + CD) - r_{CB}MT - r_{CD}CD, \tag{7.8}$$

where MD is demand deposits, MT time deposits, CD certificates of deposits, r_{CB} the time deposit rate, and r_{CD} the CD rate. It is assumed that no interest is paid on demand deposits. The time deposit rate is viewed as exogenous to the problem of choosing an optimal CD rate because of the binding effect of ceiling restrictions over most of the relevant period and the fact that time deposit rates are generally set only once a quarter, whereas CD rates fluctuate with greater frequency. Substituting equation (7.7) into

---

[c] It is also assumed that the cross partial derivative $\partial CD/\partial i \, \partial r$ is either zero or very small relative to the other parameters in the function.

equation (7.8) and differentiating, yields the first order condition for a profit maximum

$$\partial \pi / \partial r_{CD} = (ik - r_{CD})(\partial CD / \partial r_{CD}) - CD(r_{CD}, i) = 0. \tag{7.9}$$

It should be noted that the level of the time deposit rate r_{CB} does not influence the optimal CD rate. Therefore, the level of the Regulation Q ceilings on non-CD deposits has no direct impact on the CD market. From equation (7.9) it is clear that the interest rate on CDs is primarily a function of market interest rates i. The second order condition for a profit maximum is

$$\frac{\partial^2 \pi}{\partial r_{CD}^2} = (ik - r_{CD}) \frac{\partial^2 CD}{\partial r_{CD}^2} - 2 \frac{\partial CD}{\partial r_{CD}} < 0. \tag{7.10}$$

Using the implicit function rule we can solve for the effect of a change in market interest rates i on the optimal CD deposit rate

$$\frac{dr_{CD}}{di} = \frac{-\dfrac{k\partial CD}{\partial r_{CD}} + \dfrac{\partial CD}{\partial i}}{(ik - r_{CD}) \dfrac{\partial^2 CD}{\partial r_{CD}^2} - 2\dfrac{\partial CD}{\partial r_{CD}}} > 0. \tag{7.11}$$

Expression (7.11) is positive, since the numerator is negative using the signs of the partial derivatives in equation (7.7), and the denominator is negative by the second order conditions for a profit maximum. This comparative statics result indicates that an increase in market interest rates has a positive effect on the CD interest rate.

In general, during normal periods when Regulation Q ceilings are not restrictive, the interest rate on CDs is explained primarily as a function of market interest rates, that is, yields on assets held by commercial banks and interest rates on liquid assets that the public regards as substitutes for CDs. For empirical testing, the specification can be written as

$$RCD = b_0 + b_1 i_a + b_2 i_c \tag{7.12}$$

where i_a represents asset rates, and i_c competing rates. The variable RCD is the secondary yield on CDs, which is essentially identical to the offering rate on new CDs when the ceilings are not binding. Since the estimation results for the demand for CDs indicate that Treasury bills and commercial paper are the closest substitutes for CDs, the variables RTB and RCP are used to capture the effect of competing rates. Based on the sign of the comparative statics result in expression (7.11), the signs of the coefficients b_1 and b_2 should be positive.

During runoff periods when the Regulation Q ceiling on CDs is effective and the secondary rate on CDs is bid above the ceiling rate on new offerings, the CD rate is not determined by the optimization behavior of commercial banks. Instead, we hypothesize that the behavior of the CD rate is determined by movements in other short term yields through a term structure equation. The functional relationship is

$$r_{CD} = r_{CD}(i) \quad \partial r_{CD}/\partial i > 0. \tag{7.13}$$

In the empirical specification of this term structure, the variable i is proxied by the commercial paper rate RCP and the Treasury bill rate RTB, so that the equation for estimation is

$$RCD = b_0 + b_1 RTB + b_2 RCP. \tag{7.14}$$

where the coefficients b_1 and b_2 are expected to be positive.

Equations (7.12) and (7.14) are estimated jointly using dummy variables to allow the appropriate set of variables to enter for the proper time spans in the sample. The function is estimated by means of ordinary least squares over the sample period 1962.1 to 1972.4 using quarterly data. The results are reported in Table 7-2, where the numbers in parenthesis below the coefficients are the relevant t statistics.

For the normal period, where equation (7.2.1) pertains, the two competing rate variables have positive coefficients and are strongly significant. Consequently, the evidence indicates that both Treasury bills and commercial paper are strong substitutes for holdings of CDs. Although interest rates on a variety of assets found in commercial bank portfolios were tested in the equation, only the municipal bond rate $RMUN$ is statistically significant.[d] Although commercial banks hold large quantities of commercial loans and mortgages and relatively smaller amounts of long term securities, the interest rates on these assets have no statistical significance when specified in the CD rate equation.[e]

In addition, two impact variables are specified in equation (7.2.1) in order to capture the effects of short term changes in deposit and asset flows on the determination of CD rates. The first variable is the change in commercial loans ($MCL_{-1} - MCL_{-2}$). Since empirical evidence indicates that the commercial loan rate is slow to adjust to equilibrium,[f] increases in loan demand may induce commercial banks to raise CD rates as a short run

---

[d]The importance of the municipal bond rate is not surprising inasmuch as municipal bond holdings of commercial banks have increased quite rapidly in the last decade and now represent a substantial proportion of commercial bank portfolios. Data for the municipal bond holdings of commercial banks are reported in the Federal Reserve Bulletin [5].

[e]This result may be due to the multicollinearity intrinsic to the time series data for interest rate variables.

[f]A considerable literature has evolved which indicates that at least in the short run the commercial loan rate does not equilibrate the demand and supply for loans and that nonprice allocation of credit occurs. See Jaffee [35] for a recent exposition of this view of the commercial loan market.

Table 7-2
Equations for the Interest Rate on Certificates of Deposit

(7.2.1) Normal period: Regulation Q ceiling is not binding

$$RCD = 0.0518 RMUN + 0.4366 RTB$$
$$(2.04) \qquad\qquad (4.32)$$
$$+ 0.6426 RCP + 0.0350 (MCL_{-1} - MCL_{-2})$$
$$(7.20) \qquad\qquad (2.39)$$
$$- 0.4552 (QTD - QTD_{-1}) - 0.4613$$
$$(-5.00)$$

$R^2 = 0.997 \qquad SE = 0.0891 \qquad D.W. = 1.84$

(7.2.2) Runoff period: Regulation Q ceiling is binding

$$RCD = 0.5489 RTB + 0.6375 RCP - 0.8667$$
$$(3.55) \qquad\qquad (5.96)$$

buffer in order to obtain the necessary funds to meet this new loan demand instead of immediately adjusting loan rates. In order to capture this short run impact, the change in commercial loans is specified in equation (7.2.1). The variable obtains a positive coefficient that is statistically significant and indicates that the level of CD rates is in fact influenced in the short run by changes in loan demand. A second impact variable in the CD rate equation is the change in the ceiling on non-CD time deposit rates QTD. Over a considerable portion of the sample period, interest rates on non-CD deposits were at the legal maximum, so that when changes in the legal maximum were initiated, time deposit rates rapidly adjusted to the new ceilings. Therefore, we hypothesize that increases in Regulation Q can produce large inflows of deposits. Since commercial banks cannot quickly lend substantial funds for commercial loans and mortgages, the increase in bank liabilities may exceed the desired growth of earning assets in the short run. As a result commercial banks may temporarily lower the CD rate as a buffer in order to equilibrate these asset and liability flows. Consequently, the change in the ceiling on non-CD time deposit rates $(QTD - QTD_{-1})$ is specified as a variable in equation (7.2.1). The coefficient of this variable is negative as expected and quite significant. The coefficients for both impact variables provide empirical evidence that the CD rate is altered by commercial banks to balance asset and liability flows in the short run.

The specification of the CD rate equation during normal periods, when Regulation Q ceilings do not restrict CD rates, reflects the optimization behavior of commercial banks. However, during runoff periods, the offering rate on new CDs is constrained by the ceiling so that the secondary rate on marketable CDs diverges from the offering rate and is bid up to the level of competing market interest rates. For such periods, we hypothesize that the behavior of CD rates is directly related to the level of open market interest rates rather than to commercial bank behavior. The empirical results obtained for the specification that reflects this relationship are reported as equation (7.2.2). In this regression, the Treasury bill rate RTB and the commercial paper rate RCP are used to proxy open market yields. Both variables obtain large positive coefficients that are strongly significant and successfully explain the variation in the secondary CD rate.

Conclusions

In this chapter we have developed an economic model of the market for negotiable certificates of deposit. Specifically, the model indicates that demand for CDs during periods when Regulation Q ceilings are not binding is a positive function of the own rate, competing market interest rates, and income and is directly related to the level of corporate profits and inversely to changes in corporate dividends. During periods when Regulation Q is binding and a runoff in CDs occurs, the quantity of CDs is primarily a function of the volume of CDs outstanding the previous quarter, and income. During such periods, the rate of runoff in CDs accelerates as the spread widens between competing market rates and the ceiling rate. On the supply side, a deposit rate setting model of commercial bank behavior effectively explains the yield on CDs when the Regulation Q ceiling is not binding. The empirical results indicate that the CD rate is a function of rates on municipal bonds and yields on close substitutes for CDs. In addition, there is evidence that changes in commercial loans and changes in Regulation Q ceilings on non-CD time deposit rates also have an impact. Thus, the CD rate is apparently used by commercial banks in order to balance asset and liability flows in the short run. During runoff periods when the Regulation Q ceiling is binding, the secondary rate on CDs is not determined as a result of the optimization behavior of commercial banks and is instead directly related to movements in open market interest rates.

8 Regulation Q, The Credit Crunch of 1966, and the Structural Instability of the Demand for Money

In the world of neo-Keynesian economics the money market is the heart of the financial system and plays a central role in the determination of the level of aggregate demand. In neo-Keynesian macroeconomics the equilibrium level of income is established at the point at which the short term open market interest rate simultaneously clears both the product market and the money market. In the product market the desired level of savings must be sufficient to sustain the quantity of investment goods demanded at market interest rates. In the money market the public's demand for money must be equated with the stock of money. On the demand side of the money market, the quantity of money desired by the public is influenced by the level of income and the opportunity cost of holding money as measured by short term interest rates. (There is an extensive literature on the demand for money and a good summary of this research is Laidler [37]). On the supply side of the money market, the stock of money is viewed as exogenously determined by the central bank or, in more sophisticated formulations, derived from the reserve behavior of commercial banks, which are assumed to view short term interest rates as the opportunity cost of holding excess reserves. (This endogenous treatment of the money supply mechanism is found in Teigen [47] and in Modigliani, Rasche, and Cooper [43].) Consequently, the short term open market interest rate is the equilibrating price that equates the public's demand for money with the stock of money that results from the interaction of the central bank's reserve actions and commercial bank behavior.

Thus, the short term open market interest rate, which is determined through the interaction of the demand and supply for money and which in equilibrium simultaneously clears the product market, has an important role in neo-Keynesian macroeconomics as the mechanism through which changes in monetary policy are transmitted throughout the economy. In most theoretical and econometric analyses, long term interest rates are viewed as functionally related to short term open market rates through term structure relationships. (The literature on the term structure of interest rates is reviewed in Malkiel [39].) Long term rates directly influence the demand for most forms of investment, which in turn alters the level of income and other real variables such as unemployment. Consequently, the character and stability of the public's demand for money function is an important prerequisite to the determination of efficient stabilization policy in general, and monetary policy in particular. As a result, the subject of money demand has been analyzed both theoretically and empirically more than any other subject in monetary economics, with its origins traceable to the earliest development of the classical school. Nevertheless, there has been relatively little divergence among economists as to what are the major determinants of money demand. Instead, the literature has primarily dealt with the rationalization of these determinants and the analysis of their quantitative importance. In almost all of these studies the quantity of money demanded is basically assumed to be a positive function of income or wealth and a negative function of interest rates. Generally a vector of interest rates, rather than a single rate, is utilized to proxy the opportunity cost of holding money. The two most important types of yields usually included in empirical studies are an open market interest rate variable, which is specified in order to capture the substitution possibilities available to large transactors, and an interest rate on savings deposits, which is included in order to reflect the availability of alternative assets for holders of small portfolios. Consequently, the pattern of interest rates on savings deposits has a fundamental role in the behavior of the money market and therefore in the economic impact of monetary policy.

In this chapter we examine the demand for money and the impact that interest rates on savings deposits have on the behavior of the money market. In particular, we examine the stability of the demand for money and investigate whether the pattern of substitution between money and various forms of savings deposits has changed due to the behavior of savings deposit rates during the postwar period. More specifically, the pattern of interest rates on savings deposits has been affected by changes in the administration of Regulation Q. Prior to 1962 the differential between the interest rates on bank and nonbank savings deposits was quite large, ranging from 120 to 160 basis points (see Figure 6-1). This probably was due to the Regulation Q ceiling restrictions, which kept commercial bank time deposit rates low relative to nonbank rates. As a result of this rate differential, interest sensitive funds were apparently diverted into nonbank institutions rather than commercial banks. That is, holders of money balances probably considered the nonbank yield to be the opportunity cost of holding money rather than the rates at commercial banks. In 1962 these ceiling restrictions were raised by 100 basis points and the differential between bank and nonbank rates narrowed dramatically to within the range of 40 to 60 basis points. Consequently, it can be hypothesized that commercial bank time deposits and nonbank savings deposits apparently became strong substitutes only after 1961. Several recent studies of the savings market have provided considerable empirical evidence of this structural change. Modigliani [42] and Kardouche [36] found evidence that a shift in substitution characterized the demand side of the savings market. In chapter 6 of this study we found that this shift in substitution had an impact on savings deposit rate setting behavior. In an earlier study [46], we established preliminary evidence that a concomitant structural shift occurred in the demand for money.

In this chapter we extend our earlier work and more fully develop our hypothesis that the behavior of interest rates on savings deposits has had an important impact on the behavior and stability of the money market and therefore macroeconomic activity. We undertake an empirical investigation of this subject by using the standard specifications of a money demand function to demonstrate that structural instability caused by the behavior of interest rates on savings deposits characterizes the postwar money market. In addition to the shift in substitution between bank and nonbank liabilities that resulted from the 1962 rise in Regulation Q, we hypothesize that another shift occurred in 1966. During 1966 a sharp rise occurred in the level of open market interest rates which induced dislocations within the financial market and the economy as a whole. The housing industry in particular sustained a serious decline in activity. These circumstances engendered serious doubts about the ability of savings institutions to pay deposit rates sufficiently high enough to be competitive with other financial instruments and as a result the government reacted by initiating ceiling restrictions on deposit rates at nonbank institutions. These events which are reviewed in the 1966 Annual Report of the Federal Home Loan Bank Board [18], are generally referred to as the Credit Crunch of 1966. The deposit rate ceilings are administered by the Federal Home Loan Bank Board and the Federal Deposit Insurance Corporation. Since 1966 these regulatory authorities have consistently maintained a fairly constant differential between bank and nonbank deposit rates. Our contention is that these financial developments induced a shift in the structure of the public's demand for money function.

Our approach to this subject is to analyze the structural stability of the demand for money by testing a specification that has become standard in the development of large scale econometric models and by demonstrating that the function indicates that a shift in the pattern of substitution between money and near monies has occurred twice in recent years. We use the specification of money demand typified by the research of Modigliani, Rasche, and Cooper [43]. In such a formulation, money demand is specified as a function of income, open market interest rates, and the commercial bank time deposit rate. It is also assumed that money demand is characterized by partial adjustment to equilibrium. Because of the multicollinearity between interest rates and income, we first estimate the money demand equation in velocity form, that is, with the long run elasticity of income constrained to unity. This procedure allows more accurate estimation of the character of the interest rate effects on money demand. Next, we relax the income constraint in order to demonstrate that the basic character of the results are not altered even when the income elasticity of the demand for money is freely estimated.

A Velocity Specification

The basic specification of the money demand function is derived from the Latané [38] theory that

$$m^* = k(i)y \qquad \partial k/\partial i < 0 \qquad (8.1)$$

where m^* is desired holdings of nominal money balances, i is a measure of interest rates, and y is nominal income. Since it is assumed that the actual demand for money holdings m adjusts only gradually to the desired level m^*, then

$$\begin{aligned}\Delta m &= \lambda(m^* - m_{-1}) \\ &= \lambda(k(i)y - m_{-1})\end{aligned} \qquad (8.2)$$

which in logarithmic form is

$$\begin{aligned}\ln m - \ln m_{-1} &= \lambda(\ln m^* - \ln m_{-1}) \\ &= \lambda(\ln k(i) + \ln y - \ln m_{-1})\end{aligned} \qquad (8.3)$$

where λ is the speed of adjustment.[a] Solving for m and subtracting y from both sides of the equation yields the specification

$$\ln m - \ln y = \lambda \ln k(i) + (1 - \lambda)(\ln m_{-1} - \ln y). \qquad (8.4)$$

The variable $k(i)$ is approximated by a vector of yields on instruments that are assumed to be close substitutes for money balances. The competing rates in most empirical formulations are an open market interest rate, such as the commercial paper rate RCP, and an interest rate on savings deposits, such as the time deposit rate at commercial banks RTD.[b] The level of nominal income is measured by GNP in current dollars.

Throughout the empirical analysis the equations are estimated on quarterly data using the quantity of demand deposits as the dependent variable.[c] The specification of equation (8.4) for empirical testing is

---

[a]Estimation of the logarithmic form of this equation yields coefficients that are the elasticities of the variables.

[b]Regressions were also tested in which the Treasury bill rate was used as the measure of open market yields instead of the commercial paper rate. The results for the bill rate, however, were generally less significant and thus only regressions with the commercial paper rate are reported. Goldfeld's [23] findings are similar.

[c]Regressions were also tested in which the narrowly defined money supply, that is demand deposits plus currency, was used as the dependent variable. The estimation results were similar.

$$\ln(MD/GNP) = a_o + a_1 \ln RCP + a_2 \ln RTD$$
$$+ a_3 \ln(MD_{-1}/GNP). \tag{8.5}$$

The Cochrane-Orcutt [11] first order autoregressive technique is used in order to correct for serial correlation in the residuals. We begin by estimating specification (8.5) over the full sample period 1955.1-1973.4. The results are reported as equation (8.1.1) in Table 8-1. The t statistics are in parentheses below the estimated coefficients. The results for this regression are consistent with the evidence found in much of the money demand literature. The coefficients for both RTD and RCP are negative and significantly different from zero. This implies that both commercial paper and time deposits are substitutes for holdings of money balances. The long run elasticities for these interest rate variables are approximately −0.17 and −0.20.[d] The coefficient of the lagged stock variable is 0.87, which suggests that actual holdings of demand deposit balances adjust toward the desired level at a rate of 13 per cent per quarter. Although this is a fairly slow speed of adjustment, this figure is typical of the results reported throughout the money demand literature, as for example, in Modigliani, Rasche, and Cooper [43].

In order to test our hypothesis that changes in the behavior of deposit rates during the 1960s due to the administration of Regulation Q ceilings induced shifts in the structure of the demand for money function, equation (8.1.1) is reestimated over three separate time periods. These sample periods are: 1955.1 through 1961.4, a span during which yields on nonbank liabilities were sharply higher than time deposit rates at commercial banks; 1962.1 through 1966.3, a period when time deposit rates were substantially more competitive despite the absence of ceiling rate restrictions on nonbank rates; and 1966.4 through 1973.4, a time period when all savings deposit rates were under federal ceiling restrictions and the regulatory authorities sought to maintain a consistent differential between bank and nonbank deposit rates in favor of nonbank institutions. The results for these sample periods are reported as equations (8.1.2) through (8.1.4).

First, the results indicate that the time deposit rate at commercial banks RTD had no substitution effect on the demand for money prior to 1962. The value of the coefficient for this period is only −0.013 with a t value of −0.76, which clearly lacks statistical significance. In contrast, the empirical evidence for the period 1962.1 through 1966.3 indicates a substantial degree of substitution between time deposits and money. The time deposit rate variable obtains a powerful coefficient of almost −0.19 that is statistically significant. The implied long run elasticity is almost −0.47. It was during this period that the rise in time deposit rates sharply narrowed the differen-

---

[d]The long run elasticity is calculated by dividing the coefficient estimated in the equation, that is, the short run elasticity, by the speed of adjustment, which is unity minus the estimated coefficient for the lagged dependent variable.

Table 8-1
Equations for the Velocity Specification of Money Demand—Dependent Variable MD/GNP—Double Logarithmic Form

Equation	Sample Period	$\dfrac{MD_{-1}}{GNP}$	RCP	RTD	RSL	Constant	R^2 SE	D.W. Rho
(8.1.1)	1955.1 1973.4	0.8750 (37.59)	−0.0215 (−5.39)	−0.0246 (−2.86)		−0.1304 (−5.20)	0.998 0.0063	2.02 0.16
(8.1.2)	1955.1 1961.4	0.8993 (12.79)	−0.0213 (−4.70)	−0.0134 (−0.76)		−0.1040 (−1.21)	0.995 0.0042	1.99 0.31
(8.1.3)	1962.1 1966.3	0.5992 (10.41)	−0.0631 (−3.40)	−0.1878 (−2.85)		−0.3025 (−4.46)	0.996 0.0033	1.57 −0.13
(8.1.4)	1966.4 1973.4	0.9033 (12.11)	−0.0186 (−2.61)	−0.0278 (−0.66)		−0.0799 (−0.94)	0.956 0.0087	2.09 −0.01
(8.1.5)	1955.1 1961.4	0.7703 (11.66)	−0.0242 (−6.90)		−0.1000 (−2.81)	−0.1675 (−3.43)	0.996 0.0037	1.88 0.06
(8.1.6)	1962.1 1966.3	0.6213 (10.40)	−0.0561 (−2.90)	−0.1468 (−1.96)	−0.0974 (−1.19)	−0.1885 (−1.62)	0.996 0.0033	1.57 −0.12
(8.1.7)	1962.1 1966.3	0.6669 (10.66)	−0.0769 (−3.37)		−0.1481 (−1.61)	−0.2065 (−1.39)	0.995 0.0035	1.95 0.18
(8.1.8)	1966.4 1973.4	0.5919 (5.83)	−0.0307 (−3.41)		−0.1688 (−3.45)	−0.3657 (−3.09)	0.965 0.0078	2.23 0.41

tial between nonbank and bank savings deposit yields. For the sample period 1966.4 through 1973.4, however, the time deposit rate variable again fails to have any significant impact. The coefficient is −0.028 and has a t statistic of only −0.66. This suggests that in recent years there again is no significant substitution between money and time deposits at commercial banks.

Second, the results indicate that a striking change occurs in the behavior of the coefficients for the lagged dependent variable over the separate sample periods. During the period 1955.1 through 1961.4 the coefficient of the lagged stock implies a speed of adjustment of only 10 per cent compared to a speed of 40 per cent per quarter indicated for the period 1962.1 through 1966.3. For the post-1966 period a speed of 10 per cent per quarter is again estimated.

Overall, these empirical results suggest that there was a substantial degree of substitution between time deposits and money during the period between the 100 basis point increase in Regulation Q in 1962 and the Credit Crunch of 1966. This substitution, however, was inconsequential prior to 1962 and after 1966. Furthermore, the standard specification of money demand implies sharp variations in the speed of adjustment for these periods that are disguised in a full period estimation. The speed with which demand deposit holdings adjusted toward equilibrium in the middle period, 1962-1966, is 40 per cent per quarter, a result that is substantially faster than any previous research has suggested. In contrast, the standard specification implies a very slow speed of adjustment of 10 per cent per quarter for the periods 1955.1 through 1961.4 and 1966.4 through 1973.4. These results provide a strong indication of structural instability in the public's demand for money during the 1960s.

In order to evaluate more explicitly the change in the pattern of substitution between money and near monies over the period, we respecify the competing rate variable in the money demand function. Since yields on savings deposits at nonbank intermediaries were considerably higher than commercial bank time deposit rates prior to 1962, nonbank intermediaries may have dominated commercial banks in the competition for the funds of interest elastic holders of money balances. The regression results in equation (8.1.2) are consistent with this view, since the time deposit rate variable has little impact on money demand. In order to test whether deposits at nonbank institutions may have been the strongest substitute for money holdings prior to the rise in Regulation Q ceilings in 1962, equation (8.1.2) is respecified to include the yield on savings and loan shares RSL in place of the time deposit rate variable.[e] The results are reported as equation

---

[e]The mutual savings bank deposit rate and the savings and loan deposit rate work equally well in the regressions but are collinear, so that only one of these variables can be effectively estimated in the equation. Consequently, the savings and loan deposit rate should be considered a proxy for nonbank deposit rates.

(8.1.5). The savings and loan rate RSL obtains a coefficient of -0.10 and has a t statistic of -2.8. The implied long run elasticity is approximately -0.44, which indicates that prior to 1962, nonbank savings deposits rather than commercial bank time deposits were indeed a strong substitute for money holdings. Furthermore, this respecification results in a marked decrease in the standard error. In addition, the lagged dependent variable obtains a coefficient of 0.77, which implies a speed of adjustment of 23 per cent per quarter, a more reasonable result than that of equation (8.1.2).

When RSL is added to specification in equation (8.1.3) which is estimated over the sample period 1962.1 to 1966.3, the variable obtains the correct sign but is not significant, as reported in equation (8.1.6). Even when the time deposit rate is omitted from the specification, equation (8.1.7), RSL still fails in statistical significance. Although there is some evidence for substitution between money and nonbank deposits during this period, the empirical results indicate that the primary alternative for money holdings was time deposits at commercial banks. The rise in Regulation Q ceilings in 1962 evidently allowed commercial banks to offer time deposit rates sufficiently high enough to attract interest sensitive holdings of money balances. The result is reasonable given the narrowing in the differential between RSL and RTD that occurred in 1962.

During the period of disintermediation in 1966, legal ceilings were initiated on nonbank deposit rates. Since that time, the regulatory authorities have consistently maintained a spread between the ceilings on nonbank and commercial bank deposit rates in favor of nonbank institutions, (A chronology of the administration of ceiling rate changes is found in Ruebling [44].) In order to test whether interest sensitive holders of money balances have recognized that nonbank institutions are allowed to offer higher yields on savings deposits than commercial banks, the variable RSL is specified in the money demand function for the period 1966.4 through 1973.4. In contrast to the results in equation (8.1.4), where the coefficient on the time deposit rate is very weak, in equation (8.1.8) the RSL variable is quite significant. It obtains a coefficient of -0.17 and has a t statistic of -3.5. The implied long run elasticity is -0.41, which is approximately equal to the long run elasticity for the 1955.1-1961.4 sample period. An additional result of this respecification is that the coefficient of the lagged dependent variable falls from 0.90 to about 0.60. The latter figure implies a speed of adjustment of 40 per cent which is approximately the same as that obtained for the sample period 1962.1-1966.3 and faster than the 23 per cent quarter figure for the sample period 1955.1-1961.4.

Overall, the results provide further evidence that the public's demand for money function has been characterized by structural instability during the 1960s. More specifically, the pattern of substitution between money and near monies has shifted over the postwar period as a result of changes in the ceiling rate policies of the monetary authorities. Nonbank liabilities have been the primary substitute for money holdings during the 1950s and after 1966. Commercial bank time deposits were strong substitutes for money only during the period 1962.1 to 1966.3, when the sharp rise in Regulation Q ceilings enhanced the competitive capabilities of commercial banks. A second important result is that more reasonable speeds of adjustment are obtained when the specification of money demand allows for such shifts in structure. In particular, the evidence indicates that the public's demand for money since 1961 has been characterized by faster adjustment toward equilibrium than during the period of the 1950s.

Savings Deposit Rates and the Income Elasticity of Money Demand

The results in Table 8-1 are based on a velocity formulation of the demand for money function. This specification assumes that money balances are homogeneous with respect to income in the long run and permits more accurate estimation of the interest rate effects on money demand. We now relax the assumption of homogeneity and allow the income elasticity to be freely estimated. Overall, the same pattern of empirical results is obtained, which indicates that our hypothesis of structural instability in the demand for money remains appropriate. The derivation of the alternate money demand specification follows directly from equation (8.3) and can be rewritten as

$$\ln m = \lambda \ln k(i) + \lambda \ln y + (1 - \lambda)\ln m_{-1}. \tag{8.6}$$

Approximating the variable $k(i)$ by the commercial paper rate RCP and the time deposit rate at commercial banks RTD, and using nominal GNP as the measure of income, the specification for empirical purposes becomes

$$\ln MD = b_0 + b_1 \ln RCP + b_2 \ln RTD$$
$$+ b_3 \ln GNP + b_4 \ln MD_{-1}. \tag{8.7}$$

The regression results obtained by applying this specification to quarterly data for the full sample period 1955.1-1973.4 are reported as equation (8.2.1) in Table 8-2 and are similar in character to those obtained for the velocity formulation, equation (8.1.1) in Table 8-1. Both of the interest rate variables are significant and the implied speed of adjustment is 21 per cent per quarter. The long term income elasticity, reported in column eight, is 0.87, which is close to unity and provides little evidence for rejecting the hypothesis that money is homogeneous in income.

In order to test the structural stability of this function, equation (8.2.1) is reestimated over the three separate time periods, 1955.1 through 1961.4,

Table 8-2
Equations for Unconstrained Specification of Money Demand—Dependent Variable MD—Double Logarithmic Form

Equation	Sample Period	MD_{-1}	GNP	RCP	RTD	RSL	ε_{GNP}	Constant	R^2 SE	D.W. Rho
(8.2.1)	1955.1 1973.4	0.7897 (15.20)	0.1839 (4.70)	-0.0227 (-5.42)	-0.0359 (-3.36)		0.87	-0.0799 (-1.87)	0.999 0.0062	2.03 0.23
(8.2.2)	1955.1 1961.4	0.7232 (4.82)	0.1715 (1.99)	-0.0219 (-4.54)	-0.0173 (-0.95)		0.60	0.2957 (0.85)	0.987 0.0042	1.99 0.40
(8.2.3)	1962.1 1966.3	0.6238 (4.20)	0.3923 (5.23)	-0.0648 (-2.83)	-0.1888 (-2.72)		1.04	-0.3630 (-1.01)	0.995 0.0034	1.57 -0.12
(8.2.4)	1966.4 1973.4	0.5218 (3.38)	0.3365 (3.06)	-0.0246 (-3.28)	0.0817 (1.25)		0.70	0.0607 (0.55)	0.996 0.0079	2.03 0.13
(8.2.5)	1955.1 1961.4	0.7373 (6.63)	0.2386 (3.26)	-0.0242 (-6.63)		-0.0978 (-2.65)	0.91	-0.0697 (-0.28)	0.989 0.0038	1.88 0.09
(8.2.6)	1962.1 1966.3	0.5930 (4.00)	0.3877 (5.23)	-0.0535 (-2.17)	-0.1440 (-1.87)	-0.1026 (-1.15)	0.95	-0.1089 (-0.26)	0.995 0.0034	1.57 -0.13
(8.2.7)	1962.1 1966.3	0.5755 (3.18)	0.3644 (4.26)	-0.0683 (-2.33)		-0.1583 (-1.61)	0.86	0.0372 (0.08)	0.995 0.0035	1.93 0.19
(8.2.8)	1966.4 1973.4	0.5267 (3.12)	0.4341 (3.80)	-0.0297 (-3.11)		-0.1292 (-1.27)	0.92	-0.0281 (-1.25)	0.996 0.0079	2.24 0.42

1962.1 through 1966.3, and 1966.4 through 1973.4. The regressions for these sample periods are reported as equations (8.2.2), (8.2.3), and (8.2.4). The results are considerably different from the full period estimation and display the same general properties that were reported for the velocity formulation of money demand. For the sample period 1955.1-1961.4, the commercial bank time deposit rate RTD obtains only a small coefficient not significantly different from zero. For the intermediate period, however, RTD has a substantial impact on money demand. The coefficient is -0.19 with a t statistic of -2.7. In the final subperiod, 1966.4-1973.4, RTD again works poorly. The coefficient, in fact, has the incorrect positive sign and thus provides no evidence of substitution between time deposits and money. Furthermore, although the long run income elasticity of money demand is estimated to be close to unity in the full period regression, equation (8.2.1), this elasticity varies sharply when the sample periods are estimated separately. During the 1950s, the income elasticity implied by equation (8.2.2) is only 0.60. For the period 1962.1 to 1966.3, the elasticity is 1.04, but for the period 1966.4 to 1973.4 the implied long run elasticity of income is only 0.70. In addition, although the speed of adjustment implied by the full period estimation is 21 per cent per quarter, the empirical results for each of the subperiods is substantially faster than this figure. The respective speeds of adjustment are 28 per cent for the period 1955.1 to 1961.4, 38 per cent for the period 1962.4 to 1966.3, and 48 per cent for the period 1966.4 to 1973.4. In none of these subperiods is the speed of adjustment as slow as that implied by the results for a full period estimation. Thus, the specification of the money demand function in which income is explicitly included as an additional independent variable, behaves poorly when estimated separately for the three sample periods.

As in the case of the velocity formulation we reestimate each of these separate equations to test for the possibility that the deposits of nonbank intermediaries dominated those of commercial banks as a substitute for money holdings. The results are reported in equations (8.2.5) through (8.2.8). As in the velocity results, the nonbank deposit rate RSL obtains a highly significant coefficient for the sample period 1955.1-1961.4 and has an implied long run elasticity of about -0.37. In addition, more sensible results are obtained for the income variable, which has a long run elasticity of 0.91 compared to the 0.60 figure implied by equation (8.2.2), in which the time deposit rate is specified as a variable. This empirical evidence confirms that nonbank deposits, rather than time deposits at commercial banks, were the dominant substitute for money prior to the 1962 rise in Regulation Q ceilings.

When RSL is specified in the equation for 1962.1 to 1966.3, the variable obtains a large coefficient but is not significant at the 95 per cent level. Although this provides some indication of possible substitution between money and nonbank liabilities during this period, the empirical results for equation (8.2.3) suggest that time deposits were a stronger alternative for money holdings during this period.

The empirical results obtained when the nonbank rate is specified in the money demand function for the sample period 1966.4 to 1973.4 are reported in equation (8.2.8). The variable RSL has a large negative coefficient, -0.13, in contrast to the coefficient for RTD in equation (8.2.4), which has the wrong sign. Nevertheless, the t statistic for RSL is -1.27, which indicates that the coefficient is not statistically significant at the 95 per cent level. There are several possible reasons for the lack of significance for both savings deposit rates, RTD and RSL, in equations (8.2.4) and (8.2.8). One, deposit rates at savings institutions did not vary much over this period due to the restrictiveness of Regulation Q ceilings so that statistical significance is difficult to obtain. Furthermore, when income is included in the specification as a separate variable, the serious problem of multicollinearity between income and interest rates is added to the estimation difficulties. Nevertheless, the point estimates are consistent with the results reported earlier for the velocity formulation of the demand function, which indicated that since 1966 the dominant substitute for money has been nonbank deposits rather than time deposits at commercial banks. In addition, when the specification includes RSL as a variable, the long run income elasticity is estimated to be 0.92 in contrast to the low figure of 0.70 implied in equation (8.2.4) when RTD is specified as the deposit rate variable. Thus, the inclusion of the nonbank deposit rate rather than the time deposit rate produces an estimate of income elasticity that is more consistent with the pattern of the figures obtained for the earlier subperiods.

In general, the empirical results obtained by specifying a money demand function in which the income elasticity is unconstrained, also reflect the presence of structural instability in the behavior of money demand. More specifically, there is evidence that there have been several changes in the pattern of substitution between money and near monies. These estimation results are fully consistent with those derived from the velocity formulation of money demand. In addition, the unconstrained specification of the money demand function displays sharp changes in income elasticities when estimated separately over the three sample periods. However, when account is taken of the shifts in the pattern of substitution between money and near monies, long run income elasticities of close to unity are obtained in each of the sample periods. Thus, the evidence clearly suggests that the demand for money balances is homogeneous with respect to income.

Conclusions

The primary conclusion of this analysis is that there is strong empirical evidence of structural instability in the demand for money during the 1960s. More specifically, there has been a change in the pattern of substitution between money and near monies due to the administration of deposit rate ceilings by the regulatory authorities. Prior to 1962, when nonbank rates were sharply higher than bank deposit rates, holders of money balances viewed nonbank deposits as the dominant substitute for money. The sharp rise in Regulation Q ceilings in 1962, however, increased the competitiveness of commercial banks and, as a result, time deposits became the dominant substitute for money. Since 1966 the regulatory authorities have maintained a differential in rate ceilings that permits nonbank institutions to offer higher yields on savings deposits than commercial banks. As a result, the liabilities of nonbank intermediaries have again become the dominant substitute for money. Furthermore, during each subperiod, the elasticity of money demand with respect to deposit rates is sharply higher than the estimate obtained in any full period regression. This suggests that previous research has understated the impact of interest rates on savings deposits on the behavior of money demand.

A second major conclusion is that more reasonable speeds of adjustment are obtained when the specification of money demand allows for structural shifts. In addition, there is evidence that during the 1960s the speed with which the public has adjusted its holdings of money balances toward equilibrium is faster than during the previous decade.

A final major point is that similar estimation results are obtained whether or not the income elasticity is constrained in the specification of money demand in each subperiod. In the unconstrained version there are sharp variations in the long run elasticity of income. However, when the structural shifts are incorporated in the specification, the long run income elasticity is consistently estimated to be close to unity. Consequently, there is strong evidence that the demand for money is homogeneous with respect to income.

In general, we have established that interest rates on savings deposits have an important role in the behavior and stability of the money market over the postwar period. In the next chapters we investigate the impact of savings deposit rates on macroeconomic activity and the effectiveness of monetary policy.

9

Monetary Policy, Economic Activity, and Interest Rates on Savings Deposits: A Theoretical Analysis

The purpose of this chapter is to evaluate two important aspects of the economic significance of deposit rate behavior by investigating the impact of interest rates on savings deposits, on the effectiveness of monetary policy, and on the level of economic activity. First, we analyze whether the effectiveness of monetary policy is enhanced or curtailed if savings deposit rates are freely determined by the behavior of financial intermediaries or if they are restricted by the Regulation Q ceilings imposed by the regulatory authorities. Our second objective is to evaluate the macroeconomic impact that results from a change in the Regulation Q ceilings[a] on savings deposit rates, given that there is no concomitant change in any other instrument of monetary policy. Each of these questions is examined theoretically in this chapter by the derivation of the comparative statics properties of Keynesian models of income determination that incorporate savings deposit rate behavior, and empirically in the next chapter through the use of simulation experiments with the Federal Reserve-MIT-Penn (FMP) econometric model.

These policy questions have become particularly relevant in recent years as a result of the administration of ceiling rate restrictions which have sufficiently constrained the level of deposit rates so that the actual rate of interest on savings deposits can essentially be assumed to be exogenously determined by administrative action rather than by financial intermediary behavior. The purpose of this chapter is to develop theoretical models that provide qualitative evidence as to the economic consequences that result if Regulation Q ceilings remain restrictive, are completely removed, or are altered as part of a monetary program for economic stabilization.

In chapter 6 we developed savings deposit rate setting functions which demonstrated that in the absence of governmental restrictions, savings deposit rates fully respond to movements in open market interest rates. In

---

[a]Throughout chapters 9 and 10, we use the term Regulation Q to mean the legal ceiling restrictions on all savings deposit rates; that is, the ceilings on savings deposit rates at commercial banks, savings and loan associations, and mutual savings banks. Regulation Q refers to the legal ceilings administered by the Federal Reserve Board on commercial bank savings deposit rates. However, since legal ceilings on nonbank deposit rates were initiated in 1966, whenever Regulation Q has been altered by the Federal Reserve Board, the ceiling rates on nonbank savings deposits have also been altered. Ceilings at savings and loan associations and mutual savings banks are administered by the Federal Home Loan Bank Board and the Federal Deposit Insurance Corporation.

chapter 8 we presented empirical evidence that the behavior of interest rates on savings deposits has an important influence on the public's willingness to hold a given supply of money and has also affected the stability of this functional relationship. Since the behavior of the public's demand for money is central to neo-Keynesian macroeconomic analysis, the character of the relationship between deposit rates and money demand has important implications for the use of monetary policy as an instrument for stabilizing the economy. Consequently, it is clear that the manner in which interest rates on savings deposits are determined and the impact of these yields on money demand has important implications for conducting effective monetary policy. More specifically, when Regulation Q ceilings are binding, changes in monetary policy directly affect financial conditions through the money market via open market yields. There are no direct or feedback effects on savings deposit rates. In the absence of binding Regulation Q ceilings, however, changes in monetary policy not only have a direct effect on the money market and thus on open market yields but also have an indirect effect through the feedback mechanism by which savings deposit rates respond to the movements in market rates of return. Consequently, the effectiveness of monetary policy and the size of the resultant impact on macroeconomic activity is influenced by whether or not Regulation Q ceilings are binding. Furthermore, if monetary policy remains unchanged, but Regulation Q ceilings are altered at a time when they are binding, the adjustment of savings deposit rates to the new ceiling levels directly affects both the public's demand for financial assets and the level of economic activity. In this chapter we evaluate the qualitative implications of savings deposit rate behavior by using a general equilibrium framework for analyzing the interactions between savings deposit rates, economic activity, and monetary policy. In the next chapter we provide definitive quantitative evidence about these policy problems.

The general procedure in both the theoretical and empirical chapters consists of three parts, which correspond to the three basic policy alternatives for the administration of Regulation Q ceilings. In Case A, we analyze the impact of monetary policy on macroeconomic activity in a world in which Regulation Q ceilings on savings deposits are effectively binding. In such a case, a change in monetary policy has a direct effect on open market yields via the money market but has no effect on savings deposit rates. This is the simplest case and produces standard comparative statics multipliers for the impact of monetary policy. It is shown that in this case monetary policy has its greatest effectiveness because financial intermediaries are not able to offset policy through changes in deposit rates. In Case B, we evaluate the impact of the savings deposit rate behavior of financial intermediaries on the effectiveness of monetary policy by deriving similar comparative statics multipliers that reflect the absence of ceiling restrictions. In this situation, savings deposit rates are endogenously determined within the financial system as a function of open market interest rates. In Case C, we examine the economic impact of changes in Regulation Q ceilings when such restrictions are binding. We demonstrate that in such a case, changes in Regulation Q generally have a substantial impact on the level of economic activity and thus are an important potential stabilization tool of monetary policy. This case can also be viewed as an approximation to the situation that would result as part of a transition from the maintenance of binding ceilings to the elimination of such ceilings.

We begin the theoretical analysis by developing a static Keynesian model of income determination that incorporates the relevant modifications needed to reflect the impact of savings deposit rates and deposit rate ceilings. The comparative statics properties of three versions of this basic model are derived, each of which incorporates a different assumption about the central bank's choice of an exogenous monetary instrument. We assume that the central bank may control either the money supply, open market interest rates, or high powered money. These alternative assumptions are referred to as Model 1, Model 2, and Model 3, respectively. Thus we analyze Case A, Case B, and Case C and evaluate the impact for each of the three different assumptions about the central bank's choice of a monetary policy instrument. Three models are analyzed for each of the three cases in order to detail the effects of the central bank's choice of a monetary policy instrument on the economic influence of the behavior of interest rates on savings deposits.

Case A: Regulation Q Ceilings Are Binding

In this case we examine the impact of monetary policy under the assumption that Regulation Q ceilings are effectively binding. That is, we assume that the desired level of savings deposit rates is substantially above the level of the ceiling restrictions. This case yields standard comparative statics results for money multipliers because the restrictiveness of Regulation Q ceilings effectively makes savings deposit rates exogenous to the economic system. The basic Keynesian model consists of a product market and a money market. In the product market it is assumed that tax revenues t are a function of income y, and that consumption c is a function of disposable income. Investment I is specified as a negative function of the short term open market rate i.[b] Government expenditures g are assumed to be

---

[b]The model could be extended to allow investment to be a function of the long term interest rate, where such a variable would be related to the short term open market yield through a term structure equation. This would, however, complicate the model without altering any of the comparative statics results.

exogenous. In the money market, the demand and supply of money are always assumed to be in equilibrium. The demand for money m is related positively to income and negatively to the open market interest rate and to savings deposit rates at financial institutions r. Thus the product and money markets are written as

$$y = c[y - t(y)] + I(i) + g$$
$$1 > \partial c/\partial y, \ \partial t/\partial y > 0 \quad \partial I/\partial i < 0 \tag{9.A.1}$$

$$m = m(i, r, y)$$
$$\partial m/\partial i, \ \partial m/\partial r < 0 \quad \partial m/\partial y > 0. \tag{9.A.2}$$

We begin with Model 1 in which we assume that the central bank's policy instrument is the money supply $M1$, defined as demand deposits plus currency. Since the money supply is taken as the monetary policy variable, we assume that the supply of money is set at some exogenously determined level

$$m = m_0. \tag{9.A.3}$$

Equations (9.A.1) through (9.A.3) are totally differentiated so that

$$dy = (\partial c/\partial y) dy - (\partial c/\partial y)(\partial t/\partial y) dy + (\partial I/\partial i) di \tag{9.A.4}$$

and

$$dm = (\partial m/\partial i) di + (\partial m/\partial r) dr + (\partial m/\partial y) dy. \tag{9.A.5}$$

Since it is assumed that Regulation Q ceilings are binding, no change in savings deposit rates can occur so that

$$dr = 0. \tag{9.A.6}$$

With the appropriate substitutions, these equations can be rewritten in matrix form as

$$\begin{bmatrix} 1 - \dfrac{\partial c}{\partial y}\left(1 - \dfrac{\partial t}{\partial y}\right) & -\dfrac{\partial I}{\partial i} \\ \dfrac{\partial m}{\partial y} & \dfrac{\partial m}{\partial i} \end{bmatrix} \begin{bmatrix} dy \\ di \end{bmatrix} = \begin{bmatrix} 0 \\ 1 \end{bmatrix} dm. \tag{9.A.7}$$

By employing Cramer's rule, we can explicitly evaluate the relationship between monetary policy and macroeconomic activity in a world in which Regulation Q ceilings are binding. The effect of a change in the money supply on income is derived from (9.A.7) as

$$\frac{dy}{dm} = \frac{\partial I/\partial i}{\left[1 - \dfrac{\partial c}{\partial y}\left(1 - \dfrac{\partial t}{\partial y}\right)\right]\dfrac{\partial m}{\partial i} + \dfrac{\partial I}{\partial i}\dfrac{\partial m}{\partial y}} > 0. \tag{9.A.8}$$

This result is unambiguously positive, given the signs of the partial derivatives in equations (9.A.1) and (9.A.2), and indicates that an increase in the money supply by the central bank induces an increase in income. Similarly, using (9.A.7), the effect of a change in the money supply on open market interest rates is found to be

$$\frac{di}{dm} = \frac{1 - (\partial c/\partial y)(1 - \partial t/\partial y)}{\left[1 - \frac{\partial c}{\partial y}\left(1 - \frac{\partial t}{\partial y}\right)\right]\frac{\partial m}{\partial i} + \frac{\partial I}{\partial i}\frac{\partial m}{\partial y}} < 0, \qquad (9.A.9)$$

which is clearly negative, again based on the a priori signs of the partial derivatives. Thus, a rise in the money supply increases income and decreases interest rates. Furthermore, we can derive the effect of a change in the money supply on the demand for time deposits in order to evaluate the influence of monetary policy on the savings market given that savings deposit rates are constrained. We specify the demand for time deposits n as a function of relevant yields and income so that

$$n = n(i, r, y) \quad \partial n/\partial i < 0 \quad \partial n/\partial y > 0. \qquad (9.A.10)$$

Since deposit rates are bound by the ceiling, the total differential is

$$dn = (\partial n/\partial i)di + (\partial n/\partial y)dy \qquad (9.A.11)$$

and the effect of a change in the money supply, on time deposits is

$$dn/dm = (\partial n/\partial i)(di/dm) + (\partial n/\partial y)(dy/dm) > 0, \qquad (9.A.12)$$

which is positive. That is, an increase in the money supply increases the public's demand for time deposits even though deposit rates are unchanged.

Overall, in such a model the relationships between the monetary policy variable and macroeconomic activity are unambiguous. A rise in the money supply increases income, decreases open market interest rates, and also increases the demand for time deposits. An additional implication of these results is that since movements in the money supply are often more easily and quickly observed than changes in income, the money supply can be regarded as a suitable variable for targeting income. Furthermore, since $M2$ is defined as $M1$ plus time deposits, and since $M1$ has a positive effect on both income and time deposits, it is clear that the monetary aggregate $M2$ moves in the same direction as income when $M1$ is altered. In general, when Regulation Q ceilings are binding and the monetary policy variable is the money supply, the monetary aggregates and open market interest rates behave in a manner consistent with movements in income and other real variables.

In the second version of the basic Keynesian system, Model 2, the policy variable of the monetary authorities is assumed to be the level of open market interest rates. In this model open market yields are considered to be exogenous to the economic system, and the activities of the monetary authorities center on providing the money stock needed to accomodate the public's demand for money at the level of market rates determined by the central bank. The assumptions that characterize the product and money market, equations (9.A.1) and (9.A.2) are retained. However, we replace expression (9.A.3) with the equation

$$i = i_0 \tag{9.A.13}$$

where i_0 is the exogenously set path of open market interest rates. We investigate the impact of a change in monetary policy under the assumption that the central bank's monetary policy instrument is the level of open market interest rates and that deposit rate ceilings prevent any induced changes in the rate of interest offered on savings deposits. In this model we take the total differentials of equations (9.A.1), (9.A.2), and (9.A.13) and arrange the derivatives in matrix form to yield

$$\begin{bmatrix} 1 - \dfrac{\partial c}{\partial y}\left(1 - \dfrac{\partial t}{\partial y}\right) & 0 \\ -\dfrac{\partial m}{\partial y} & 1 \end{bmatrix} \begin{bmatrix} dy \\ dm \end{bmatrix} = \begin{bmatrix} \dfrac{\partial I}{\partial i} \\ \dfrac{\partial m}{\partial i} \end{bmatrix} di, \tag{9.A.14}$$

where the level of income and the money supply are the endogenous variables. By Cramer's rule, the effect of a change in open market interest rates on income is derived as

$$\frac{dy}{di} = \frac{\partial I / \partial i}{1 - (\partial c / \partial y)(1 - \partial t / \partial y)} < 0, \tag{9.A.15}$$

which is unambiguously negative, given the a priori signs of the partial derivatives. That is, open market interest rates and income are inversely related so that decreases in interest rates result in increases in income. In a similar manner, the effect of a policy change in open market interest rates on the narrowly defined money supply $M1$ is

$$\frac{dm}{di} = \frac{\left(\dfrac{\partial m}{\partial i}\right)\left[1 - \dfrac{\partial c}{\partial y}\left(1 - \dfrac{\partial t}{\partial y}\right)\right] + \dfrac{\partial m}{\partial y}\dfrac{\partial I}{\partial i}}{1 - (\partial c / \partial y)(1 - \partial t / \partial y)} < 0, \tag{9.A.16}$$

which is also negative. Thus, a given policy change in interest rates induces an inverse effect on $M1$, which indicates that $M1$ moves in the same direction as income. The effect of a policy change in interest rates on time deposits can be similarly derived. We retain the specification of the market for time deposits contained in equation (9.A.10) and the appropriate total differential, equation (9.A.11). Then the effect of a change in open market yields on time deposits is

$$dn/di = \partial n/\partial i + (\partial n/\partial y)(dy/di) < 0, \qquad (9.A.17)$$

which is unambiguously negative, so that an increase in open market yields lowers the public's demand for time deposits. Since a change in open market rates has a negative impact on both $M1$ and the demand for time deposits, it is clear that interest rates and $M2$ are negatively related. Consequently, the monetary aggregate $M2$ moves in the same direction as income in response to a change in monetary policy.

The character of the relationships between monetary variables and income when the level of open market interest rates is the policy instrument, is quite clear. A rise in the open market interest rate decreases income, $M1$, time deposits, and $M2$. This implies that movements in $M1$, $M2$, or open market interest rates each appear to move in a direction indicative of developments in the real sector of the economy.

In Model 3 we assume that the monetary authorities operate in the market for reserves. In this case the supply of money and open market interest rates are both determined endogenously as a result of the interaction of the Federal Reserve, the commercial banking system, and the behavior of the public. Consequently, the relationship between the supply of money and unborrowed reserves provided through Federal Reserve open market operations, depends upon the public's preferences for currency, demand deposits, and time deposits and on the commercial banking sector's desire to hold excess reserves and borrowed reserves through the discount mechanism. In this model, the policy variable of the monetary authorities is high powered money, which is defined as the quantity of unborrowed reserves plus currency. Although this version requires the development of a more complicated financial sector, the basic assumptions that characterize the product market are retained from the earlier models, and the demand for money is still required to equal the supply of money.

The product market specification in equation (9.A.1) remains unchanged. However, money demand is disaggregated into the demand for demand deposits and the demand for currency so that

$$MD = MD(i, r_{CB}, r_{NB}, y)$$

$$\frac{\partial MD}{\partial i}, \frac{\partial MD}{\partial r_{CB}}, \frac{\partial MD}{\partial r_{NB}} < 0 \qquad \frac{\partial MD}{\partial y} > 0 \qquad (9.A.18)$$

$$MC = MC(i, r_{CB}, r_{NB}, y)$$

$$\frac{\partial MC}{\partial i}, \frac{\partial MC}{\partial r_{CB}}, \frac{\partial MC}{\partial r_{NB}} < 0 \qquad \frac{\partial MC}{\partial y} > 0 \qquad (9.A.19)$$

where MD is demand deposits and MC is currency held by the public. Savings deposit rates are also disaggregated into the time deposit rate at commercial banks r_{CB}, and the nonbank deposit rate r_{NB}, which includes the rate at savings and loan associations and mutual savings banks. Furthermore, the demand for time deposits MT is also a function of relevant yields and income, so that

$$MT = MT(i, r_{CB}, r_{NB}, y)$$

$$\frac{\partial MT}{\partial i}, \frac{\partial MT}{\partial r_{NB}} < 0 \quad \frac{\partial MT}{\partial y}, \frac{\partial MT}{\partial r_{CB}} > 0. \qquad (9.A.20)$$

On the money supply side, the willingness of the commercial banking sector to supply demand deposits depends on the availability of reserves and reserve ratios required by the central bank. Unborrowed reserves UR are defined as the sum of required reserves RR and excess reserves ER minus borrowed reserves BR, that is

$$UR = RR + ER - BR. \qquad (9.A.21)$$

By definition, free reserves FR is excess reserves minus borrowed reserves

$$FR = ER - BR, \qquad (9.A.22)$$

and the quantity of required reserves is

$$RR = z_D MD + z_T MT \qquad (9.A.23)$$

where z_D and z_T are the reserve requirements on demand and time deposits respectively. Substituting for FR and RR in the expression for unborrowed reserves yields

$$UR = z_D MD + z_T MT + FR. \qquad (9.A.24)$$

Rearranging terms, the identity that relates demand deposits and reserves becomes

$$MD = \frac{UR - z_T MT - FR}{z_D}. \qquad (9.A.25)$$

Within this identity, free reserves are assumed to be an endogenous function of open market interest yields and the discount rate d,[c] so that

$$FR = FR(i, d) \quad \partial FR/\partial i < 0 \quad \partial FR/\partial d > 0. \qquad (9.A.26)$$

Rearranging the terms in the definition for high powered money, which is unborrowed reserves plus currency, yields

$$UR = HP - MC, \qquad (9.A.27)$$

---

[c] See, for example, Goldfeld and Kane [26] and Modigliani, Rasche, and Cooper [43].

where the quantity of currency *MC* held by the public is assumed to be demand determined as specified in equation (9.A.19).

In order to solve for the various comparative statics results, we specify and differentiate the equilibrium conditions in the product and money market. In the financial sector, equilibrium depends on the interaction of the public's demand for demand deposits and the commercial banking sector's willingness to supply those deposits. Equating this demand and supply yields

$$MD(i, r_{CB}, r_{NB}, y) = \frac{UR - z_T MT - FR}{z_D}. \quad (9.A.28)$$

Equilibrium in the product market is described in equation (9.A.1). Therefore, the total differentials of equation (9.A.1) and (9.A.28) are

$$dy = \frac{\partial c}{\partial y} dy - \frac{\partial c}{\partial y} \frac{\partial t}{\partial y} dy + \frac{\partial I}{\partial i} di \quad (9.A.29)$$

$$\frac{\partial MD}{\partial y} dy + \frac{\partial MD}{\partial i} di + \frac{\partial MD}{\partial r_{CB}} dr_{CB} + \frac{\partial MD}{\partial r_{NB}} dr_{NB}$$

$$= \frac{1}{z_D}(dUR - z_T dMT - dFR)$$

$$= \frac{1}{z_D}(dHP - dMC - z_T dMT - dFR). \quad (9.A.30)$$

We assume that the quantity of high powered money is exogenously set by the central bank and that the discount rate is kept constant. Furthermore, Regulation Q ceilings are still assumed to be binding, so that there can be no induced effects on deposit rates, that is, $dr = 0$. Consequently, by substituting the total differentials for currency *dMC*, time deposits *dMT*, and free reserves *dFR*, we can rewrite equation (9.A.30) as

$$\frac{\partial MD}{\partial y} dy + \frac{\partial MD}{\partial i} di = \frac{1}{z_D} \Big(dHP - \frac{\partial MC}{\partial y} dy - \frac{\partial MC}{\partial i} di$$

$$- z_T \frac{\partial MT}{\partial y} dy - z_T \frac{\partial MT}{\partial i} di - \frac{\partial FR}{\partial i} di \Big). \quad (9.A.31)$$

Employing shorthand notation in writing equations (9.A.29) and (9.A.31) in matrix form, yields

$$\begin{bmatrix} Dy & Di \\ My & Mi \end{bmatrix} \begin{bmatrix} dy \\ di \end{bmatrix} = \begin{bmatrix} 0 \\ 1 \end{bmatrix} dHP \quad (9.A.32)$$

where

$$Dy = 1 - \frac{\partial c}{\partial y}\left(1 - \frac{\partial t}{\partial y}\right)$$

$$Di = -\frac{\partial I}{\partial i}$$

$$My = z_D\frac{\partial MD}{\partial y} + \frac{\partial MC}{\partial y} + z_T\frac{\partial MT}{\partial y}$$

$$Mi = z_D\frac{\partial MD}{\partial i} + \frac{\partial MC}{\partial i} + z_T\frac{\partial MT}{\partial i} + \frac{\partial FR}{\partial i}$$

Using Cramer's rule on expression (9.A.32) gives the ceteris paribus effect of a change in high powered money on income

$$\frac{dy}{dHP} = \frac{-Di}{DyMi - DiMy} > 0, \qquad (9.A.33)$$

which is unambiguously positive, since Di, Dy and My are positive, and Mi is negative based on the a priori signs of the partial derivatives. Thus, an increase in unborrowed reserves supplied through open market operations raises the level of national income. Similarly, the effect of a policy change in high powered money on open market interest rates is derived as

$$\frac{di}{dHP} = \frac{Dy}{DyMi - DiMy} < 0, \qquad (9.A.34)$$

which is clearly negative. Therefore, an increase in high powered money is expansionary, inducing a decline in open market interest rates and a rise in income.

The effect of a change in high powered money on the two monetary aggregates $M1$ and $M2$ can be obtained by using the signs of expressions (9.A.33) and (9.A.34). Since $M1$ is defined as the sum of demand deposits MD and currency MC, the total differential is

$$dM1 = dMD + dMC$$
$$= \frac{\partial MD}{\partial i}di + \frac{\partial MD}{\partial y}dy + \frac{\partial MC}{\partial i}di + \frac{\partial MC}{\partial y}dy. \qquad (9.A.35)$$

The effect of a change in high powered money on $M1$ is

$$\frac{dM1}{dHP} = \frac{\partial MD}{\partial i}\frac{di}{dHP} + \frac{\partial MD}{\partial y}\frac{dy}{dHP}$$
$$+ \frac{\partial MC}{\partial i}\frac{di}{dHP} + \frac{\partial MC}{\partial y}\frac{dy}{dHP} > 0, \qquad (9.A.36)$$

which is clearly positive. This indicates that changes in $M1$ are positively related to changes in the central bank's reserve policy. Since reserve behavior and income are also positively related, $M1$ and income move in the same direction as a result of a change in reserves. A similar result characterizes the case of time deposits MT and therefore $M2$. The total differential of equation (9.A.20) yields

$$dMT = (\partial MT/\partial i)di + (\partial MT/\partial y)dy. \qquad (9.A.37)$$

The effect of a change in high powered money on MT is

$$\frac{dMT}{dHP} = \frac{\partial MT}{\partial i}\frac{di}{dHP} + \frac{\partial MT}{\partial y}\frac{dy}{dHP} > 0, \qquad (9.A.38)$$

which is positive. Consequently, the effect of a change in reserves policy on $M2$, which is the combined effect of this policy on $M1$ and MT, is also positive.

Overall, the macroeconomic effects of a change in the central bank's willingness to supply reserves is straightforward in this version of the Keynesian model. A change in the level of reserves has an inverse effect on the level of open market interest rates and a positive impact on income. Furthermore, a change in reserves has a positive impact on movements in $M1$, the public's holdings of time deposits, and $M2$, so that these monetary variables respond to movements in reserves in a manner that is consistent with the direction in which income is altered.

In summary, when Regulation Q ceilings are effectively binding, interest rates on savings deposits can be considered exogenous to financial behavior. In such a case, the macroeconomic impact of a change in monetary policy yields the standard money market multipliers. This result is invariant to which monetary variable is taken as the central bank's policy instrument. Furthermore, the comparative statics results indicate that financial variables are altered in response to changes in monetary policy in a manner that is consistent with the changes that occur in income and real variables. Since movements in monetary variables may be more observable in the short run than income and other real variables, such as investment, these standard results imply that any of these monetary variables may usefully serve as an indicator or intermediate target for pursuing the desired levels of economic activity. These results, however, are appropriate only for the case when Regulation Q ceilings are binding and no change in savings deposit rates occurs. In subsequent analyses, this assumption of binding ceilings is relaxed so that deposit rates are free to fluctuate in response to changing financial conditions. Different comparative statics results are obtained, which have implications for the magnitude of money multipliers, and thus the conduct of monetary policy.

Case B: Regulation Q Ceilings Are Not Effective

In this second case, we completely relax the assumption that Regulation Q ceilings bind interest rates on savings deposits so that we can analyze the macroeconomic impact of monetary policy when the savings deposit rate behavior of financial intermediaries is not subject to any legal restrictions.[d] We continue to use the three versions of the simple Keynesian model, each of which incorporates a different assumption about monetary policy; that is, the monetary authorities control the money supply, open market interest rates, or high powered money. Again we retain the assumptions that characterize the product and money markets in the previous case, so that

$$y = c[y - t(y)] + I(i) + g$$
$$1 > \partial C/\partial y, \; \partial t/\partial y > 0 \quad \partial I/\partial i < 0, \tag{9.B.1}$$
$$m = m(i, r, y)$$
$$\partial m/\partial i, \; \partial m/\partial r < 0 \quad \partial m/\partial y > 0. \tag{9.B.2}$$

Since ceiling rates are completely absent in this case, savings deposit rates r are assumed to be endogenously determined by financial intermediary behavior. Our previous theoretical and econometric analyses in chapters 2 through 6 have fully established the character of this deposit rate setting behavior. We demonstrated that financial intermediary behavior can be well explained by a model of profit maximization and that the level of deposit rates can primarily be viewed as a positive function of open market interest rates. Consequently, to complete the system we specify an additional equation in which deposit rates are determined endogenously as a function of open market rates

$$r = r(i) \quad \partial r/\partial i > 0. \tag{9.B.3}$$

In Model 1 the monetary policy instrument is the money supply so that

$$m = m_0. \tag{9.B.4}$$

Taking the total differentials of equations (9.B.1)-(9.B.4), we obtain

$$dy = (\partial c/\partial y)dy - (\partial c/\partial y)(\partial t/\partial y)dy + (\partial I/\partial i)di \tag{9.B.5}$$
$$dm = (\partial m/\partial i)di + (\partial m/\partial r)dr + (\partial m/\partial y)dy \tag{9.B.6}$$
$$dr = (\partial r/\partial i)di. \tag{9.B.7}$$

---

[d]The termination of ceiling restrictions on savings deposit rates is one of the primary recommendations prepared by the Hunt Commission [50].

Making the appropriate substitutions, we can arrange these equations in matrix form as

$$\begin{bmatrix} 1 - \dfrac{\partial c}{\partial y}\left(1 - \dfrac{\partial t}{\partial y}\right) & -\dfrac{\partial I}{\partial i} \\ \dfrac{\partial m}{\partial y} & \left(\dfrac{\partial m}{\partial i} + \dfrac{\partial m}{\partial r}\dfrac{\partial r}{\partial i}\right) \end{bmatrix} \begin{bmatrix} dy \\ di \end{bmatrix} = \begin{bmatrix} 0 \\ 1 \end{bmatrix} dm. \quad (9.\text{B}.8)$$

Applying Cramer's rule to expression (9.B.8) we can evaluate the effect of a change in the money supply on income in a world in which there are no ceilings to restrict deposit rate setting by financial intermediaries:

$$\dfrac{dy}{dm} = \dfrac{\partial I/\partial i}{\left[1 - \dfrac{\partial c}{\partial y}\left(1 - \dfrac{\partial t}{\partial y}\right)\right]\left[\dfrac{\partial m}{\partial i} + \dfrac{\partial m}{\partial r}\dfrac{\partial r}{\partial i}\right] + \dfrac{\partial I}{\partial i}\dfrac{\partial m}{\partial y}} > 0. \quad (9.\text{B}.9)$$

This result is positive, given the signs of the partial derivatives in equations (9.B.1)-(9.B.3), and indicates that income is positively related to movements in the money supply. However, this comparative statics multiplier differs from the result obtained for Case A in which savings deposit rates are effectively bound at the ceiling and are assumed exogenous. The difference is due to the term $(\partial m/\partial r)(\partial r/\partial i)$ which enters additively with $\partial m/\partial i$ in the denominator. The presence of this term reflects the impact of the additional channel through which a change in monetary policy influences the money market if deposit rate behavior is endogenous in the model. A change in the money supply not only affects the equilibrium level of open market rates through the direct response of the public's demand for money to changes in open market yields $\partial m/\partial i$, but also through the sensitivity of money demand to deposit rate changes $\partial m/\partial r$. This is because any movement in open market yields produces a concomitant change in deposit rates $\partial r/\partial i$. Thus, for any given change in the money supply, the induced change in open market rates needed to clear the money market is moderated because any change in monetary policy induces a movement in deposit rates which has a subseqeunt feedback into the money market. More specifically, in chapters 5 and 6, our empirical results indicated that $\partial r/\partial i$, the effect of a change in market interest rates on savings deposit rates is quite large and in fact close to unity. That is, profit maximizing financial intermediaries transmit movements in market rates of return to their depositors through changes in savings deposit rates. Furthermore, our previous empirical work on money demand, chapter 8, suggested that the effect of a change in deposit rates on desired money holdings $\partial m/\partial r$ is substantially larger than the influence of open market rates $\partial m/\partial i$ on money demand. Thus, since $\partial r/\partial i$ is close to unity and $\partial m/\partial r > \partial m/\partial i$, the effect of the additional term is to make the denominator substantially larger than the denominator for the standard money multiplier, equation (9.A.8) in Case A. Consequently, the size of the multiplier dy/dm is reduced by incorporating the endogeneity of deposit rates into the model. This result is fairly intuitive. An increase in the stock of money produces a decline in open market rates sufficient to induce the public to hold the new, larger stock of money. As a result of this decline in interest rates, investment rises and aggregate demand is stimulated. However, if a change in open market rates induces a concomitant movement in savings deposit rates at financial institutions, there is a feedback effect on money demand. As a result, a smaller decline in open market rates is required to induce the public to hold the new supply of money. Because the overall change in market interest rates is moderated, the effect of a given change in the money supply on income is lessened.

In order to demonstrate that the change in monetary policy induces a smaller response in open market yields, the comparative statics result is obtained from (9.B.8) as

$$\frac{di}{dm} = \frac{1 - \frac{\partial c}{\partial y}\left(1 - \frac{\partial t}{\partial y}\right)}{\left[1 - \frac{\partial c}{\partial y}\left(1 - \frac{\partial t}{\partial y}\right)\right]\left[\frac{\partial m}{\partial i} + \frac{\partial m}{\partial r}\frac{\partial r}{\partial i}\right] + \frac{\partial I}{\partial i}\frac{\partial m}{\partial y}} < 0. \quad (9.B.10)$$

The result is clearly negative and indicates that a rise in the money supply increases income and decreases interest rates. However, the additional term $(\partial m/\partial r)(\partial r/\partial i)$ in the denominator of (9.B.10) has the effect of reducing the size of the impact of a change in the money supply on interest rates relative to the impact that occurs when ceiling rates are binding. A similar result also applies to the demand for time deposits. Assuming that the demand for time deposits n is taken as

$$n = n(i, r, y)$$
$$(\partial n/\partial i) < 0 \quad (\partial n/\partial y) > 0 \quad (\partial n/\partial r) \geq 0, \quad (9.B.11)$$

where the effect of the own rate on time deposits is assumed to either dominate or equal the effect of the nonbank rate. It is clear that the effect of a change in the money supply on the public's holdings of time deposits is

$$\frac{dn}{dm} = \left(\frac{\partial n}{\partial i} + \frac{\partial n}{\partial r}\frac{\partial r}{\partial i}\right)\frac{di}{dm} + \frac{\partial n}{\partial y}\frac{dy}{dm} > 0. \qquad (9.B.12)$$

Since the absolute size of each of the money multipliers di/dm and dy/dm is reduced by allowing deposit rates to be market determined rather than bound by ceiling restrictions, the multiplier effect on time deposits and $M2$ is also decreased.

In general, in an economic environment in which there are no interest rate ceilings and savings deposit rates are endogenously determined by financial intermediaries, the macroeconomic impact of a change in the money supply is reduced compared to the case of restrictive ceilings that is, the absolute size of the money multipliers is decreased and the power of a given change in monetary policy is diminished if there are no interest rate ceilings. These results complement the argument of Tobin and Brainard's Regime III [49].

In Model 2, open market interest rates are taken as the monetary policy instrument of the central bank. Expression (9.B.4) is replaced by

$$i = i_0. \qquad (9.B.13)$$

Arranging the total differentials of equations (9.B.1), (9.B.2), (9.B.3) and (9.B.13) in matrix form, yields

$$\begin{bmatrix} 1 - \frac{\partial c}{\partial y}\left(1 - \frac{\partial t}{\partial y}\right) & 0 \\ -\frac{\partial m}{\partial y} & 1 \end{bmatrix} \begin{bmatrix} dy \\ dm \end{bmatrix} = \begin{bmatrix} \frac{\partial I}{\partial i} \\ \frac{\partial m}{\partial i} + \frac{\partial m}{\partial r}\frac{\partial r}{\partial i} \end{bmatrix} di \qquad (9.B.14)$$

Employing Cramer's rule makes it clear that this set of equations yields a comparative statics result for dy/di that is identical to the one obtained when deposit rates are exogenous, expression (9.A.15). Consequently, when the monetary authorities use open market interest rates as the policy instrument, a given change in interest rates has the same negative impact on aggregate demand regardless of whether deposit rates are exogenous, as in Case A with binding restrictions, or endogenous. The only effect of allowing for endogenous deposit rates in this model is to increase the impact of a change in monetary policy on the demand for money since the comparative statics result

$$\frac{dm}{di} = \frac{\left(\frac{\partial m}{\partial i} + \frac{\partial m}{\partial r}\frac{\partial r}{\partial i}\right)\left[1 - \frac{\partial c}{\partial y}\left(1 - \frac{\partial t}{\partial y}\right)\right] + \frac{\partial m}{\partial y}\frac{\partial I}{\partial i}}{1 - \frac{\partial c}{\partial y}\left(1 - \frac{\partial t}{\partial y}\right)} < 0 \qquad (9.\text{B}.15)$$

has the additional term $(\partial m/\partial r)(\partial r/\partial i)$ in the numerator, compared to expression (9.A.16) in Case A. This result reflects the fact that a change in open market interest rates is reinforced by a concomitant change in savings deposit rates. There is an opposite effect on time deposits. Assuming that savings deposit rates are endogenous, a policy change in open market interest rates has an effect on the demand for time deposits, which follows from expression (9.B.11)

$$\frac{dn}{di} = \frac{\partial n}{\partial i} + \frac{\partial n}{\partial r}\frac{\partial r}{\partial i} + \frac{\partial n}{\partial y}\frac{dy}{di} < 0, \qquad (9.\text{B}.16)$$

This result is smaller than expression (9.A.17) in Case A, unless the effects of the own rate and the nonbank rate on the demand for time deposits are equal.

In general, a policy change in open market yields has the same negative effect on income whether or not savings deposit rates are bound by ceilings. If interest rates on savings deposits are free to fluctuate, however, a policy change in open market rates has a larger impact on the public's demand for money and a smaller impact on time deposits than if ceilings are restrictive. Consequently, although *M*1 and *M*2 still move in the same direction as economic developments in the real sector, given a change in monetary policy, movements in these monetary aggregates are altered by the endogeneity of deposit rates, although the size of the income response is unaffected.

In Model 3, the central bank operates on monetary policy by altering the supply of high powered money so that the supply of money and open market interest rates are endogenously determined. We retain the disaggregated description of the money market, contained in equations (9.A.18)-(9.A.27). Thus, the expression that equates the demand and supply of money is

$$MD(i, r_{CB}, r_{NB}, y) = (UR - z_T MT - FR)/z_D. \qquad (9.\text{B}.17)$$

In addition we disaggregate the savings deposit rate function, equation (9.B.3), into separate rate equations for banks and nonbanks, so that

$$r_{CB} = r_{CB}(i) \qquad \partial r_{CB}/\partial i > 0 \qquad (9.\text{B}.18)$$

$$r_{NB} = r_{NB}(i) \qquad \partial r_{NB}/\partial i > 0.^e \qquad (9.B.19)$$

The total differential of equation (9.B.1), which describes equilibrium in the product market, and equations (9.B.17), (9.B.18) and (9.B.19), which reflect the behavior of the money market, are

$$dy = \frac{\partial c}{\partial y} dy - \frac{\partial c}{\partial y} \frac{\partial t}{\partial y} dy + \frac{\partial I}{\partial i} di \qquad (9.B.20)$$

$$\frac{\partial MD}{\partial y} dy + \frac{\partial MD}{\partial i} di + \frac{\partial MD}{\partial r_{CB}} dr_{CB} + \frac{\partial MD}{\partial r_{NB}} dr_{NB}$$

$$= \frac{1}{z_D} (dUR - z_T dMT - dFR)$$

$$= \frac{1}{z_D} (dHP - dMC - z_T dMT - dFR) \qquad (9.B.21)$$

$$dr_{CB} = \frac{\partial r_{CB}}{\partial i} di \qquad (9.B.22)$$

$$dr_{NB} = \frac{\partial r_{NB}}{\partial i} di \qquad (9.B.23)$$

It is assumed that the quantity of high powered money is an exogenous variable set by the central bank and that the discount rate is kept constant. By substituting the total differentials for deposit rates, currency, time deposits, and free reserves, equation (9.B.21) can be written as

$$\frac{\partial MD}{\partial y} dy + \frac{\partial MD}{\partial i} di + \frac{\partial MD}{\partial r_{CB}} \frac{\partial r_{CB}}{\partial i} di + \frac{\partial MD}{\partial r_{NB}} \frac{\partial r_{NB}}{\partial i} di$$

$$= \frac{1}{z_D} \bigg(dHP - \frac{\partial MC}{\partial y} dy - \frac{\partial MC}{\partial i} di - \frac{\partial MC}{\partial r_{CB}} \frac{\partial r_{CB}}{\partial i} di$$

$$- \frac{\partial MC}{\partial r_{NB}} \frac{\partial r_{NB}}{\partial i} di - z_T \frac{\partial MT}{\partial y} dy - z_T \frac{\partial MT}{\partial i} di$$

$$- z_T \frac{\partial MT}{\partial r_{CB}} \frac{\partial r_{CB}}{\partial i} di - z_T \frac{\partial MT}{\partial r_{NB}} \frac{\partial r_{NB}}{\partial i} di - \frac{\partial FR}{\partial i} di \bigg) \qquad (9.B.24)$$

---

[e]It could also be assumed that the savings deposit rate is a function of deposit rates at competing institutions as well as open market rates so that $r_{CB} = r_{CB}(i, r_{NB})$ and $r_{NB} = r_{NB}(i, r_{CB})$ where $\partial r_{NB}/\partial r_{CB} > 0$ and $\partial r_{CB}/\partial r_{NB} > 0$. However, if it is assumed that $\partial r_{CB}/\partial r_{NB} < 1$ and $\partial r_{NB}/\partial r_{CB} < 1$, then these functions reduce to (9.B.18) and (9.B.19). The estimation results presented in chapter 6 indicate that the assumptions about $\partial r_{CB}/\partial r_{NB}$ and $\partial r_{NB}/\partial r_{CB}$, which are essential for stability, are in accord with the empirical evidence.

Employing shorthand notation, equations (9.B.20) and (9.B.24) are written in matrix form as

$$\begin{bmatrix} Dy & Di \\ My & Mi \end{bmatrix} \begin{bmatrix} dy \\ di \end{bmatrix} = \begin{bmatrix} 0 \\ 1 \end{bmatrix} dHP \qquad (9.B.25)$$

where

$$Dy = 1 - \frac{\partial c}{\partial y}\left(1 - \frac{\partial t}{\partial y}\right)$$

$$Di = -\partial I/\partial i$$

$$My = z_D \frac{\partial MD}{\partial y} + \frac{\partial MC}{\partial y} + z_T \frac{\partial MT}{\partial y}$$

$$Mi = z_D \left(\frac{\partial MD}{\partial i} + \frac{\partial MD}{\partial r_{CB}} \frac{\partial r_{CB}}{\partial i} + \frac{\partial MD}{\partial r_{NB}} \frac{\partial r_{NB}}{\partial i}\right)$$

$$+ \frac{\partial MC}{\partial i} + \frac{\partial MC}{\partial r_{CB}} \frac{\partial r_{CB}}{\partial i} + \frac{\partial MC}{\partial r_{NB}} \frac{\partial r_{NB}}{\partial i}$$

$$+ z_T \left(\frac{\partial MT}{\partial i} + \frac{\partial MT}{\partial r_{CB}} \frac{\partial r_{CB}}{\partial i} + \frac{\partial MT}{\partial r_{NB}} \frac{\partial r_{NB}}{\partial i}\right) + \frac{\partial FR}{\partial i}$$

Using Cramer's rule, we obtain the effect of a change in high powered money on income as

$$\frac{dy}{dHP} = \frac{-Di}{Dy\, Mi - Di\, My} > 0, \qquad (9.B.26)$$

which is positive, since the denominator must be negative by the stability conditions for static equilibrium. Thus an increase in unborrowed reserves induces a rise in aggregate demand. The sign of the result is the same as in Case A, in which ceiling rates are restrictive, but the size of the multiplier is altered because of the additional terms in Mi that reflect the impact of endogenous deposit rate setting behavior. The effect of the inclusion of these factors is ambiguous because five of the additional terms tend to increase the size of Mi while one term, $z_T(\partial MT/\partial r_{CB})(\partial r_{CB}/\partial i)$, is positive and thus tends to decrease the size of Mi. If the following condition holds

$$\left| z_D \frac{\partial MD}{\partial r_{CB}} \frac{\partial r_{CB}}{\partial i} + z_D \frac{\partial MD}{\partial r_{NB}} \frac{\partial r_{NB}}{\partial i} + \frac{\partial MC}{\partial r_{CB}} \frac{\partial r_{CB}}{\partial i} + \frac{\partial MC}{\partial r_{NB}} \frac{\partial r_{NB}}{\partial i} \right.$$

$$\left. + z_D \frac{\partial MT}{\partial r_{NB}} \frac{\partial r_{NB}}{\partial i} \right| > \left| z_T \frac{\partial MT}{\partial r_{CB}} \frac{\partial r_{CB}}{\partial i} \right|, \qquad (9.B.27)$$

the size of *Mi* and therefore the denominator is increased. Under these conditions, the comparative statics multiplier is reduced. If condition (9.B.27) does not hold, then the multiplier is increased. Consequently, unless the effect of the own rate on the demand for time deposits is unusually strong, a change in reserves alters income by a smaller amount if savings deposit rates are free to fluctuate than if savings deposit rates are bound by restrictive ceilings. Similarly, the effect of a change in high powered money on open market interest rates is

$$\frac{di}{dHP} = \frac{Dy}{Dy\,Mi - Di\,My} < 0, \qquad (9.B.28)$$

which is negative. Again, however, the size of the denominator of expression (9.B.28) compared to the case of restrictive ceilings is increased by the inclusion of the additional terms in *Mi*, if condition (9.B.27) holds, so that a given change in the quantity of reserves has a smaller impact on the level of open market interest rates. More definitive conclusions require empirical evidence.

Next we derive the effect of a change in high powered money on the monetary aggregates *M*1 and *M*2. Since the total differential for *M*1 is the sum of the differentials for currency and demand deposits, the effect of a change in high powered money on *M*1 is

$$\frac{dM1}{dHP} = \left(\frac{\partial MD}{\partial i} + \frac{\partial MD}{\partial r_{CB}} \frac{\partial r_{CB}}{\partial i} + \frac{\partial MD}{\partial r_{NB}} \frac{\partial r_{NB}}{\partial i} \right) \frac{di}{dHP} + \frac{\partial MD}{\partial y} \frac{dy}{dHP}$$

$$+ \left(\frac{\partial MC}{\partial i} + \frac{\partial MC}{\partial r_{CB}} \frac{\partial r_{CB}}{\partial i} + \frac{\partial MC}{\partial r_{NB}} \frac{\partial r_{NB}}{\partial i} \right) \frac{di}{dHP}$$

$$+ \frac{\partial MC}{\partial y} \frac{dy}{dHP} > 0. \qquad (9.B.29)$$

This comparative statics result is positive, based on the signs of expressions (9.B.26) and (9.B.28) and the a priori signs of the partial derivatives. Nevertheless it is not clear whether the size of this impact on *M*1 is larger or smaller than the impact that occurs when the ceilings constrain movements in savings deposit rates. The effects of open market rates on savings deposit rates tend to increase the overall impact of a change in the quantity of reserves, but as demonstrated in equations (9.B.26) and (9.B.28), the comparative statics multipliers, dy/dHP and di/dHP, may each be smaller and tend to reduce the impact of high powered money on *M*1. Consequently, whether the effect of high powered money on *M*1 is increased or decreased as a result of endogenous deposit rate setting, depends on the size of each of the partial derivatives. In order to derive more definitive results, explicit empirical evidence must be used. This question is reconsidered in the next chapter. A similar result applies to the demand for time deposits and $M2$. The effect of a change in high powered money on the quantity of time deposits, is

$$\frac{dMT}{dHP} = \left(\frac{\partial MT}{\partial i} + \frac{\partial MT}{\partial r_{CB}} \frac{\partial r_{CB}}{\partial i} + \frac{\partial MT}{\partial r_{NB}} \frac{\partial r_{NB}}{\partial i} \right) \frac{di}{dHP}$$
$$+ \frac{\partial MT}{\partial y} \frac{dy}{dHP} > 0, \qquad (9.B.30)$$

which is smaller than expression (9.A.38) in Case A, again on the assumption that the effect of the own rate on time deposits either dominates or equals the effect of the nonbank rate. It is not clear whether the effect of a change in high powered money on $M2$ is enhanced or diminished by allowing deposit rates to be market determined. A more definitive evaluation of this question can only be obtained quantitatively.

In general, when Regulation Q ceilings are not binding and savings deposit rates are endogenously determined, the macroeconomic impact of changes in the quantity of reserves supplied by the central bank is similar in direction to the effects when Regulation Q ceilings are restrictive, Case A. An increase in high powered money increases income, decreases open market yields, and increases $M1$ and $M2$. Nevertheless endogenous determination of deposit rates does decrease the size of the money multipliers for income and open market interest rates. That is, for a given increase in high powered money there is a smaller impact on aggregate demand when deposit rates are unconstrained than when Regulation Q ceilings prevent adjustments in deposit rates. The qualitative impact on $M1$ and $M2$ is unclear and more definitive statements must await quantitative evidence.

In summary, the comparative statics properties of Case B, in which interest rates on savings deposits are freely determined by financial intermediaries, are similar in sign to the properties derived in Case A in which Regulation Q ceilings are effectively binding. Nevertheless, the results for these two cases clearly indicate that the impact of changes in monetary policy on economic activity is less effective if savings deposit rates are endogenously determined. The only exception to this result occurs when the central bank uses the level of open market interest rates as its policy instrument. Consequently, we can conclude that the presence of binding Regulation Q ceilings on deposit rates enhances the effectiveness of monetary policy.

Case C: Regulation Q Ceilings Are Changed

In this section we use the economic models developed previously in order to analyze explicitly the impact on the economy that results from a change in the ceilings on interest rates on savings deposits. We assume that when Regulation Q ceilings are altered there is no concomitant change in any other monetary policy instrument. Such a change in Regulation Q may be viewed as part of an economic stabilization program or the initial step in a program seeking the ultimate elimination of legal ceilings on deposit rates. In this analysis we assume the ceiling is binding at the time a change in Regulation Q is initiated and that, as a result of this change, deposit rates move immediately to the new ceiling. If deposit rates are not effectively restricted, then a change or even the removal of the ceilings has no macroeconomic impact, since a change in the ceiling can only affect the economy if it alters savings deposit rates. We again utilize the basic Keynesian model of income determination and obtain comparative statics results for three models each of which incorporates a different assumption about the monetary policy variable controlled by the central bank: the money supply, open market interest rates, or high powered money. The assumptions that characterize the product and money markets are retained from the previous cases

$$y = c[y - t(y)] + I(i) + g \tag{9.C.1}$$

$$1 > \partial c/\partial y, \ \partial t/\partial y > 0 \qquad \partial I/\partial i < 0$$

$$m = m(i, r, y) \qquad \partial m/\partial i, \ \partial m/\partial r < 0 \qquad \partial m/\partial y > 0. \tag{9.C.2}$$

In Model 1, the policy variable of the monetary authorities is the money supply, which is exogenous, so that

$$m = m_0. \tag{9.C.3}$$

Taking the total differentials of equation (9.C.1), (9.C.2), and (9.C.3) yields

$$dy = \frac{\partial c}{\partial y} dy - \frac{\partial c}{\partial y} \frac{\partial t}{\partial y} dy + \frac{\partial I}{\partial i} di \tag{9.C.4}$$

$$dm = \frac{\partial m}{\partial i} di + \frac{\partial m}{\partial r} dr + \frac{\partial m}{\partial y} dy \tag{9.C.5}$$

$$dm = dm_0 = 0. \tag{9.C.6}$$

Expression (9.C.6) indicates that there is no policy change in the money supply when ceilings are altered. With the appropriate substitutions, equations (9.C.4) and (9.C.5) can be rewritten in matrix form as

$$\begin{bmatrix} 1 - \dfrac{\partial c}{\partial y}\left(1 - \dfrac{\partial t}{\partial y}\right) & -\dfrac{\partial I}{\partial i} \\[1em] \dfrac{\partial m}{\partial y} & \dfrac{\partial m}{\partial i} \end{bmatrix} \begin{bmatrix} dy \\[1em] di \end{bmatrix} = \begin{bmatrix} 0 \\[1em] -\dfrac{\partial m}{\partial r} \end{bmatrix} dr. \tag{9.C.7}$$

Applying Cramer's rule, we can use expression (9.C.7) to obtain comparative statics results that describe the macroeconomic impact of changes in Regulation Q ceilings. We begin by solving for the effect of a ceiling rate change on income

$$\frac{dy}{dr} = \frac{-(\partial I/\partial i)(\partial m/\partial r)}{\left[1 - \frac{\partial c}{\partial y}\left(1 - \frac{\partial t}{\partial y}\right)\right]\frac{\partial m}{\partial i} + \frac{\partial I}{\partial i}\frac{\partial m}{\partial y}} > 0. \quad (9.C.8)$$

This result is positive given the signs of the partial derivatives in equations (9.C.1) and (9.C.2). Consequently, an increase in deposit rates induced by a rise in Regulation Q ceilings has an expansionary impact on the economy. This result may initially appear to be contradictory, since higher savings deposit rates are usually associated with higher open market yields, lower investment, and a decline in the level of national income. However, the expansionary results are explained as follows. A rise in savings deposit rates lowers the public's desired money balances. Since the money supply is exogenously set by the central bank, open market interest rates must fall in order to equilibrate money demand and supply. This fall in market rates generates a rise in investment and an expansion in national income. Thus the comparative statics multiplier dy/dr indicates that an increase in Regulation Q ceiling induces a rise in income despite the fact that there has been no policy change in the money supply, that is, $dm = 0$. As a result, the narrowly defined money supply $M1$ is a misleading indicator for movements in income since it does not reflect the induced changes occurring in the real sector of the economy. Similarly, the comparative statics effect of a change in savings deposit rate ceilings on open market interest rates can be derived as

$$\frac{di}{dr} = \frac{-\left[1 - \frac{\partial c}{\partial y}\left(1 - \frac{\partial t}{\partial y}\right)\right]\frac{\partial m}{\partial r}}{\left[1 - \frac{\partial c}{\partial y}\left(1 - \frac{\partial t}{\partial y}\right)\right]\frac{\partial m}{\partial i} + \frac{\partial I}{\partial i}\frac{\partial m}{\partial y}} < 0, \quad (9.C.9)$$

which is negative, based on the signs of the partial derivatives in equations (9.C.1) and (9.C.2). Thus, when Regulation Q ceilings are increased in an environment in which the central bank uses the money supply as its policy instrument, income rises and open market rates fall despite the absence of a change in the money supply. In this situation, open market interest rates provide a more appropriate indication of the ensuing effects on the real sector than the level of the money supply.

Furthermore, we can evaluate the effect of a change in Regulation Q ceilings on the quantity of time deposits at commercial banks. In order to do so, it is necessary to disaggregate interest rates on savings deposits into the time deposit rate at commercial banks r_{CB} and the savings deposit rate at nonbanks r_{NB}. The total differential for time deposits is

$$dn = \frac{\partial n}{\partial i} di + \frac{\partial n}{\partial y} dy + \frac{\partial n}{\partial r_{CB}} dr_{CB} + \frac{\partial n}{\partial r_{NB}} dr_{NB} \qquad (9.\text{C}.10)$$

where $\dfrac{\partial n}{\partial r_{CB}} > 0, \quad \dfrac{\partial n}{\partial r_{NB}} < 0.$

The change in the demand for time deposits that results from an increase in Regulation Q is

$$\frac{dn}{dr} = \frac{\partial n}{\partial i} \frac{di}{dr} + \frac{\partial n}{\partial y} \frac{dy}{dr} + \frac{\partial n}{\partial r_{CB}} + \frac{\partial n}{\partial r_{NB}}. \qquad (9.\text{C}.11)$$

The first three terms of (9.C.11) have the effect of increasing time deposits, while the last term, which reflects the substitution effect of nonbank rates on the demand for time deposits, tends to reduce time deposits, so that the sign of (9.C.11) is not clear. Nevertheless, since it seems unreasonable that the effect of nonbank deposit rates on time deposits is greater than the own rate effect, the sign of expression (9.C.11) is positive. Since there is no effect on $M1$, the effect of Regulation Q changes on $M2$, which is the sum of $M1$ and time deposits, should also be positive. This suggests that when Regulation Q ceilings are increased the quantity of time deposits is likely to rise, so that the monetary aggregate $M2$ is probably a better indicator for income than $M1$ but still not as consistent a reflection of aggregate demand as open market interest rates.

In general, the macroeconomic impact of a rise in Regulation Q ceilings is expansionary even though the monetary policy variable $M1$ is held constant. Furthermore, the behavior of interest rates provides a more accurate indication of the induced rise in the economic activity in the real sector than the behavior of the monetary aggregates $M1$ and $M2$.

Next we assume that the policy variable of the monetary authorities is the level of open market interest rates. For Model 2 we retain expressions (9.C.1) and (9.C.2), which describe the product and money market, and replace equation (9.C.3) with

$$i = i_0 \qquad (9.\text{C}.12)$$

where i_0 is the exogenously set open market interest rate and the central bank stands prepared to supply the quantity of money needed to accommodate the public's demand at the policy determined level of market rates. Differentiating equations (9.C.1), (9.C.2) and (9.C.12) and arranging in matrix form yields

$$\begin{bmatrix} 1 - \dfrac{\partial c}{\partial y}\left(1 - \dfrac{\partial t}{\partial y}\right) & 0 \\ \\ -\dfrac{\partial m}{\partial y} & 1 \end{bmatrix} \begin{bmatrix} dy \\ \\ dm \end{bmatrix} = \begin{bmatrix} 0 \\ \\ \dfrac{\partial m}{\partial r} \end{bmatrix} dr \qquad (9.C.13)$$

since $di = 0$.

These equations are solved for the ceteris paribus effect of a change in savings deposit rates on income by using Cramer's rule, so that

$$\frac{dy}{dr} = \frac{0}{1 - \dfrac{\partial c}{\partial y}\left(1 - \dfrac{\partial t}{\partial y}\right)} = 0. \qquad (9.C.14)$$

This indicates that when monetary policy is directed at controlling open market interest rates, changes in savings deposit rates due to changes in Regulation Q have no impact on the level of macroeconomic activity. This is because in a Keynesian model financial developments affect the level of aggregate demand through the interest rate mechanism. The only impact of a change in savings deposit rates in this model is an appropriate change in the money supply without any effect on income. The comparative statics multiplier which demonstrates that a change in Regulation Q ceilings has an appreciable effect on the money supply is

$$dm/dr = \partial m/\partial r < 0. \qquad (9.C.15)$$

The result is negative and indicates that a rise in Regulation Q ceilings induces a decline in the money supply despite the fact that there is no impact on income. This is because the rise in deposit rates induces the public to economize on its holdings of money. In such a situation $M1$ is again a poor indicator of developments in the real sector of the economy. The impact of a change in Regulation Q on $M2$ is ambiguous. Since there is no change in either short term interest rates or income, it follows from expression (9.C.10) that the effect on the demand for time deposits is simply

$$dn/dr = \partial n/\partial r_{CB} + \partial n/\partial r_{NB} \qquad (9.C.16)$$

In this expression the first term is positive while the second is negative, so that the overall effect on time deposits is unclear. However, again making the reasonable assumption that the own rate effect outweighs the effect of the competing rate, we can conclude that the effect of Regulation Q ceiling changes on the demand for time deposits is positive. Nevertheless, the impact on $M2$ is the combined effects of a change in Regulation Q on both $M1$ and time deposits, which in this model are negative and positive respectively. Consequently, the total effect is unclear and further evaluation requires quantitative evidence.

In general, in a world in which the monetary authorities control open market interest rates, a rise in Regulation Q ceilings induces a decline in the supply of money but the level of income remains unaltered. As a result, $M1$ is again a poor indicator of movements in aggregate demand. The broader monetary aggregate $M2$ is also likely to be a poor indicator of income since the effect of a change in ceiling rates on $M2$ is ambiguous.

In Model 3, we assume that the monetary authorities operate in the market for reserves and that the supply of money and open market interest rates are determined endogenously. The disaggregated description of the money market is retained from the previous cases for this model so that the equation that equates the demand and supply of money is

$$MD(i, r_{CB}, r_{NB}, y) = (UR - z_T MT - FR)/z_D. \qquad (9.C.17)$$

Equilibrium in the product market is described in equation (9.C.1). Therefore, the total differentials of equations (9.C.1) and (9.C.17) are

$$dy = \frac{\partial c}{\partial y} dy - \frac{\partial c}{\partial y} \frac{\partial t}{\partial y} dy + \frac{\partial I}{\partial i} di \qquad (9.C.18)$$

$$\frac{\partial MD}{\partial y} dy + \frac{\partial MD}{\partial i} di + \frac{\partial MD}{\partial r_{CB}} dr_{CB} + \frac{\partial MD}{\partial r_{NB}} dr_{NB}$$

$$= \frac{1}{z_D} (dUR - z_T dMT - d\dot{F}R). \qquad (9.C.19)$$

Again assuming that high powered money and the discount rate are exogenously set by the central bank and substituting the total differentials for unborrowed reserves, time deposits, and free reserves, equation (9.C.19) can be rewritten as

$$\frac{\partial MD}{\partial y} dy + \frac{\partial MD}{\partial i} di + \frac{\partial MD}{\partial r_{CB}} dr_{CB} + \frac{\partial MD}{\partial r_{NB}} dr_{NB}$$

$$= \frac{1}{z_D} \bigg(-\frac{\partial MC}{\partial y} dy - \frac{\partial MC}{\partial i} di - \frac{\partial MC}{\partial r_{CB}} dr_{CB} - \frac{\partial MC}{\partial r_{NB}} dr_{NB} - z_T \frac{\partial MT}{\partial y} dy$$

$$- z_T \frac{\partial MT}{\partial i} di - z_T \frac{\partial MT}{\partial r_{CB}} dr_{CB} - z_T \frac{\partial MT}{\partial r_{NB}} dr_{NB} - \frac{\partial FR}{\partial i} di \bigg). \qquad (9.C.20)$$

Employing shorthand notation in writing equations (9.C.18) and (9.C.20) in matrix form, yields

$$\begin{bmatrix} Dy & Di \\ My & Mi \end{bmatrix} \begin{bmatrix} dy \\ di \end{bmatrix} = \begin{bmatrix} 0 \\ Mr_{CB} \end{bmatrix} dr_{CB} + \begin{bmatrix} 0 \\ Mr_{NB} \end{bmatrix} dr_{NB} \qquad (9.C.21)$$

where

$$Dy = 1 - \frac{\partial c}{\partial y}\left(1 - \frac{\partial t}{\partial y}\right)$$

$$Di = -\partial I/\partial i$$

$$My = z_D \frac{\partial MD}{\partial y} + \frac{\partial MC}{\partial y} + z_T \frac{\partial MT}{\partial y}$$

$$Mi = z_D \frac{\partial MD}{\partial i} + \frac{\partial MC}{\partial i} + z_T \frac{\partial MT}{\partial i} + \frac{\partial FR}{\partial i}$$

$$Mr_{CB} = -z_D \frac{\partial MD}{\partial r_{CB}} - \frac{\partial MC}{\partial r_{CB}} - z_T \frac{\partial MT}{\partial r_{CB}}$$

$$Mr_{NB} = -z_D \frac{\partial MD}{\partial r_{NB}} - \frac{\partial MC}{\partial r_{NB}} - z_T \frac{\partial MT}{\partial r_{NB}}$$

By Cramer's rule the effect on income caused by a change in deposit rate ceilings is

$$\frac{dy}{dr} = \frac{dy}{dr_{CB}} + \frac{dy}{dr_{NB}} = \frac{-Di(Mr_{CB} + Mr_{NB})}{Dy\, Mi - Di\, My}. \qquad (9.C.22)$$

Dividing both numerator and denominator by $(-Di)$, this expression can be rewritten as

$$\frac{dy}{dr} = \frac{Mr_{CB} + Mr_{NB}}{(Dy\, Mi/-Di) + My}. \qquad (9.C.23)$$

Based on the a priori signs of the partial derivatives, the denominator of (9.C.23) is positive and the Mr_{NB} term in the numerator is also positive. However, the sign of Mr_{CB} is ambiguous because one of the components, $-z_T(\partial MT/\partial r_{CB})$ is negative. Consequently, if the following condition holds

$$\left| z_D \frac{\partial MD}{\partial r_{CB}} + \frac{\partial MC}{\partial r_{CB}} + z_D \frac{\partial MD}{\partial r_{NB}} + \frac{\partial MC}{\partial r_{NB}} + z_T \frac{\partial MT}{\partial r_{NB}} \right| > \left| z_T \frac{\partial MT}{\partial r_{CB}} \right|, \qquad (9.C.24)$$

then the numerator and hence the total derivative is positive, and an increase in ceiling rates is expansionary. If the reverse holds, then the effect is contractionary. More intuitively, a rise in savings deposit rates reduces the demand for demand deposits and currency, which releases reserves as indicated by the first four terms in condition (9.C.24). The rise in the time deposit rate increases the demand for time deposits, which absorbs reserves, the right hand side term. Consequently, whether there is a net increase or decrease in the demand for reserves depends on the relative size of all these parameters and the relevant reserve requirements,

z_D and z_T. Generally, the reserve requirement for demand deposits has been about 0.14 while that on time deposits has been about 0.04. Unless the relative effect of the own rate on the demand for time deposits is unusually strong, the overall impact of an increase in the Regulation Q ceiling is expansionary.

It is interesting to note another important implication of equation (9.C.23). Increases in savings deposit rate ceilings at nonbank intermediaries are clearly expansionary if ceilings on time deposit rates at commercial banks are unchanged. In such circumstances, dr_{CB} equals zero and

$$\frac{dy}{dr} = \frac{Mr_{NB}}{\dfrac{Dy\ Mi}{-Di} + My} > 0. \qquad (9.C.25)$$

In this case the sign of each term is positive and a rise in nonbank deposit rates, ceteris paribus, increases income. This is the case studied by Gurley and Shaw [29] during the 1950s.

In a similar manner we can derive the comparative statics effect of a change in deposit rate ceilings on the level of open market rates. From expression (9.C.21), we obtain

$$\frac{di}{dr} = \frac{Dy\ (Mr_{CB} + Mr_{NB})}{Dy\ Mi - Di\ My}. \qquad (9.C.26)$$

Based on the signs of the partial derivatives given previously, the sign of the denominator is negative. In the numerator the signs for Dy and Mr_{NB} are positive, but as in the comparative statics result for dy/dr, the sign of Mr_{CB} is ambiguous. Nevertheless, if we retain the assumption that Mr_{CB} is likely to be positive, then the overall sign of di/dr is negative and an increase in Regulation Q ceilings induces a decline in open market rates and an increase in income.

Finally, we can analyze the effect of a change in deposit rate ceilings on the monetary aggregates, $M1$ and $M2$. In the case of $M1$ the comparative statics effect of a change in ceiling rates is the sum of the effects on demand deposits and currency. The effect of ceiling changes on demand deposits is

$$\frac{dMD}{dr} = \frac{\partial MD}{\partial i}\frac{di}{dr} + \frac{\partial MD}{\partial y}\frac{dy}{dr} + \frac{\partial MD}{\partial r_{CB}} + \frac{\partial MD}{\partial r_{NB}}. \qquad (9.C.27)$$

If we assume that a rise in the ceiling is expansionary, that is, there is an increase in income and a decrease in open market rates, then the first two terms of (9.C.27) are positive, reflecting the effect of the expansion in aggregate demand, but the last two terms are negative, reflecting the rise in the opportunity cost of holding money as a result of the rise in savings deposit rates. The comparative statics result for currency is symmetrical so that the overall effect of changes in Regulation Q ceilings on $M1$ is ambiguous. Consequently, even if a rise in savings deposits rates is expansionary, that is $dy/dr > 0$ and $di/dr < 0$, the narrowly defined money supply may not rise at all and may in fact decline. Therefore, $M1$ is likely to be a poor indicator of movements in income and other real variables. For $M2$ the comparative statics effect of changes in Regulation Q is the sum of the effect on $M1$ and time deposits where the effect on time deposits is

$$\frac{dMT}{dr} = \frac{\partial MT}{\partial i}\frac{di}{dr} + \frac{\partial MT}{\partial y}\frac{dy}{dr} + \frac{\partial MT}{\partial r_{CB}} + \frac{\partial MT}{\partial r_{NB}}. \quad (9.\text{C}.28)$$

The first three terms are positive if we assume that a rise in Regulation Q is expansionary, $di/dr < 0$ and $dy/dr > 0$. However, the effect of nonbank rates on the demand for time deposits, the last term, is negative. Therefore the sign of the expression (9.C.28), like that if (9.C.27), is not clear unless there is empirical information on the relative size of these derivatives. Consequently, both monetary aggregates, $M1$ and $M2$, are likely to be poor variables for targeting income when ceiling rates are changed. In a world in which the monetary authorities follow a reserves policy, only open market interest rates definitely provide a good indication of the movements in income.

Overall, in a model in which the central bank controls reserves, the comparative statics results suggest that if Regulation Q ceiling rates are changed there is likely to be an expansionary impact on income with a concomitant fall in open market rates. However, the effect of the ceiling change on the monetary aggregates, $M1$ and $M2$, is ambiguous with the sign depending upon the relative size of the effects from the change in aggregate demand and upon the sensitivity of the public's demand for deposits to variations in savings deposit rates. In such a model, $M1$ and $M2$ are likely to be poor indicators of macroeconomic activity. Only open market rates consistently provide an accurate reflection of developments in the real sector of the economy.

In summary, these three theoretical models suggest that the macroeconomic effect of raising legal interest rate ceiling restrictions on savings deposit rates depends on which financial variable is used by the central bank as its policy instrument. If the monetary instrument is the money supply and Regulation Q ceilings are raised, then the effect on income is clearly expansionary even though the supply of money is unaltered. If monetary policy centers on open market interest rates, the level of income is not affected by changes in deposit rate ceilings. The major impact in this model is an inverse effect on the supply of money. If high powered money is the policy instrument, then the macroeconomic impact of Regulation Q changes is not clear. The results are either expansionary or contractionary depending on the relative impact of deposit rates on the demand for demand deposits, currency, and time deposits and depending on the reserve requirements on these liabilities. A further implication of the theoretical results is that when Regulation Q ceilings are changed, the usefulness of the monetary aggregates, $M1$ and $M2$, as indicators of macroeconomic activity is reduced and in fact can be misleading. If the central bank controls the money supply or open market interest rates, the behavior of $M1$ provides a misleading indication of the movements in income, while the behavior of $M2$ is ambiguous. If the central bank's policy variable is high powered money, then the behavior of $M1$ and $M2$ is ambiguous. In general, the theoretical results suggest that open market interest rates are the only monetary variable that uniformly behaves in a manner consistent with the induced effects on aggregate demand when changes in Regulation Q ceilings are implemented. This result applies regardless of which monetary variable the central bank uses as its policy instrument.

Conclusions

The behavior of interest rates on savings deposits has an important influence on the effectiveness of monetary policy and on the level of economic activity, which depends on the impact of these deposit rates on the money market and on the administration of the legal deposit rate ceilings. Thus, the comparative statics properties of the three Keynesian models of income determination provide considerable theoretical information that is relevant for the general conduct of monetary policy. In Case A, where Regulation Q ceilings are binding, savings deposit rate setting behavior is exogenous and the macroeconomic impact of a change in monetary policy is described by the standard money multipliers. This result holds, regardless of whether the central bank uses the money supply, open market interest rates, or high powered money as its policy instrument. Furthermore, given the conditions of this case, the behavior of each major monetary variable is consistent with developments in the real sector of the economy. Since these monetary variables are more easily and quickly observable in the short run than movements in income, they may usefully serve as indicators of economic activity in any program of stabilization policy.

In Case B, Regulation Q ceilings are not effective and savings deposit rates are freely determined by the profit maximizing behavior of financial intermediaries. The signs of the comparative statics multipliers for monetary policy in this case are similar to the standard results for Case A. However, the size of each of the money multipliers in Case B is likely to be smaller than in Case A. This suggests that the impact of monetary policy on economic activity is less effective if savings deposit rates are determined by market behavior than if legal ceilings are binding. The only clear exception to this conclusion is if the policy instrument is open market interest rates. In this event, the macroeconomic impact of a change in monetary policy is the same whether or not deposit rate ceilings are binding. Nevertheless, regardless of which policy instrument is used by the central bank in this case, each of the major monetary variables is a consistent indicator of movements in national income.

In Case C, Regulation Q ceilings are altered without any concomitant change in the monetary policy instruments. In this case the macroeconomic impact of changing Regulation Q depends on which monetary variable is considered to be the policy instrument of the central bank. If Regulation Q ceilings are raised when the policy variable is the money supply, the macroeconomic impact is expansionary. If monetary policy centers on open market rates, then macroeconomic activity is not affected by a change in ceiling rates. If high powered money is the policy instrument, the impact of changing Regulation Q is ambiguous in the absence of quantitative evidence. Furthermore, when Regulation Q ceilings are altered, the usefulness of the monetary aggregates $M1$ and $M2$ is curtailed, and in some cases $M1$ actually moves in an opposite direction from income. Only the behavior of open market interest rates consistently reflects movements in national income.

In order to assess the quantitative importance of these conclusions, empirical evidence is essential. Consequently, in the next chapter simulation experiments with the Federal Reserve-MIT-Penn econometric model provide definitive evidence to complement these theoretical results.

10 Monetary Policy, Economic Activity, and Interest Rates on Savings Deposits: An Empirical Analysis with the FMP Model

This chapter presents empirical evidence about the comparative statics properties of the theoretical models derived in the previous chapter in order to assess the validity of the results and determine the magnitude of their importance. Furthermore, since some of the signs of the theoretical results are ambiguous, this analysis provides specific information about the relative size of the unknown parameters. Overall, empirical evidence must be used in order to yield more definitive insight into the character of the economic effects that result from an exogenous change in monetary policy or in Regulation Q ceilings on savings deposit rates. The source for this quantitative evidence is simulation experiments with the Federal Reserve-MIT-Penn (FMP) econometric model.

The FMP model is a large scale simultaneous system of structural equations embodying neo-Keynesian theory. The model is characterized by a well developed financial sector and strong links between monetary phenomena and aggregate demand. At the heart of the financial sector are equations that explain the demand and supply of money. It is assumed that the money market is always cleared and that the Treasury bill rate is the price that equilibrates demand and supply. Long term interest rates are determined as a function of short term market rates through term structure relationships. It is primarily through such movements in interest rates that monetary policy is transmitted to the remainder of the economy via cost of capital effects on investment and the impact of changes in wealth on consumer spending. In addition, the FMP model incorporates the influence of credit rationing in the housing sector so that residential investment is a function of the flow of funds into various intermediaries. Thus in the FMP model, monetary developments affect investment through cost of capital, credit rationing, and wealth channels. Of course, this is a more complex and detailed treatment of investment than is specified in the theoretical models in chapter 9, in which all investment is a function of open market interest rates in order to keep the mathematical analysis tractable. Since the FMP model incorporates these complexities in its structural equations, it provides a particularly appropriate framework for empirically analyzing the impact of the behavior of savings deposit rates on the effectiveness of monetary policy, the distribution of investment, and the level of economic activity. Therefore, the results for full model simulations with the FMP model provide useful quantitative insight into the general equilibrium impact of savings deposit rate behavior and serve as an important complement to the theoretical results derived earlier.

Although a complete description of the FMP model is not available in any comprehensive form, background information about several sectors that are most relevant to this analysis is published. A description of a very early version of the model is found in de Leeuw and Gramlich [13,14]. The model has been substantially developed and reformulated since that time, however. The equations of the savings deposit, mortgage, and housing sectors are described in Gramlich and Jaffee [28]. The equations that determine the interest rates on savings deposits are explained in chapter 6 in this volume. The development of the money market equations is found in Modigliani, Rasche, and Cooper [43]. However, in the simulation work in this study we use somewhat different estimated coefficients for these money demand equations than those reported in Modigliani, Rasche, and Cooper. Since the money market equations are central to the FMP model, it is important to note the character of the equations used in this study. In chapter 8 we presented considerable evidence that over the postwar years money demand functions have been characterized by structural instability due to the administration of Regulation Q ceilings on deposit rates, which has affected the competitiveness of banks and nonbanks and altered the pattern of substitution between money and near monies. Furthermore, our empirical results suggest that the money demand equations found throughout the literature, including the Modigliani, Rasche, and Cooper specification, have seriously underestimated the impact of movements in savings deposit rates on money demand. Although the equations we use in the simulation work in this chapter do not fully incorporate the character of these structural shifts, so that the deposit rate elasticities are relatively low, we do allow for a degree of substitution between nonbank savings deposit rates and currency that is somewhat larger for the period prior to 1962 than is usually found in the literature. Nevertheless, the properties of both the demand deposit and currency equations for the time span after 1962, the sample period over which these simulations experiments are conducted, are quite similar to those found in the equations estimated by Modigliani, Rasche, and Cooper. Thus, the impact of savings deposit rate behavior on economic activity and monetary policy as indicated in the following simulation results should be regarded as minimum estimates which would be substantially enhanced in size if the coefficients for money demand fully reflected the effects of the structural shifts described in chapter 8. For convenience, the reestimated equations are reported in Table 10-1. (For an explanation of these equations, see Slovin and Sushka [46].) The t statistics are found in parentheses below the coefficients.

The simulation analysis is divided into three parts, each of which corresponds to the three theoretical cases in chapter 9. A set of simulations

Table 10-1
Equations for Demand Deposits and Currency Used in the Simulation Experiments

(10.1.1)

$$\ln \frac{MD}{GNP} = -\underset{(-2.52)}{0.02566} \ln RTD - \underset{(-5.26)}{0.02565} \ln RTB + \underset{(28.02)}{0.85203} \ln \frac{MD_{-1}}{GNP}$$

$$+ \underset{(2.21)}{0.02247} \ln \frac{RDIS}{RDIS_{-1}} - \underset{(-4.78)}{0.16413} + 0.4086 \, u_{-1}$$

$R^2 = 0.9988$
$SE = 0.0049$
$DW = 1.93$ Sample Period: 1955.1 to 1969.4

(10.1.2)

$$\ln \frac{MC}{EPCE} = -\underset{(-3.35)}{0.04774} \ln RTD^*Q - \underset{(-2.16)}{0.00374} \ln RTB - \underset{(-5.40)}{0.14331} \ln RSL^*(1-Q)$$

$$+ \underset{(21.63)}{0.79351} \ln \frac{MC_{-1}}{EPCE} - \underset{(-5.58)}{0.29610} - \underset{(-5.52)}{0.13827} \, Q$$

$R^2 = 0.9992$
$SE = 0.0028$ $Q = \begin{cases} 0 & \text{if } TIME \leq 1962.1 \\ 1.0 & \text{if } TIME > 1962.1 \end{cases}$
$DW = 1.55$ Sample Period: 1955.1 to 1969.4

is conducted first for Case A in which Regulation Q ceilings are binding, next for Case B in which Regulation Q ceilings are not effective, and finally for Case C in which Regulation Q ceilings are raised. Each of the three sets of simulations are divided into three experiments, each of which incorporates one of the three potential instruments of monetary policy examined in the theoretical models. In the first experiment the money supply is the policy variable, in the second open market interest rates, and in the third high powered money.

Case A: Regulation Q Ceilings Are Binding

In this section, the quantitative impact of monetary policy is evaluated under the assumption that Regulation Q ceilings are binding, so that savings deposit rates are essentially exogenous to the economic system. More specifically, three simulation experiments are conducted in order to evaluate the quantitative impact of a contractionary change in the central bank's monetary policy variable when ceilings are fully binding and no effect on savings deposit rates can be induced as a result of the response of financial intermediaries to economic contraction. In the first experiment the money supply is the exogenous policy variable, in the second open market rates, and in the third high powered money. In the first simulation of each experiment, historical values of all the exogenous variables are used. The model is then simulated a second time incorporating a contractionary change in monetary policy. The solution values from the first simulation are subtracted from the results for the second simulation in order to obtain the multipliers[a] that correspond to the comparative statics results derived in the previous chapter. Consequently, in each graph it is the difference between two simulations that is plotted. In each simulation deposit rates are maintained at their historical levels in order to reflect the assumption that Regulation Q ceilings are binding. The sample period used for this analysis is 1964.4 through 1966.3. The initial quarter is chosen because the data indicate that deposit rates were not at the ceiling in 1964.4.

The first experiment corresponds to Model 1 in Case A of the previous chapter, in which the central bank's policy instrument is the money supply. In this experiment the money supply is decreased by $3 billion compared to its historical level. The theoretical results indicated that when the money supply is the policy variable and Regulation Q ceilings are binding, a decrease in $M1$ should decrease income and $M2$, and increase open market interest rates. The simulation evidence graphed in Figure 10-1 clearly confirms these results. By the end of the simulation period, the level of nominal income *GNP* is decreased by approximately $35 billion and real income falls by more than $20 billion. The decrease in income is accompanied by a sharp jump in the commercial paper rate *RCP* for several quarters after which it returns to a level below its historical value. Long term interest rates *RCB* also rise but display a smoother pattern. This rise in open market rates induces a fairly sharp decline in the demand for time deposits so that $M2$ falls. Consequently, as suggested by the comparative statics results of Model 1, a decline in $M1$ induces a substantial fall in income and $M2$ and a rise in open market interest rates.

In the next experiment the central bank's policy instrument is taken as open market interest rates, so that in order to simulate a change in monetary policy the Treasury bill rate is increased 50 basis points over its historical level again maintaining the assumption that savings deposit rates are effectively bound by ceiling restrictions. The corresponding theoretical results for Model 2 indicated that such a policy change produces a decrease in income and an attendant fall in both $M1$ and $M2$. The empirical findings, graphed in Figure 10-2, confirm these results. By the end of the simulation

---

[a]As is standard in multiplier analyses, the coefficients of the lagged error terms in each equation in the model are set equal to zero for each simulation.

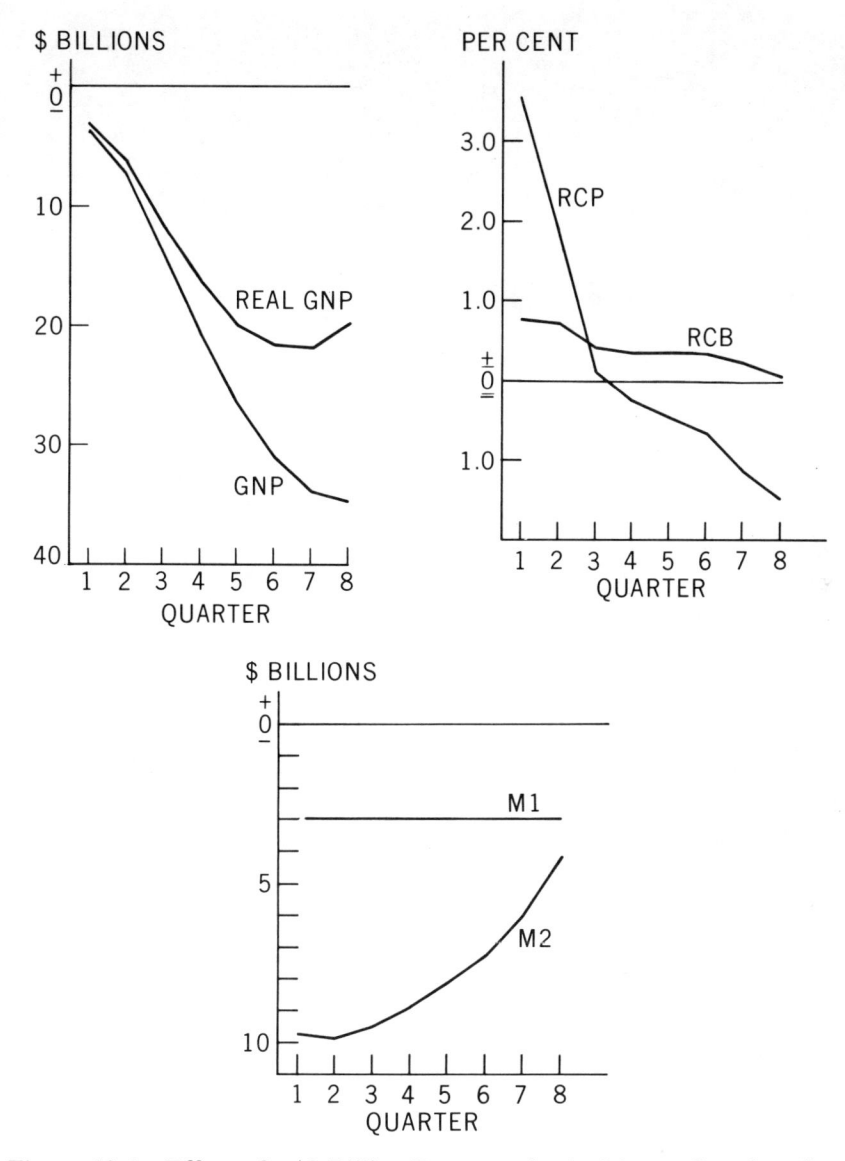

Figure 10-1. Effect of a $3 Billion Decrease in the Money Supply—Case A: Regulation Q Ceilings Are Binding.

period, nominal income is about $15 billion below its historical level and real income is decreased by $10 billion. At the same time, the narrowly defined money supply $M1$ falls by more than $3 billion. The demand for time deposits is also decreased, so that a concomitant fall occurs in the broader monetary aggregate $M2$. As predicted in the theoretical work,

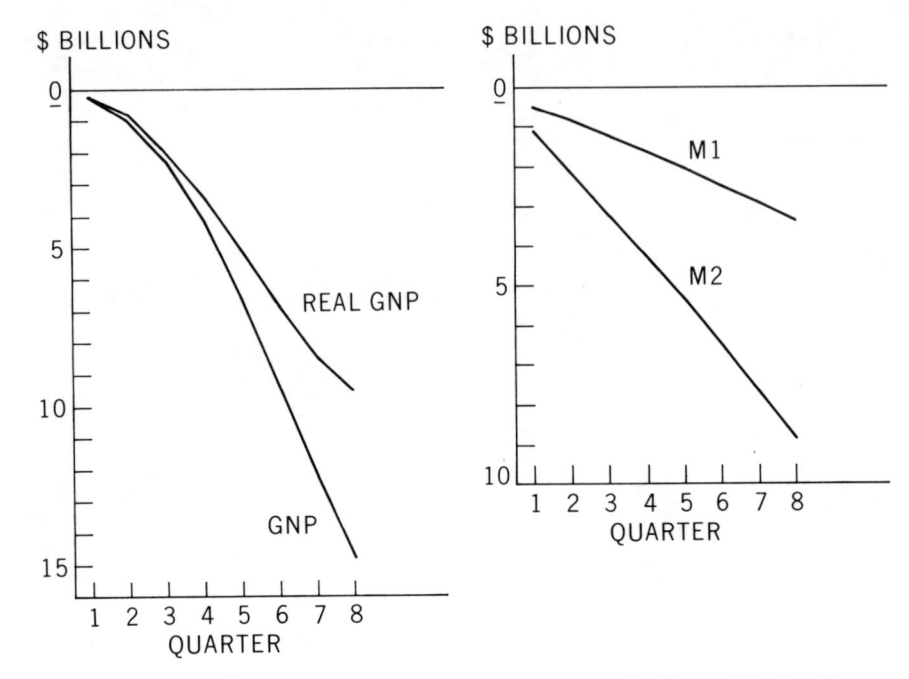

Figure 10-2. Effect of a 50 Basis Point Increase in Open Market Rates —Case A: Regulation Q Ceilings Are Binding.

when the monetary policy instrument of the central bank is open market rates, a contraction in monetary policy induces a decline in macroeconomic activity and the monetary aggregates, $M1$ and $M2$.

Last, a simulation experiment is performed in which the quantity of unborrowed reserves plus currency, that is, high powered money, is assumed to be the monetary variable through which the central bank pursues its policy objectives. These results correspond to the theoretical Model 3, in which both open market interest rates and the money supply are endogenously determined as a result of the interaction of the behavior of the central bank, the commercial banking system, and the public. In this experiment, the quantity of reserves is lowered by $1 billion compared to its historical path. The empirical results, reported in Figure 10-3, confirm the comparative statics findings presented earlier that such a policy lowers the level of income and simultaneously decreases $M1$ and $M2$ while increasing open market rates. By the end of the simulation, nominal income is decreased by $18 billion with a decline in real terms of over $10 billion. At the same time, $M1$ declines by approximately $3 billion. In addition, there is a moderate decrease in the level of time deposits so that $M2$ also falls. Open market rates rise sharply throughout the first year after the change in monetary policy before returning to historical levels by the end of the

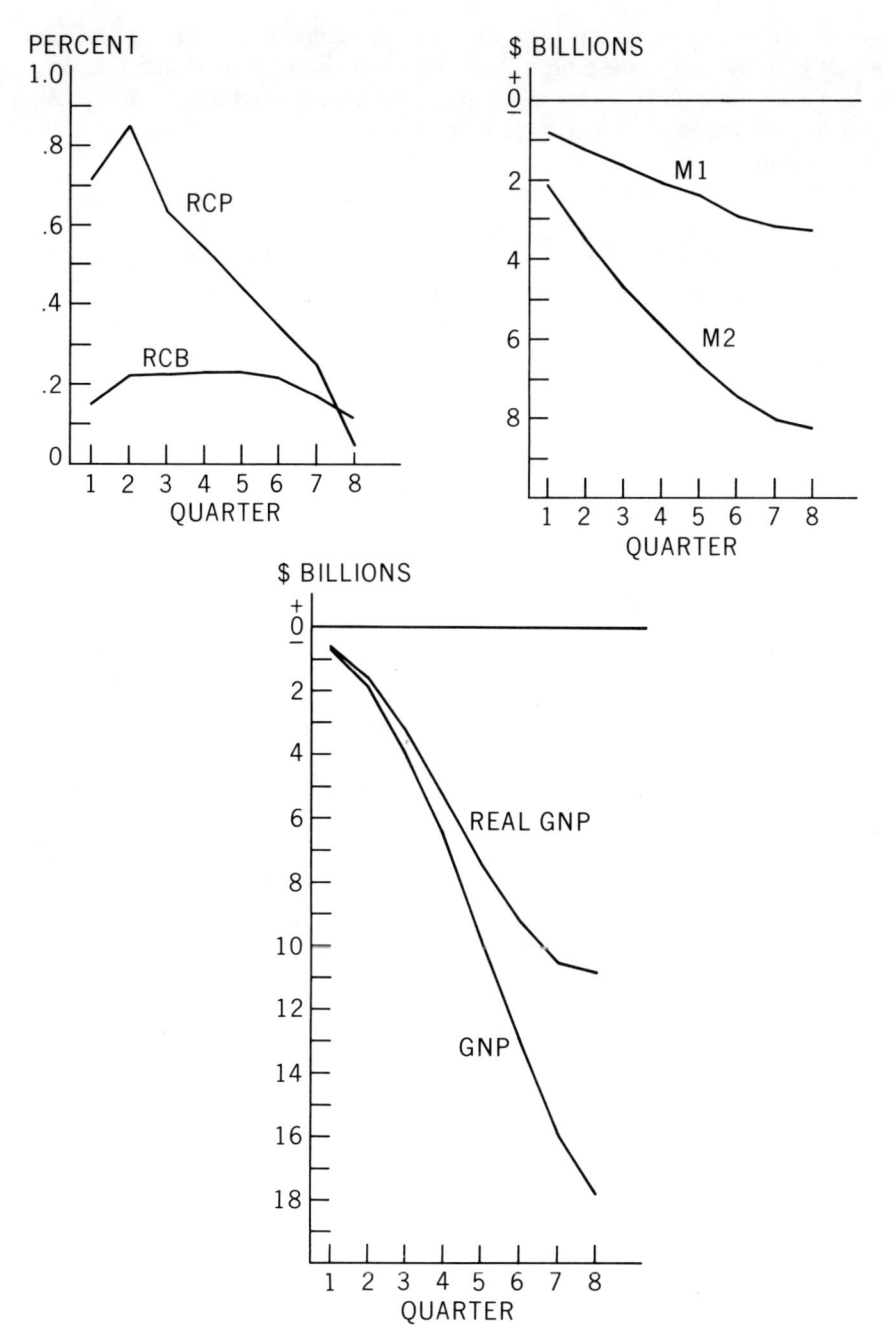

Figure 10-3. Effect of a $1 Billion Decrease in High Powered Money —Case A: Regulation Q Ceilings Are Binding.

period as indicated by the path of the commercial paper rate *RCP*. The effect is more moderate on long term interest rates *RCB*, which rise only about 20 basis points. Thus, a decline in high powered money induces a contraction in economic activity, a rise in interest rates, and a decline in the major monetary aggregates.

In general, these three simulation experiments provide evidence that supports the standard results of the theoretical models developed earlier. When Regulation Q ceilings are binding, a contractionary change in monetary policy induces the expected results of a decline in income, and the monetary aggregates, *M*1 and *M*2, and an increase in open market yields. These results hold regardless of whether the money supply, open market rates, or high powered money is the policy instrument used by the monetary authorities.

Case B: Regulation Q Ceilings Are Not Effective

In this section the quantitative impact of monetary policy is evaluated under the assumption that financial intermediaries are free to adjust the interest rates on savings deposits in accordance with changing financial conditions. In this case, savings deposit rates are endogenously determined within the framework of the model as a result of financial intermediary behavior. These simulation results, when compared with the findings for Case A in the previous section, provide evidence about the quantitative impact that the endogenous determination of savings deposit rates has on the effectiveness of monetary policy in an economic system without legal interest rate ceilings. The sample period remains 1964.4 through 1966.3. Since deposit rate ceilings did not have a restrictive effect on deposit rates at the beginning of this period, there is no transition effect produced by the release of the ceilings as would be the case if such ceilings had kept deposit rates artificially low. The character of this transition effect, which is observed if ceilings are raised in a period when they are effectively binding, is analyzed separately in the next section. The objective in this section is to evaluate the permanent impact that the induced behavior of savings deposit rates has on the overall effectiveness of monetary policy.

Once again each of the three potential instruments of monetary policy is incorporated into a separate simulation experiment. This procedure is important because the theoretical results demonstrated that the effect of endogenous deposit rate setting on the impact of monetary policy varies with the central bank's choice of a policy variable. In the first experiment the money supply is assumed to be the central bank's policy variable, in the second the Treasury bill rate is used, while in the third the quantity of high powered money is taken as the policy instrument. In the first simulation of each experiment, historical values of all the exogenous variables are used. The model is then simulated a second time incorporating the same assumptions of a contractionary change in monetary policy as in Case A. In both simulations interest rates on savings deposits are determined endogenously through the behavior of deposit rate functions. The solution values from the first simulation are subtracted from the results for the second simulation in order to obtain the multiplier impact of a change in monetary policy. The multipliers are reported in the graphs and labeled Case B. The symmetrical results obtained in the previous section for the case of exogenous deposit rates are also graphed in the figures and are labeled Case A. In order to facilitate comparison of the results, the difference between the multipliers for both cases is also charted.

In the first experiment the money supply, which is the central bank's policy variable, is lowered by $3 billion. As a result, in Figure 10-4 nominal *GNP* falls substantially, but by an amount almost $8 billion less than if savings deposit rates are bound by ceiling restrictions. For real *GNP* the difference in the two multipliers amounts to about $5 billion. This indicates that the endogeneity of savings deposit rates lowers the impact of a given change in monetary policy by about 25 per cent. This is because the induced rise in savings deposit rates caused by the monetary contraction lessens the degree to which open market interest rates *RCP* must rise in order to clear the money market. As a result, the rise in long term interest rates *RCB* is also curtailed by about 10 basis points. Furthermore, the decline in time deposits and thus *M2* is diminished by $2 billion. These results are consistent with the comparative statics results obtained in the previous chapter. The contraction in monetary policy induces a rise in deposit rates at financial intermediaries. This effect, when permitted by the absence of Regulation Q ceilings, lowers the extent to which open market rates must adjust in order to induce the public to hold the altered supply of money. Consequently, the size of the money multipliers is reduced compared to Case A in which deposit rates are bound at the ceiling.

In the next experiment the Treasury bill rate, which is assumed to be the central bank's policy instrument, is raised by 50 basis points over its historical values. The theoretical results for Model 2 indicated that if the central bank pursues an open market interest rate policy, the endogeneity of savings deposit rates does not alter the impact of a change in open market rates on the level of economic activity. The simulation results in Figure 10-5 confirm this finding. The decline in both nominal and real *GNP* is almost identical to the case in which deposit rates are exogenous. In fact, the difference in the multipliers is less than half a billion dollars. This is because in a neo-Keynesian model, financial behavior affects the level of economic activity through the interest rate mechanism. Therefore, if the central bank pursues a policy centered on interest rates, the endogeneity of savings

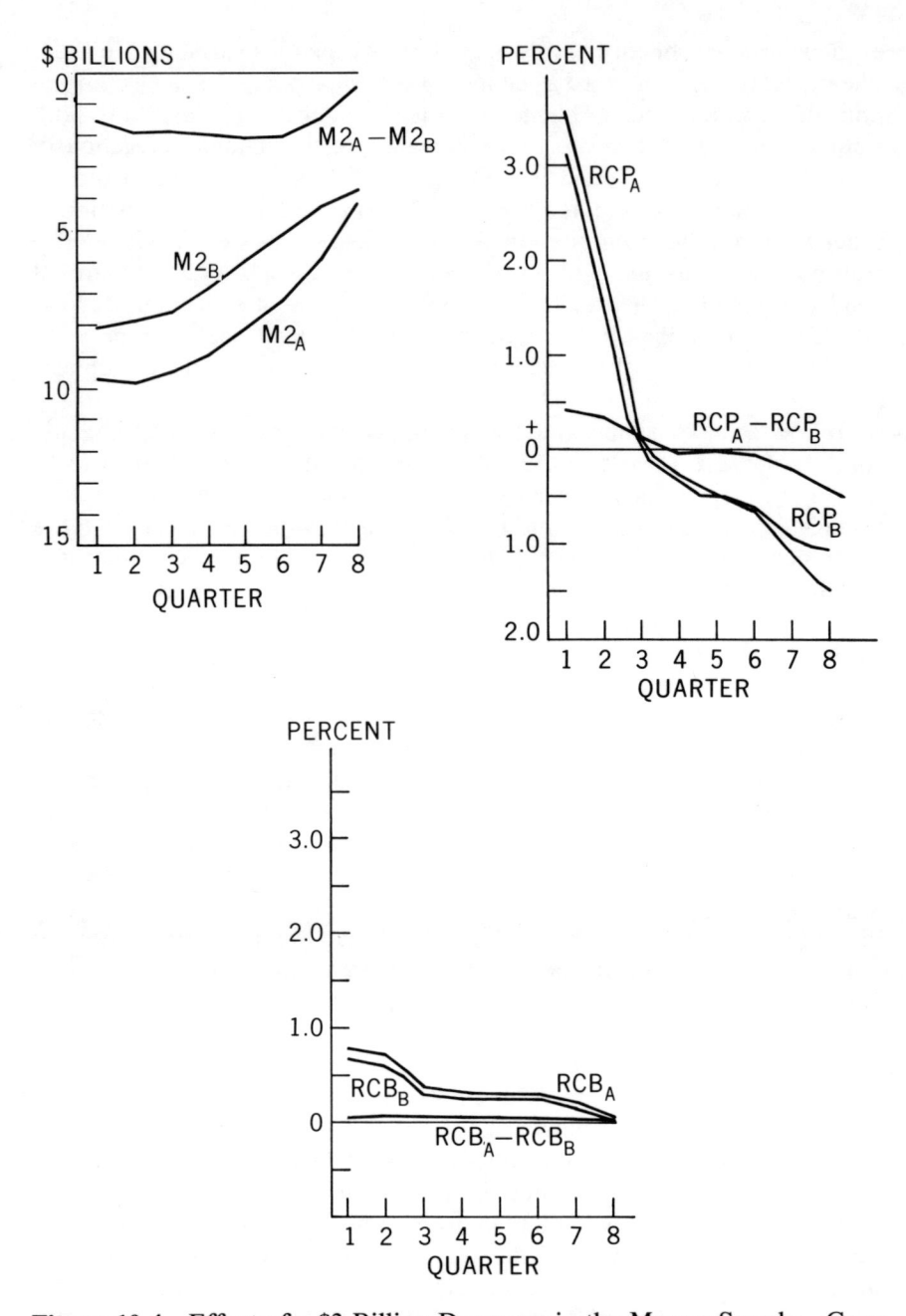

Figure 10-4. Effect of a $3 Billion Decrease in the Money Supply—Case B: Regulation Q Ceilings Are Not Effective; Case A: Regulation Q Ceilings Are Binding.

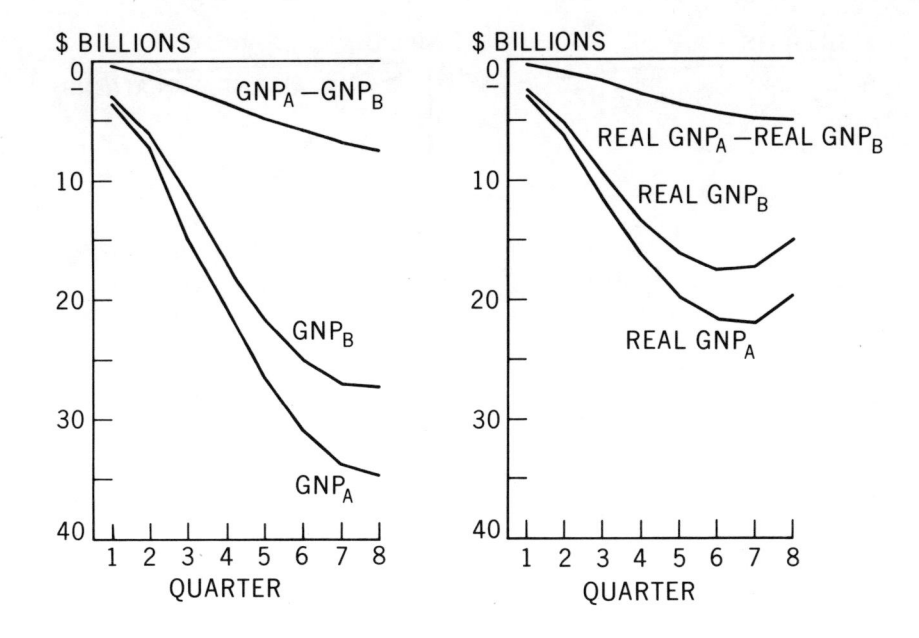

Figure 10-4 (continued)

deposit rates cannot affect open market interest rates. The only major impact of the endogenous rise in deposit rates in this case is to produce a somewhat sharper decrease in the demand for money although the effect is relatively mild. The induced rise in deposit rates, however, diminishes the decline in time deposits and $M2$, compared to the case of exogenous deposit rates.

In the last experiment, the central bank's monetary policy variable is assumed to be the quantity of high powered money, which is reduced by $1 billion compared to its historical level. The character of the simulation results confirm the comparative statics derived earlier for Model 3. As reported in Figure 10-6, the decline in nominal and real *GNP* is lessened by about $2 billion and $1.75 billion respectively, which is a reduction of about 10 per cent in the size of the multiplier. The multipliers are smaller because the induced rise in savings deposit rates lessens the degree to which open market interest rates must increase in order for the public and the commercial banking sector to adjust to the lowered availability of reserves. Consequently, the rise in short term rates is reduced by about 10 basis points. The rise in long term rates is lessened by a smaller amount. It is interesting to note that in the previous chapter, the theoretical results were ambiguous as to whether the endogeneity of savings deposit rates lowers or increases the

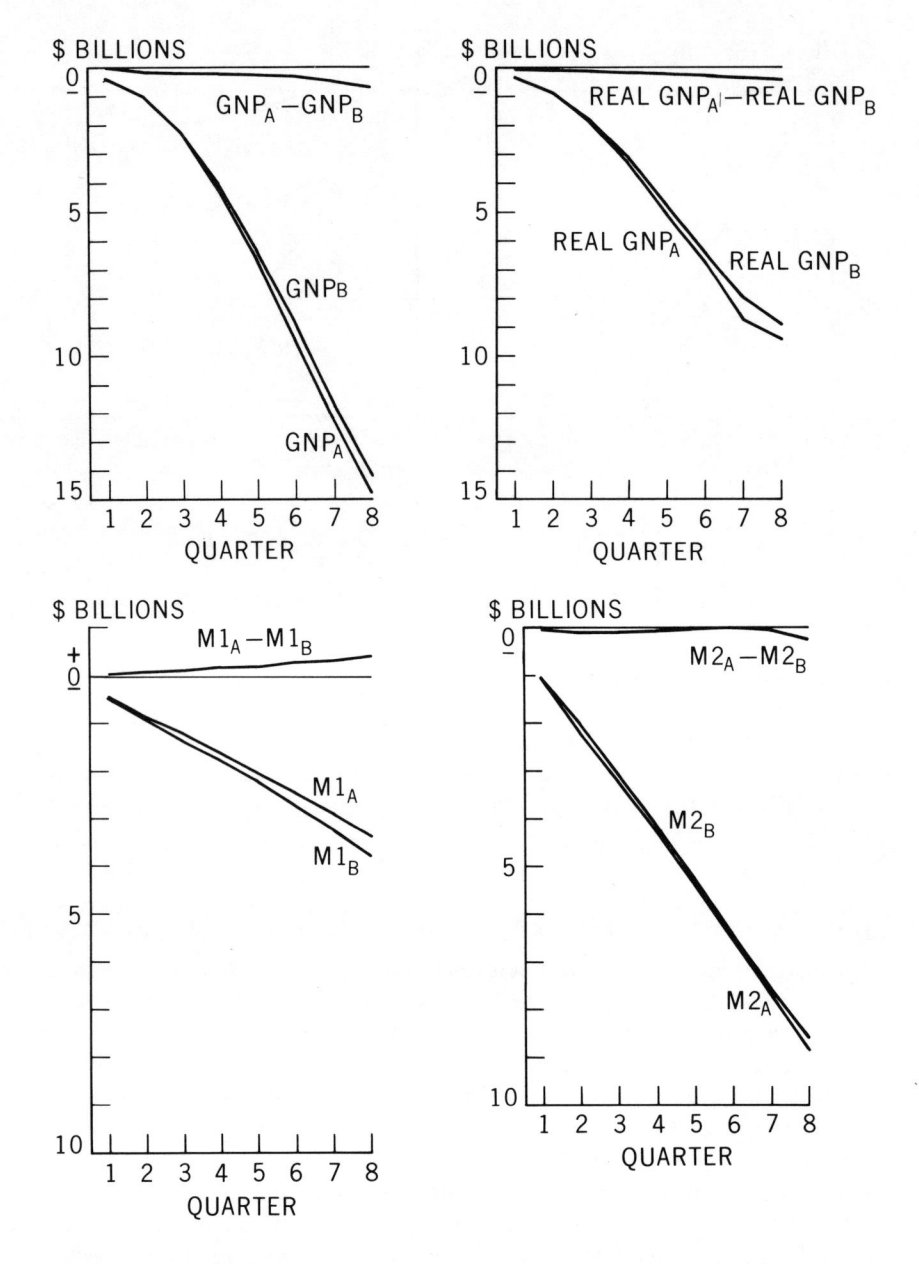

Figure 10-5. Effect of a 50 Basis Point Increase in Open Market Rates —Case B: Regulation Q Ceilings Are Not Effective; Case A: Regulation Q Ceilings Are Binding.

degree to which the money supply responds to a given change in reserves. The simulation evidence indicates that endogenous savings deposit rates induce a larger decline in $M1$, although the size of the effect is relatively minor. Nevertheless, the rise in deposit rates moderates the outflow of time deposits from commercial banks caused by the decrease in reserves, so that the decline in $M2$ is about a billion dollars less than if deposit rates are bound by the ceilings.

In general, the simulation evidence indicates that the impact of the endogeneity of savings deposit rates on the effectiveness of monetary policy depends upon which monetary variable the central bank uses as a policy instrument. If the central bank pursues a policy centered on open market interest rates, then the effectiveness of monetary policy remains essentially unchanged when interest rates on savings deposits are free to fluctuate in response to changes in financial conditions. If the central bank views its monetary policy variable as either the money supply or the quantity of high powered money, then the endogeneity of deposit rates lessens the magnitude of the money multipliers. In such a case, the removal of Regulation Q ceilings on savings deposit rates reduces the effectiveness of a given change in monetary policy.

Case C: Regulation Q Ceilings Are Changed

In this final set of experiments we analyze the economic impact that results from a change in Regulation Q ceilings on deposit rates. The theoretical results developed for Case C in the previous chapter indicated that the character of these effects varies depending upon which monetary variable the central bank regards as its policy instrument. The comparative statics results indicated that if the monetary instrument is the money supply, then the macroeconomic effect is expansionary. If monetary policy centers on open market interest rates, then there is no impact on aggregate demand and the only result is a change in the monetary aggregates, $M1$ and $M2$. If high powered money is the policy instrument, then the results are either expansionary or contractionary depending on the relative impact of deposit rates on the demand for demand deposits, currency, and time deposits. In general, the simulation evidence supports these theoretical conclusions and provides more definitive information about the theoretical results that are ambiguous.

The simulation period is 1970.3 through 1972.2, a different sample period than that used in the previous two sections, because in order for a change in the ceilings on deposit rates to have any economic impact, the

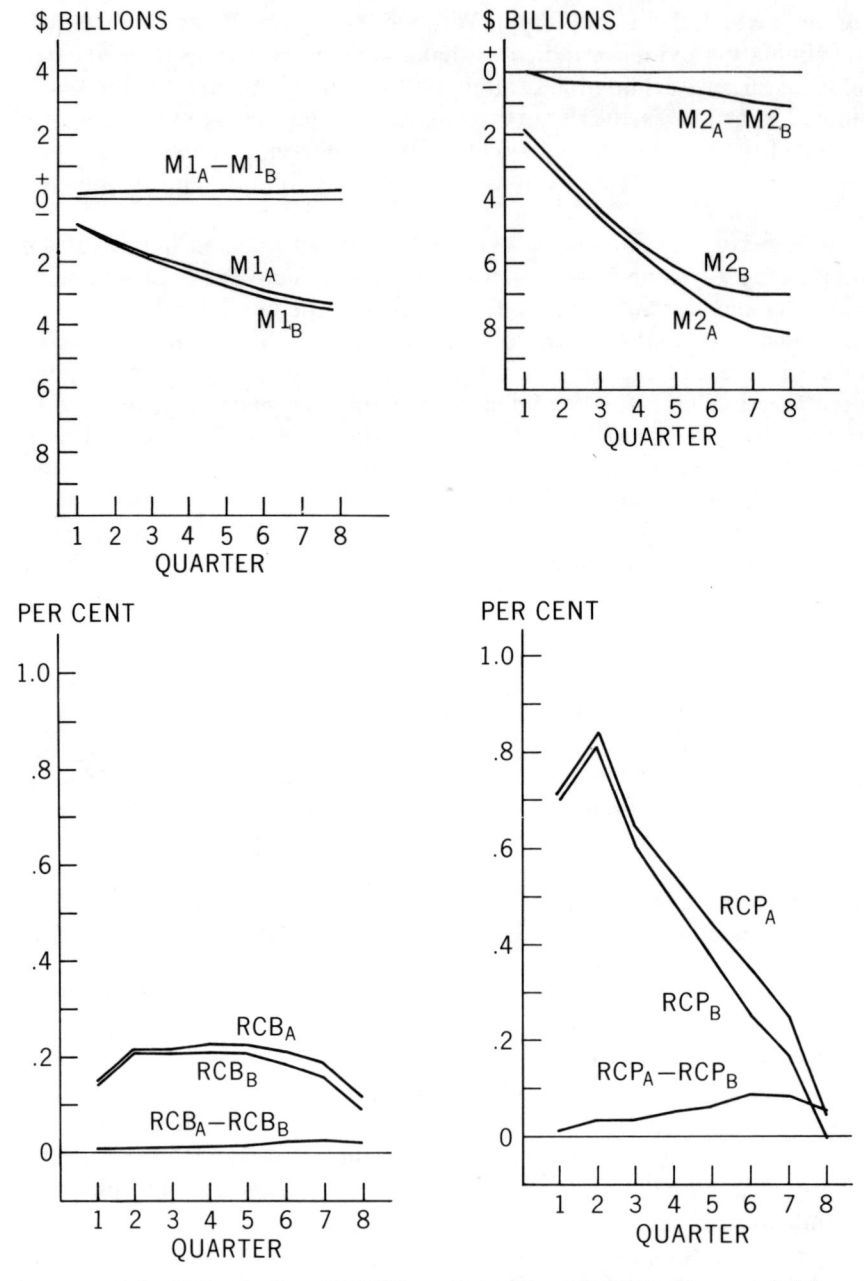

Figure 10-6. Effect of a $1 Billion Decrease in High Powered Money—Case B: Regulation Q Ceilings Are Not Effective; Case A: Regulation Q Ceilings Are Binding.

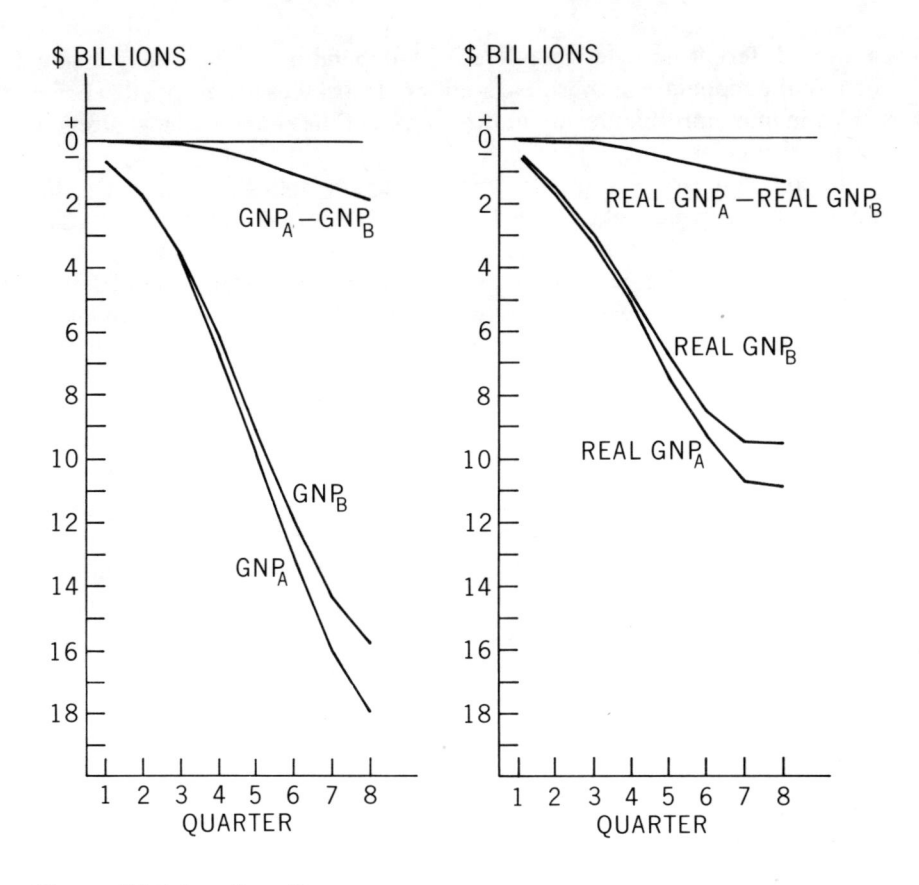

Figure 10-6 (continued)

ceilings must be binding at the time the change is initiated. Consequently, 1970.3 is chosen as the starting quarter because the ceiling rates on both bank and nonbank deposits were clearly binding at the time. In the first experiment the money supply is the exogenous variable, in the second the Treasury bill rate, and in the third high powered money. In the first simulation of each experiment, historical values of all the exogenous variables are used. The model is then simulated a second time, incorporating an increase of 100 basis points in the ceilings on all savings deposit rates. There is no change in any other exogenous monetary policy instrument. The solution values from the first simulation are then subtracted from the results for the second simulation in order to obtain the multipliers that correspond to the comparative statics results derived in the previous chapter. Thus in each of the reported graphs it is the difference between the simulations that is plotted. Because a change in the ceilings on deposit rates induces different macroeconomic effects depending on the policy instrument of the monetary authorities, additional variables are graphed in order to obtain more information about the sectors of the economy most affected by these policies.

In the first experiment, the central bank's policy instrument is the money supply, which takes on its historical values in both simulations. The impact of a 100 basis point rise in all ceiling rates is graphed in Figure 10-7. The comparative statics results obtained previously from Model 1 indicated that the rise of deposit rates to the new ceilings induces an expansion in aggregate demand despite the fact that the supply of money is not altered by central bank policy. The simulation evidence confirms this result. Since the money supply is fixed, the rise in savings deposit rates causes a sharp decline in short term open market interest rates in order to induce the public to hold the given money supply, as indicated by the pattern of *RCP*. Since savings deposit rates are a function of current and past open market rates, the feedback effect of the decline in open market rates eventually lowers savings deposit rates at the financial intermediaries. The fall in open market rates also induces a decline in the long term bond rate, and as a result investment is stimulated and income rises. The growth in income, however, eventually increases the demand for money, and the decline in *RCP* is gradually arrested. Overall, nominal income rises by about $12 billion over

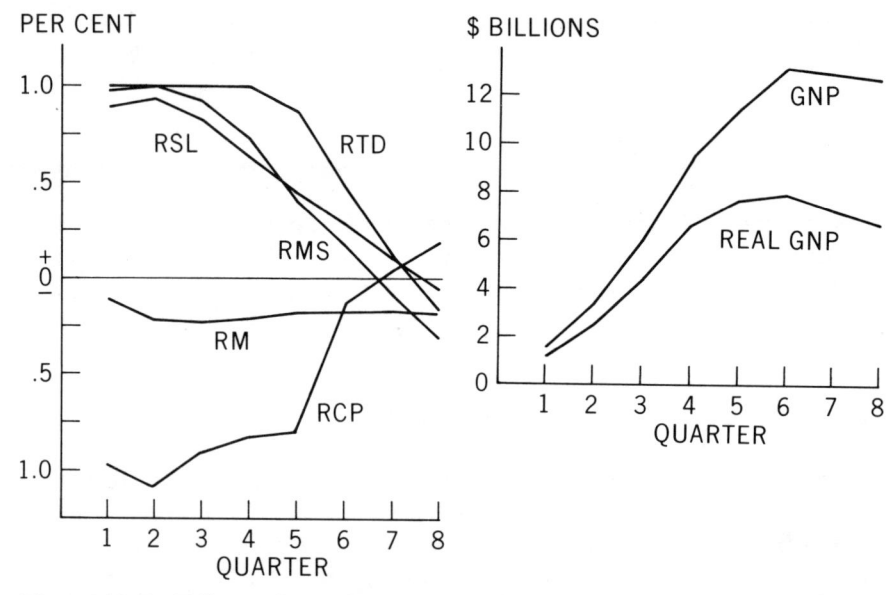

Figure 10-7. Effect of a 100 Basis Point Increase in Regulation Q Ceilings—Money Supply Maintained at Historical Values.

its historical level, while the increase in real income is about half this amount. As a result, there is a lower rate of unemployment and a higher rate of inflation. The combination of an increase in savings deposit rates and lower open market rates induces a large increase in the flow of savings

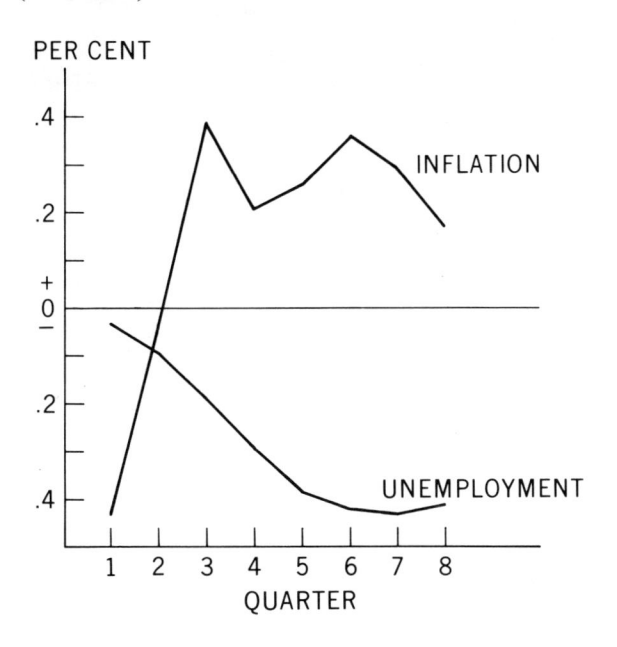

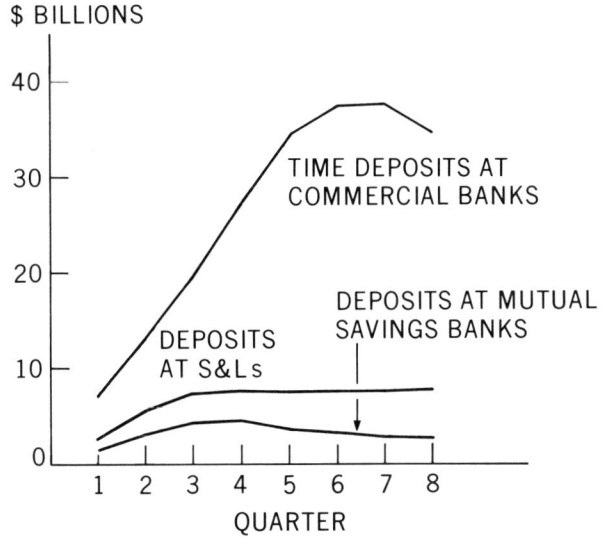

Figure 10-7 (continued)

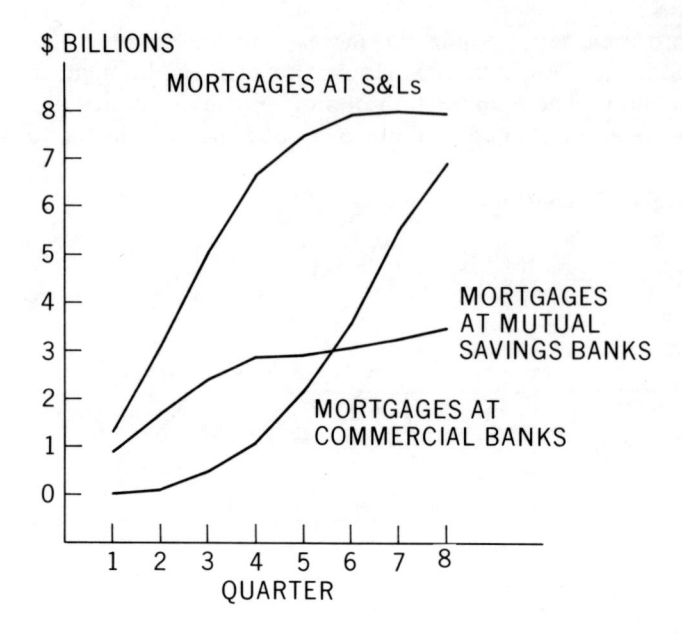

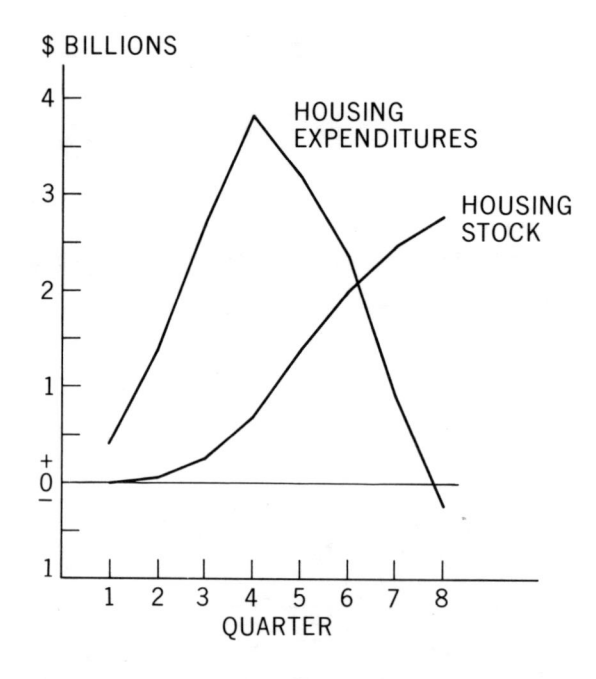

Figure 10-7 (continued)

deposits at financial intermediaries. Commercial bank time deposits grow by over $37 billion, while deposits at savings and loan associations rise by over $7 billion, and mutual savings bank deposits rise by about $4 billion. As a result of the decline in open market yields and the increase in the supply of funds at financial intermediaries, the mortgage rate RM falls by about 20 basis points. Thus, the rise in savings deposit rates increases the supply of mortgage funds and lowers the mortgage rate. The mortgage holdings of commercial banks rise by $7 billion, mortgages at savings and loan associations rise by about $8 billion, while those at mutual savings banks increase by over $3 billion. In the FMP model the housing sector incorporates the influence of credit rationing so that housing investment is partially constrained by the availability of mortgage funds. Since the rise in Regulation Q ceilings induces a substantial increase in mortgage funds supplied by financial intermediaries, an expansion occurs in residential investment. More specifically, expenditures on housing construction rise by about $4 billion before declining to their historical level. As a result of this increased investment, the stock of completed housing rises by almost $3 billion by the end of the simulation.

Overall, the simulation evidence confirms the comparative statics results derived earlier that if the ceilings on savings deposit rates are raised while the central bank is pursuing a monetary policy centered on $M1$, an economic expansion occurs despite the absence of any policy increase in the money supply. Nevertheless, the increase in economic activity is not as large as indicated by the rapid growth in $M2$. Consequently, the only monetary variable that appropriately reflects the degree of expansion in income is the pattern of open market interest rates.

In the next experiment it is assumed that Regulation Q ceilings are raised 100 basis points while the central bank's policy instrument is the level of open market interest rates, which remains fixed at historical values. The comparative statics results derived for Model 2 in the previous chapter indicated that a rise in ceiling rates has no impact on the level of economic activity. Instead, the only major result of higher savings deposit rates is a reduction in the money supply. The pattern of the empirical results indicated in Figure 10-8 is generally consistent with the relevant comparative statics multipliers for this case. More specifically, when the ceilings are raised 100 basis points, savings deposit rates at all financial institutions rise sharply. Since the central bank is assumed to stabilize open market rates, the decrease in the public's desired money holdings caused by the rise in deposit rates is reflected in a decline in $M1$, which falls by about $4 billion. Since short term open market interest rates are exogenous, long term bond rates take on historical values and thus no stimulus is provided to corporate investment. Nevertheless, in contrast to the theoretical results, the simula-

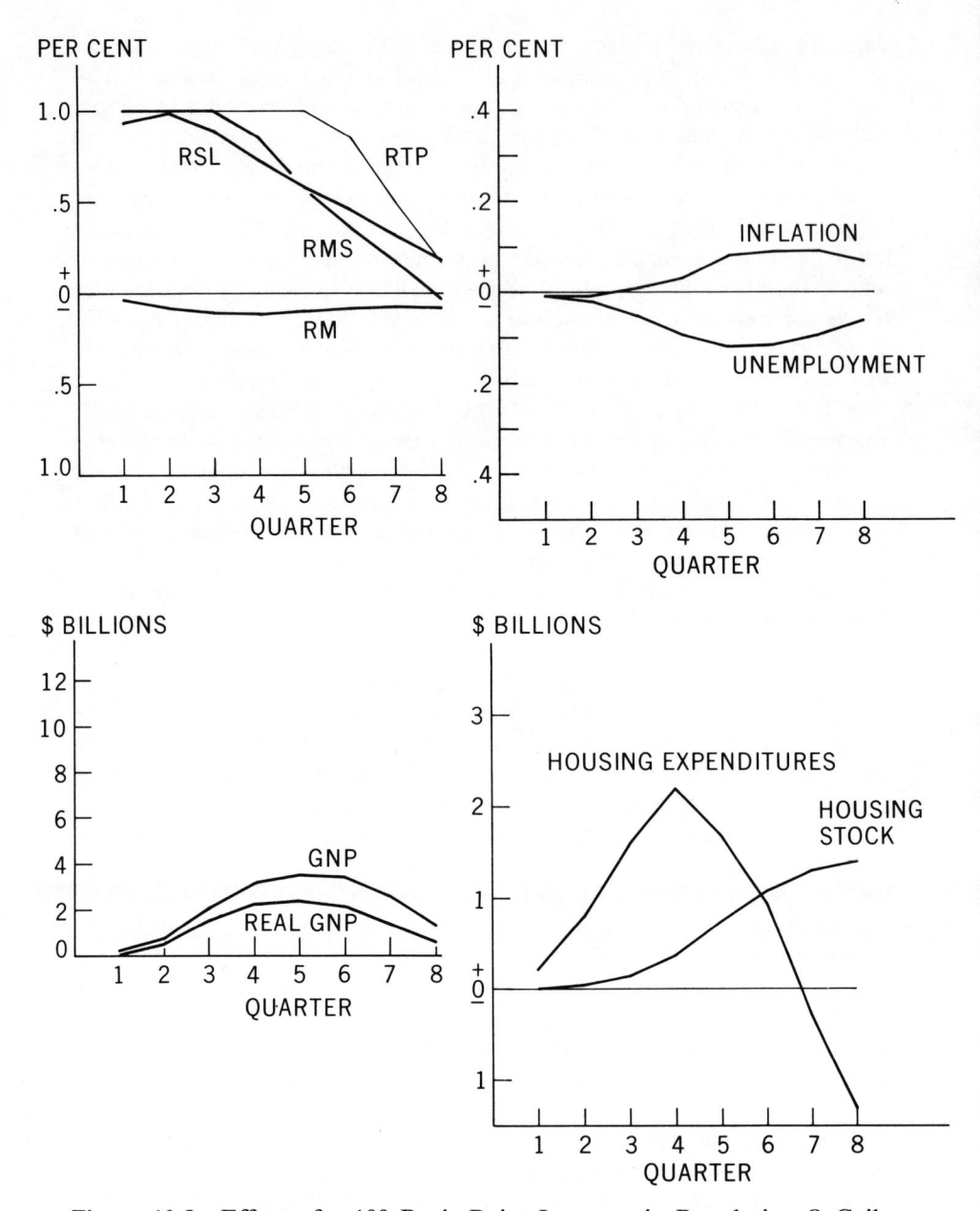

Figure 10-8. Effect of a 100 Basis Point Increase in Regulation Q Ceilings—Open Market Interest Rates Maintained at Historical Values.

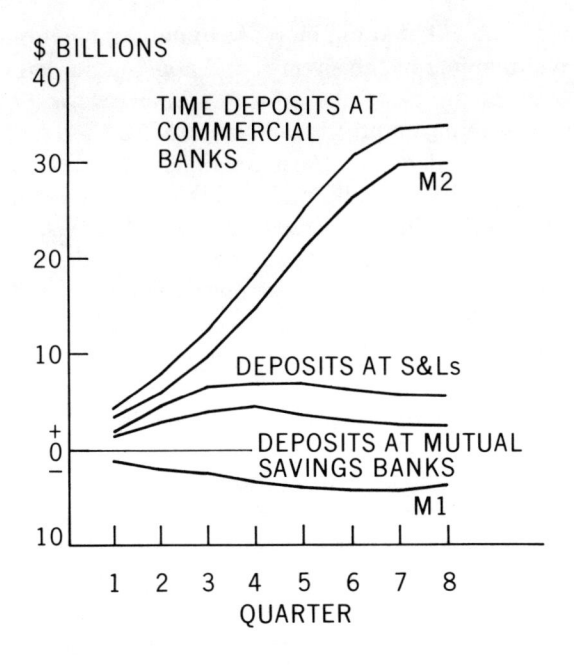

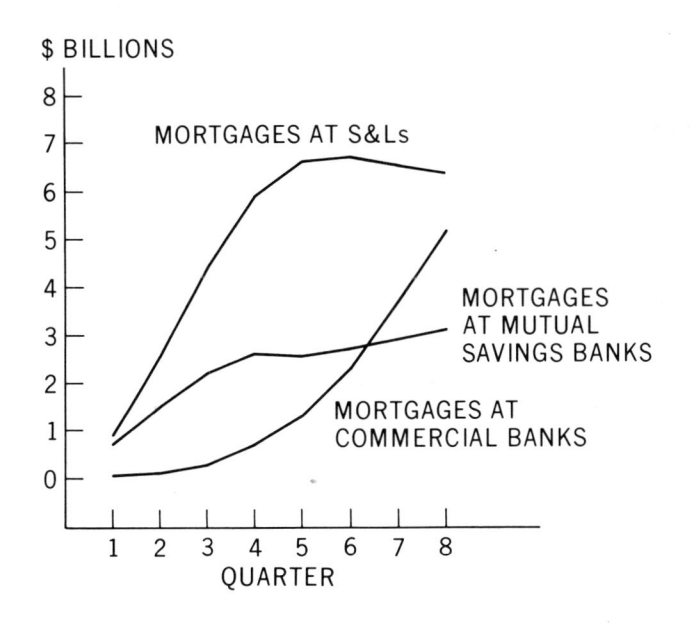

tion evidence indicates that some increase in national income does occur because of developments in the savings and housing markets. The rise in interest rates on savings deposits induces an increase in both bank and nonbank deposits totaling about $34 billion and $10 billion respectively. As a result of this inflow of deposits, these financial institutions increase total holdings of mortgages by $15 billion. This increase in the supply of mortgages results in a drop in the mortgage rate of about 10 basis points, which stimulates a rise in expenditures for housing construction. It is this growth in residential investment that induces a mild rise in income of $3.5 billion in nominal terms and about $2 billion in constant dollars. As a result, the unemployment rate falls slightly, although there is only a minimal effect on inflation.

In general, the simulation evidence confirms the pattern of the comparative statics results for the case in which Regulation Q ceiling rates are raised and the central bank uses open interest rates as the instrument for monetary policy. There is relatively little impact on economic activity as a result of an increase in ceiling rates. However, there is some expansionary effect due to the impact of savings inflows on residential investment, a channel of monetary policy that is usually omitted from a simple theoretical Keynesian model. However, both major monetary aggregates, $M1$ and $M2$, fail to reflect these economic developments, since $M1$ actually falls, while the growth in $M2$, caused by the inflows of time deposits at commercial banks, is far in excess of the growth in income. Only the pattern of open market interest rates provides an appropriate reflection of the movements in macroeconomic activity.

In the final experiment Regulation Q ceilings are raised while the central bank's policy instrument is the quantity of high powered money, defined as unborrowed reserves plus currency. The comparative statics results for this model were generally ambiguous. If we assumed, however, that the effect of savings deposit rates on the demand for money plus the effect of competing nonbank rates on the demand for time deposits outweighs the own rate effect on time deposits, then the comparative statics result for an increase in ceiling rates is expansionary. The simulation evidence as reported in Figure 10-9 indicates that this assumption is valid. The rise in savings deposit ceiling rates induces a decline in open market rates RCP of about 75 basis points after three quarters. This impact on short term interest rates is more moderate than for the experiment in which the policy variable is the money supply. This is because, ceteris paribus, any decline in open market rates induces commercial banks to hold larger quantities of free reserves, so that the banks are less willing to supply demand deposits. Consequently, despite the increase in aggregate demand, the monetary aggregate, $M1$, actually remains below its historical values throughout the simulation and a less extreme decline in open market rates is needed to equate money demand and supply for the given level of unborrowed reserves. The decline in open market interest rates stimulates investment and income rises. Eventually the increase in income brings about a sufficient increase in the public's demand for money so that higher market interest rates result. Nominal *GNP* rises by $9 billion after six quarters, with the increase in real *GNP* about two thirds of this size. As a result of this economic expansion, unemployment falls by 0.3 per cent, while the rate of inflation rises by an about 0.3 per cent. The quantitative results for the savings and housing sectors are quite similar to the case in which the central bank regards the supply of money as the exogenous variable. Time deposits at commercial banks rise by $36 billion, while savings and loan shares and mutual savings bank deposits rise by about $7 billion and $4 billion respectively. As a result of these inflows of savings deposits, mortgage holdings at commercial banks rise by $6 billion, by $7 billion at savings and loan associations, and $3 billion at mutual savings banks. Because of the increased supply of mortgages and the reduction in open market rates, the mortgage rate falls by 20 basis points. Consequently, expenditures on housing construction are stimulated, with the stock of completed housing approximately $2.25 billion higher by the end of the simulation.

In general, the simulation evidence indicates that the impact of a rise in Regulation Q ceilings is expansionary if the central bank regards high powered money as its policy instrument. These results complement the comparative statics findings presented earlier. Furthermore, the quantitative results indicate that the monetary aggregate $M1$ fails to reflect the changes in macroeconomic activity, since the quantity of demand deposits plus currency actually falls substantially. In contrast, the growth in the broader monetary aggregate $M2$ is so large that if $M2$ were used as an economic indicator, it would overstate the rise in aggregate demand. Consequently, both $M1$ and $M2$ are misleading indicators of movements in income. Only open market interest rates behave in a manner that consistently reflects the character of the economic changes induced by the rise in Regulation Q ceilings.

Conclusions

The empirical evidence provided by simulation experiments with the FMP model closely parallels the comparative statics results derived from the theoretical models in chapter 9. In general, the impact of endogenous saving deposit rate behavior on the effectiveness of monetary policy and the impact of a change in Regulation Q ceilings on the level of economic

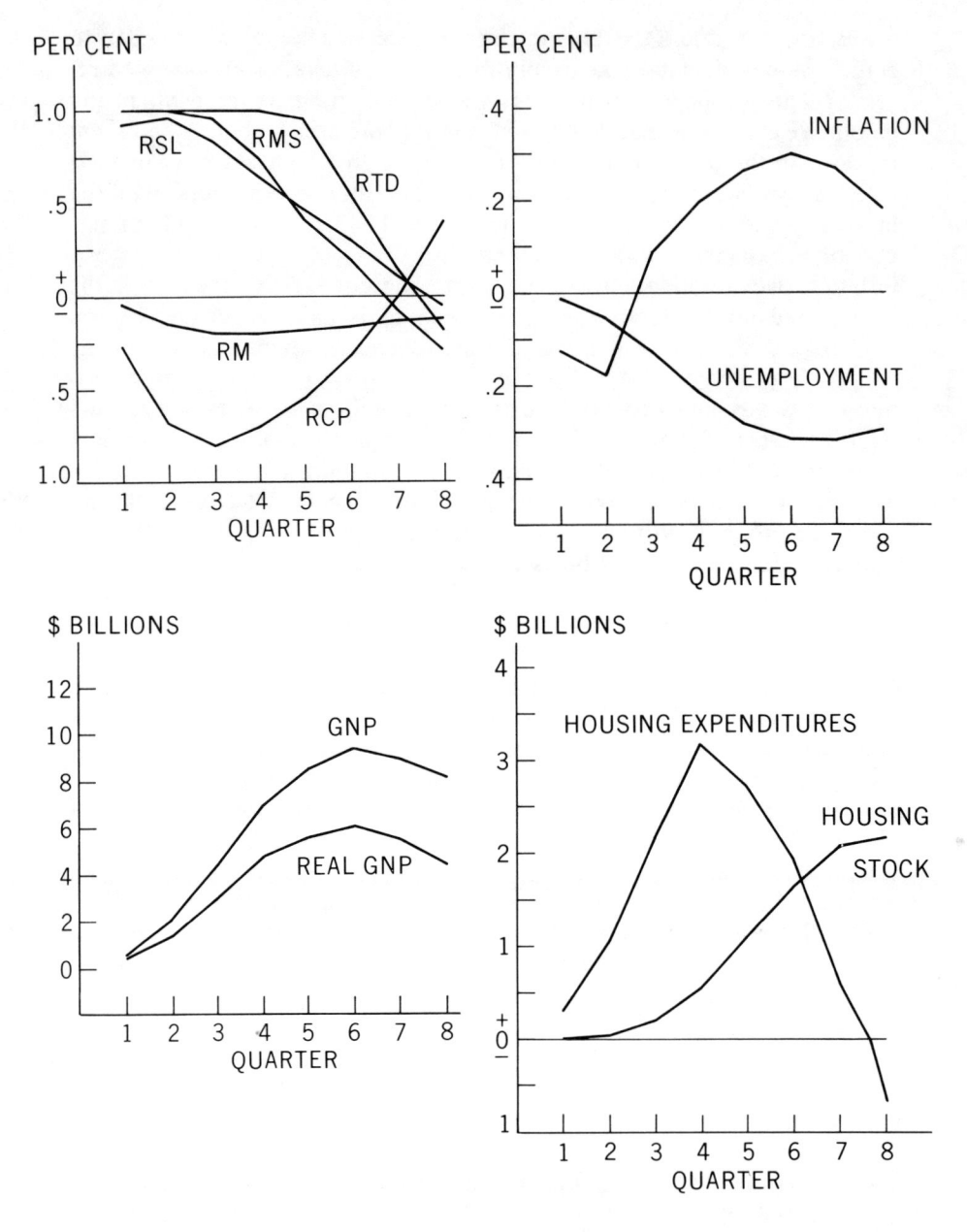

Figure 10-9. Effect of a 100 Basis Point Increase in Regulation Q Ceilings—High Powered Money Maintained at Historical Values.

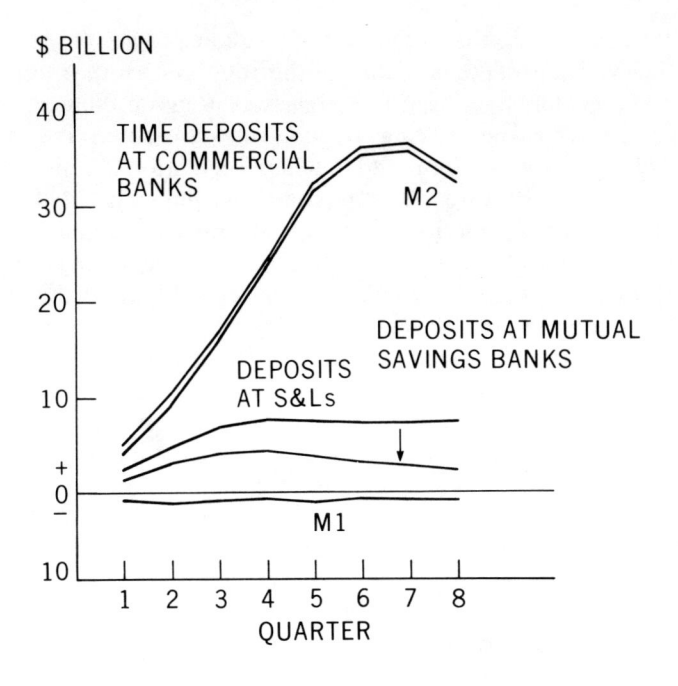

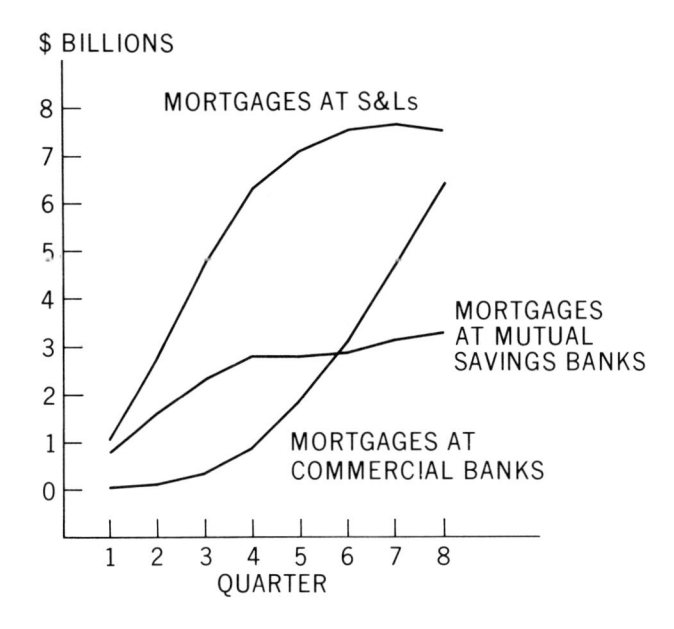

activity, depend upon the central bank's choice of a policy instrument. If the policy variable of the monetary authorities is either the money supply or high powered money, the effectiveness of a given change in monetary policy is reduced when savings deposit rates are determined by financial intermediary behavior compared to when Regulation Q ceilings effectively bind savings deposit rates. That is, monetary policy has its largest money multipliers when Regulation Q ceilings are restrictive and financial intermediaries cannot offset policy changes by altering savings deposit rates. However, if the policy instrument of the central bank is the level of open market interest rates, the economic impact of monetary policy is not influenced by the manner in which savings deposit rates are determined. Furthermore, the monetary aggregates, $M1$ and $M2$, or open market interest rates are useful indicators of movements in national income regardless of the central bank's choice of a policy instrument and regardless of whether or not Regulation Q ceilings are binding.

In general, an increase in the level of Regulation Q ceilings has a significant expansionary impact on aggregate demand whether the central bank uses the money supply, open market interest rates, or high powered money as the policy variable. However, the sharpest increase in macroeconomic activity occurs when the money supply is the policy instrument of the monetary authorities. A significant expansion also occurs if the quantity of high powered money is the control variable, although the rise in macroeconomic activity appears to be somewhat smaller than if the money supply is exogenous. If the central bank pursues a monetary policy centered on the level of open market interest rates, the economic stimulus is mild and is mostly due to the increased flow of funds to financial intermediaries, which spurs residential construction. Overall, the effect of an increase in ceiling rates is favorable for the housing sector regardless of which monetary variable is the central bank's policy instrument. Each of the savings institutions increases its holdings of mortgages and, as a result, the mortgage rate falls and housing expenditures rise. Finally, the usefulness of the monetary aggregates $M1$ and $M2$ as indicators of the level of economic activity is sharply curtailed when Regulation Q is altered. An increase in the ceilings produces a sharp rise in $M2$ that greatly exceeds the increase in economic activity. The monetary aggregate $M1$ generally declines, which is a movement in the opposite direction to movements in income. Only the behavior of open market interest rates provides a consistent reflection of the pattern of economic activity.

Glossary

a — amount of advertising
a_1 — ratio of advertising expenditures to deposits
a_2 — number of branches
A — advertising expenditures
BR — borrowed reserves
c — consumption
C — costs
CD — quantity of certificates of deposit
d — discount rate
D — deposits
DIV — corporate dividends
$EPCE$ — consumer expenditures
ER — excess reserves
FR — free reserves
g — government expenditures
GNP — Gross National Product
HP — quantity of high powered money
i — open market rate of return
i_a — asset rates
i_c — competing rates
i_1 — current mortgage rate
i_2 — current mortgage fees
i_3 — average yield on an institution's mortgages
i_4 — commercial bank time deposit rate
I — investment
k — ratio of interest earning assets to deposits
k_1 — ratio of reserves plus surplus to deposits

k_2 — ratio of mortgages in default to total mortgages
K — capital
m — money supply, narrowly defined
MC — quantity of currency outside banks
MCL — quantity of commercial and industrial loans at commercial banks
MD — demand deposits at commercial banks
$MKCB$ — stock of mortgages at commercial banks
$MKMS$ — stock of mortgages held by mutual savings banks
$MKSL$ — stock of mortgages held by savings and loan associations
MMS — mutual savings bank deposits
MSL — savings and loan association deposits
MT — time deposits at commercial banks, excluding negotiable certificates of deposit
$M1$ — narrowly defined money supply, demand deposits plus currency
$M2$ — broadly defined money supply, demand deposits plus currency, plus time deposits, excluding negotiable certificates of deposit
n — commercial bank time deposits
P — quantity of interest earning assets
$PCON$ — consumer price index
$PROFIT$ — corporate profits plus depreciation allowances
π — profits
QCD — legal ceiling on certificates of deposit interest rates
QTD — legal ceiling on commercial bank time deposit rates
r — savings deposit rate
r_{CB} — commercial bank time deposit rate
r_{CD} — certificate of deposit interest rate
r_{NB} — savings deposit rate at nonbank intermediaries

R — revenue
RCB — corporate bond rate
RCL — commercial loan rate
RCP — commercial paper rate
$RDIS$ — Federal Reserve discount rate
RM — mortgage rate
RMS — mutual savings bank deposit rate
$RMUN$ — municipal bond rate
RR — required reserves
RSL — savings and loan deposit rate
RTB — Treasury bill rate
RTD — commercial bank time deposit rate
s — shift variable
s_1 — taxable income per capita
s_2 — ratio of savings and loan association offices to population
s_3 — ratio of commercial bank employees to population
t — tax revenues
U — utility
UR — unborrowed reserves
w — minimum required rate of return on capital
x_1 — change in mortgages scaled by deposits
x_2 — ratio of fee income to total income
x_3 — logarithm of total assets
y — income
z_D — reserve requirement on demand deposits
z_T — reserve requirement on time deposits
$ZAFH$ — advances from the Federal Home Loan Bank Board to savings and loan associations

Bibliography

[1] Almon, Shirley. "The Distributed Lag Between Capital Appropriations and Expenditures," *Econometrica*, Vol. 33, No. 1 (January 1965) pp. 178-196.

[2] American Bankers Association. *Results of 1964 Survey of Certificates of Deposit and Savings Certificates*. New York, 1965.

[3] Baumol, William. *Business Behavior, Value, and Growth*. New York: Harcourt, Brace, and World, 1967.

[4] Baumol, William. *Economic Theory and Operations Analysis*. Third Edition, Englewood Cliffs, New Jersey: Prentice-Hall, 1972.

[5] Board of Governors of the Federal Reserve System. *Federal Reserve Bulletin*. Washington, D.C.: Board of Governors of the Federal Reserve System, various issues.

[6] Board of Governors of the Federal Reserve System. *The Federal Reserve System: Purposes and Functions*. Washington, D.C.: Board of Governors of the Federal Reserve System, 1974.

[7] Brigham, Eugene, and R. Richardson Pettit. "Effects of Structure on Performance in the Savings and Loan Industry," in Irwin Friend, ed., *The Savings and Loan Industry*. Washington, D.C.: Government Printing Office, 1969.

[8] Bureau of the Census. *County Business Patterns*. Washington, D.C.: Government Printing Office, various years.

[9] Bureau of the Census. *Statistical Abstract of the United States*. Washington, D.C.: Government Printing Office, various years.

[10] Chow, Gregory. "Tests of Equality between Sets of Coefficients in Two Linear Regressions," *Econometrica*, Vol. 28, No. 3 (July 1960), pp. 591-605.

[11] Cochrane, D. and G. Orcutt, "Application of Least Squares Regression to Regressions Containing Autocorrelated Errors," *Journal of the American Statistical Association,* Vol. 44, No. 1 (March 1949), pp. 32-61.

[12] de Leeuw, Frank. "A Model of Financial Behavior," in James S. Duesenbery et al., eds., *The Brookings Quarterly Econometric Model of the United States*. Chicago: Rand-McNally and Co., 1965.

[13] de Leeuw, Frank, and Edward Gramlich. "The Channels of Monetary Policy," *Federal Reserve Bulletin,* Vol. 56, No. 6 (June 1969), pp. 472-491.

[14] de Leeuw, Frank, and Edward Gramlich. "The Federal Reserve-MIT

Econometric Model," *Federal Reserve Bulletin,* Vol. 56, No. 1 (January 1968), pp. 11-40.

[15] Dhrymes, Phoebus, and Paul Taubman. "An Empirical Analysis of the Savings and Loan Industry," in Irwin Friend, ed., *Study of the Savings and Loan Industry.* Washington, D.C.: Government Printing Office, 1969.

[16] Fand, David. "Financial Regulation and Allocative Efficiency of Our Capital Markets," *The National Banking Review*, Vol. 3 (September 1965), pp. 55-63.

[17] Federal Home Loan Bank Board. *News.* Washington, D.C.: Federal Home Loan Bank Board, various issues.

[18] Federal Home Loan Bank Board. *Report of the Federal Home Loan Bank Board, 1966.* Washington, D.C.: Federal Home Loan Bank Board, 1967.

[19] Feige, Edgar L. *The Demand for Liquid Assets: A Temporal Cross Section Analysis.* Englewood Cliffs, New Jersey: Prentice-Hall, 1963.

[20] Frederickson, E. Bruce. "The Geographic Structure of Residential Mortgage Yields," in Jack Guttentag, ed., *Essays on Interest Rates, Volume II.* New York: Columbia University Press, 1971.

[21] Galbraith, John Kenneth. *The New Industrial State.* Boston: Houghton Mifflin Co., 1967.

[22] Goldfeld, Stephen M. *Commercial Bank Behavior and Economic Activity.* Amsterdam: North Holland Press, 1966.

[23] Goldfeld, Stephen M. "The Demand for Money Revisited," *Brookings Papers on Economic Activity,* No. 3 (1973), pp. 557-638.

[24] Goldfeld, Stephen M. "Savings and Loan Associations and the Market for Savings," in Irwin Friend, ed., *Study of the Savings and Loan Industry.* Washington, D.C.: Government Printing Office, 1969.

[25] Goldfeld, Stephen M. and Dwight Jaffee. "The Determinants of Deposit Rate Setting by Savings and Loan Associations," *Journal of Finance*, Vol. 25, No. 3 (June 1970), pp. 615-632.

[26] Goldfeld, Stephen, and Edward Kane. "The Determinants of Member Borrowing," *Journal of Finance,* Vol. 21, No. 3 (September 1966), pp. 499-514.

[27] Gramlich, Edward and David Hulett. "The Demand and Supply of Savings Deposits in the FRB-MIT Econometric Model," in Edward Gramlich and Dwight Jaffee, eds., *Savings Deposits, Mortgages, and Housing.* Lexington, Mass.: Lexington Books, D.C. Heath and Co., 1972.

[28] Gramlich, Edward, and Dwight Jaffee. *Savings Deposits, Mortgages*

and Housing. Lexington, Mass.: Lexington Books, D.C. Heath and Co., 1972.

[29] Gurley, John and Edward Shaw. *Money in a Theory of Finance.* Washington, D.C.: Brookings Institute, 1959.

[30] Hamburger, Michael. "Household Demand for Liquid Assets," *Econometrica*, Vol. 36, No. 1 (January 1968), pp. 97-118.

[31] Heebner, A. Gilbert. "Negotiable Certificates of Deposit: The Development of a Money Market Instrument," New York University Institute of Finance, *Bulletin,* Vol. 69-70, No. 53-54 (February 1969).

[32] Henderson, James M. and Richard Quandt. *Microeconomic Theory: A Mathematical Approach.* New York: McGraw-Hill Book Co., 1958.

[33] Hendershott, Patric H. "Recent Developments in the Financial Sector of Econometric Models," *Journal of Finance,* Volume 23 (March 1968).

[34] Hester, Donald. *Stock and Mutual Associations in the Savings and Loan Industry.* Washington, D.C.: Federal Home Loan Bank Board, 1968.

[35] Jaffee, Dwight. *Credit Rationing and the Commercial Market.* New York: John Wiley & Sons, 1971.

[36] Kardouche, George K. *The Competition for Savings.* New York: National Industrial Conference Board, Inc., 1969.

[37] Laidler, David. *The Demand for Money: Theories and Evidence.* Scranton, Pennsylvania; International Textbook Co., 1969.

[38] Latané, Henry, "Cash Balances and the Interest Rate—A Pragmatic Approach," *Review of Economics and Statistics*, Vol. 36, No. 4 (November 1954), pp. 456-460.

[39] Malkiel, Burton. *The Term Structure of Interest Rates: Expectations and Behavior Patterns.* Princeton: Princeton University Press, 1966.

[40] Markowitz, Harry. *Portfolio Selection: Efficient Diversification of Investments.* New York: John Wiley & Sons, 1959.

[41] Meyer, Paul. "Comment," *Journal of Finance,* Vol. 33, No. 4 (September 1967), pp. 467-470.

[42] Modigliani, Franco. "The Dynamics of Portfolio Adjustment and the Flow of Savings Through Financial Intermediaries in the FMP Model," in Edward Gramlich and Dwight Jaffee, eds., *Savings Deposits, Mortgages and Housing.* Lexington, Mass.: Lexington Books, D.C. Heath and Co., 1972.

[43] Modigliani, Franco, Robert Rasche, and J. Phillip Cooper. "Central Bank Policy, the Money Supply and the Short Term Rate of Interest,"

Journal of Money, Credit and Banking, Vol. 2 (May 1970), pp. 166-218.

[44] Ruebling, Charlotte. "The Administration of Regulation Q," *Federal Reserve Bank of St. Louis Review,* Vol. 52, No. 2 (February 1970), pp. 29-40.

[45] Silber, William. *Portfolio Behavior of Financial Institutions.* New York: Holt, Rhinehart & Winston, 1970.

[46] Slovin, Myron B. and Marie Elizabeth Sushka. "The Structural Shift in the Demand for Money," *Journal of Finance,* Vol. 30, No. 3 (June 1975).

[47] Teigen, Ronald. "The Demand for and the Supply of Money," in Ronald Teigen and Warren Smith, eds., *Money, National Income and Stabilization Policy.* Homewood, Illinois: Richard Irwin and Co., 1965.

[48] Tobin, James. "Commercial Banks as Creators of 'Money'," in Deane Carson, ed., *Banking and Monetary Studies.* Homewood, Illinois: Richard Irwin and Co., 1966.

[49] Tobin, James and William Brainard. "Financial Intermediaries and the Effectiveness of Controls," *American Economic Review,* Vol. 53 (May 1963), pp. 383-400.

[50] United States President's Commission on Financial Structure and Regulation. *Report of the President's Commission on Financial Structure and Regulation.* Washington, D.C.: Government Printing Office, 1972.

[51] Weber, Gerald S. "Interest Rates on Mortgages and Dividend Rates on Savings and Loan Shares," *Journal of Finance,* Vol. 21, No. 3 (September 1966), pp. 515-521.

Index

Index

advertising, 11, 13-15, 24, 25-26, 32, 33n, 36n, 37, 41, 45, 45n
Almon, 64
American Bankers Association, 82n
asset and liability flows, 46, 64, 65-68, 70, 72, 73-76, 77, 81, 89, 90
asset rates, 5, 6n, 8, 9, 19, 21-22, 23, 26, 37, 40, 43, 45, 60, 61, 62, 64, 65, 70, 71, 72, 73, 86, 87

bank regulation, 33, 33n
Baumol, 17, 19n, 20n
Brainard, 119
Brigham, 3

Census Bureau, 41n
certificates of deposit, large denomination negotiable, 2, 3, 73; definition, 79; demand for, 79, 80-84, 89-90; dichotomy in behavior, 79-80; supply of, 79, 85-89, 90
chartering status, 5, 38-39, 52-57, 59
Chow test, 54
Chochrane-Orcutt, 65, 95
commercial banks, 1, 38, 68-70, 85, 87, 89, 90, 91, 103; deposit rates at, 1, 3, 40, 40n, 42, 47, 50, 59-60, 61, 62, 68-76, 77, 85, 86, 93, 94, 95, 97, 98, 99, 101, 102, 112, 127, 131
commercial loan rate, 70, 87, 87n
commercial loans, 70, 87, 89, 90
commercial paper rate, 80, 82, 86, 87, 89, 94, 94n, 95, 99, 138, 142, 143, 150, 156
competing rates, 5, 6n, 21-22, 23, 26, 37, 40, 43, 45, 60, 61-62, 64, 65, 68, 70, 71, 72, 73, 84, 86, 87, 89, 90, 94, 97, 156
composite variable weights, 61-62, 62n, 68, 70, 70n, 71
constrained maximization, 19, 32
Cooper, 91, 93, 95, 112n, 136
corporate behavior, 5, 17-18, 27, 82-84
corporate bond rate, 61, 62, 138, 142, 143
corporate profits, 82-83, 89
cost of capital, 135
Credit Crunch of 1966, 93, 97, 98
credit rationing, 87n, 135, 153

de Leeuw, 1, 60, 80, 136
demand for liquid liabilities, 5, 6, 37, 79, 80-81; shift variables, 11, 12, 15, 24, 26, 32-33, 35, 37, 38, 41, 42, 43, 45, 47-52, 56

deposit insurance, 18, 18n, 46
deposit maximization 2, 17-26, 27, 33n, 37-38, 42, 45, 48, 52, 56, 59
deposit rate setting behavior, 1-3; commercial banks, 38, 59-60, 68-78, 79, 85-89; impact on monetary policy, 116-124, 142-147; mutual savings banks, 59-60, 61-68; savings and loan associations, 38-40, 42-58, 60-68, 77-78; theoretical models, 5-16, 17-26, 27-36. *See also* certificates of deposit; deposit maximization; profit maximization; Regulation Q; utility maximization
Dhrymes, 39, 43
differential between bank and nonbank deposit rates, 62, 71, 92, 95, 98, 102
discount rate, 72, 76, 111, 112, 113, 121, 137
distributed lags, 64, 65, 72, 76, 77
dividends, 8n, 22n, 30n, 42n, 82, 84, 90

economies of scale, 1, 5, 41, 47, 57
effectiveness of monetary policy, 2, 3, 105, 106, 118, 119, 120, 124, 133-134, 135, 142, 147, 157, 160
expectations, 11, 32, 40, 60, 62, 64, 65, 72, 73, 77

Fand, 9
Federal Home Loan Bank Board, 2, 3, 39n, 40n, 52, 68, 93, 105n
Federal Reserve Board, 33n, 40n, 62, 79, 105n, 111
Federal Reserve-MIT-Penn model (FMP), 4, 105-107, 134; description, 135-137; simulation experiments, 137-160
Feige, 1, 79
financial intermediary, 1, 5, 17-18, 19, 33, 57. *See also* commercial banks; mutual savings banks; savings and loan associations
Frederickson, 7

Galbraith, 17
geographical variation of interest rates, 5, 7, 39, 40, 47, 48, 56, 61
Goldfeld, 1, 5, 38, 39, 40, 43, 46, 53, 80, 94n, 112n
Gramlich, 60, 68, 80, 136
Gross National Product, 80, 94
Gurley, 1n, 131

Hamburger, 1, 79

171

Heebner, 79
Hendershott, 60
Henderson, 11, 32
Hester, 38, 40, 43, 45, 46, 53
high powered money. *See* monetary policy instrument
housing investment, 93, 135, 136, 153, 156, 157, 160
Hulett, 60, 68, 80
Hunt Commission, 3, 116n

income, 12, 15, 24, 33, 37, 38, 41, 42, 48, 80, 81, 84, 91, 92, 93, 94, 99, 101, 102, 107, 108, 109, 110, 111, 114, 115, 117, 118, 119, 120, 122, 124, 126, 128, 129, 131, 132, 134, 138, 139, 140, 142, 143, 145, 150-151, 153, 157, 160
inflation, 151, 156, 157
intermediate monetary variables, 109, 111, 115, 120, 124, 126, 127, 128, 129, 132, 133, 134, 142, 153, 156, 157, 160

Jaffee, 5, 87n, 136

Kane, 112n
Kardouche, 1, 92
Keynesian models of income determination, 4, 107, 116, 125, 133
Kuhn-Tucker conditions, 19, 19n

Laidler, 91
Latané, 94
liquidity ratio, 6, 11-12, 15, 24, 26, 32, 35, 37, 40-41, 45-46

Malkiel, 91
Markowitz, 27
Meyer, 5
Modigliani, 1, 61, 62, 79, 91, 93, 95, 112n, 136
monetary policy. *See* effectiveness of monetary policy
monetary policy instrument, 107, 133, 137, 160; high powered money, 107, 111-115, 116, 120-124, 125, 129-133, 134, 137, 138, 140-142, 145-147, 156, 157, 160; market interest rates, 107, 109-111, 119-120, 127-129, 132-133, 138-140, 143-145, 153-156, 160; money supply, 107, 108-109, 116-119, 125-127, 133, 138, 143, 150-153, 160
money demand, 2, 3; determinants of, 91-92, 94-95, 99; effect of savings deposit rates on, 3, 92, 94, 103; income elasticity, 99-102; speed of adjustment, 93-97, 98, 99, 101, 103; structural stability, 3, 91-93, 97, 98, 102, 103, 106, 136-137

money multipliers, 106, 107, 115, 118, 119, 122, 123, 124, 133, 138, 138n, 143, 145, 147, 149, 160
mortgage commitments, 68
mortgage fees, 40, 40n, 42, 45, 50
mortgage rate, 7, 9n, 40, 40n, 42, 45, 50, 61, 65, 70, 153, 156, 157, 160
multicollinearity, 42, 45, 47, 61, 64, 70, 82, 87n, 93, 102
municipal bond rate, 70, 87, 87n, 90
mutual institutions. *See* chartering status
mutual savings banks, 1-2, 3, 17, 64, 68; savings deposit rates at, 60, 61-68, 71, 72, 77, 78, 97n, 112

opportunity cost of money, 91, 92, 131
own rate, 6, 80, 82, 85, 89, 120, 123, 124, 127, 128, 131, 156

Pettit, 3
planning horizon, 8, 22, 29; single period, 7-9, 10, 15, 21-23, 26, 29-30, 35, 37, 38, 40, 45, 50, 52, 57, 60, 61, 65, 71, 73, 77; multiperiod, 9-11, 15, 23n, 26, 30-32, 35, 37, 38, 40, 45, 50, 52, 57, 60, 63-64, 65, 72, 73, 77
portfolio, 1, 5; behavior, 1, 5, 6, 6n, 7, 11, 21, 22, 57, 58, 60, 73-76, 80, 87; holdings, 37, 46, 61, 64, 69, 70, 70n, 77; inherited, 8, 9, 11, 15, 22, 23, 26, 29, 30, 37, 38, 40, 45
price leadership, 72
product market, 91, 107, 110, 111, 116, 121, 125, 127, 129
profit maximization, 2-3, 5-15, 17, 20, 21-22, 23, 24, 25, 26, 27, 28, 29, 30, 32, 33, 34, 35, 36, 42-43, 45, 48, 50, 52, 54, 56, 56n, 59-61, 63-65, 71, 73, 77, 79, 85-86, 116, 117, 133

quadratic utility function, 27, 33-36
Quandt, 11, 32

Rasche, 91, 93, 95, 112n, 136
rate of return on capital, 2, 18, 19
Regulation Q, 3, 62, 71, 73, 76, 77, 79, 89, 97, 105-107, 115, 116, 124, 133, 142, 156
reserve ratio, 37, 45
reserve requirements, 112, 130-131
risk premium, 37, 40-41, 45-46
Ruebling, 98
runoff period, 80, 81, 81n, 82, 84, 86-87, 89, 90. *See also* certificates of deposit

savings and loan associations, 17, 38, 54-58; deposit rates at, 38-40, 42, 43-58, 59,

60, 61-68, 77-78, 92, 97-98, 99, 101-102, 103
savings deposit rates. *See* deposit rate setting behavior
savings market, 5, 57, 62, 70, 79, 92, 109, 110-111, 112, 115, 118-119, 120, 124, 126-127, 128, 132, 136, 156
Shaw, 1n, 131
Silber, 1, 80
Slovin, 136
stabilization policy, 3, 91-92, 105, 106, 107, 125, 133
stock institutions. See chartering status
Sushka, 136

Taubman, 39, 43

Teigen, 91
term structure of interest rates, 85, 87, 89, 90, 91, 107n, 135
Tobin, 1n, 119
Treasury bill rate, 61, 62, 71, 80, 82, 86, 87, 89, 94n, 138, 142, 143

unemployment, 151, 156, 157
utility maximization, 2, 27-36, 37, 42, 45, 56, 56n, 59, 60

variable rate mortgages, 9, 9n, 23, 30, 35
velocity of money, 93, 94-99, 101, 102

Weber, 5

About the Authors

Myron B. Slovin received the B.A., degree from the University of Michigan where he was elected to membership in Phi Beta Kappa. He received the M.A. and Ph.D. degrees in economics from Princeton University and also studied at the London School of Economics. Dr. Slovin is an economist with the Board of Governors of the Federal Reserve System. He is the author of journal articles in monetary economics and macroeconomics.

Marie Elizabeth Sushka received the B.A. degree from Sweet Briar College where she was elected to membership in Phi Beta Kappa. She received M.A. degrees in both Russian Area Studies and economics, and the Ph.D. degree in economics from Georgetown University. Dr. Sushka is an economist with the Board of Governors of the Federal Reserve System and was on the staff of the RAND Corporation. She is the author of journal articles in monetary economics and economic history.

DATE DUE

AP 25 '77			
MAY 10 '77			
DEC 5 '77			
MAY 5 '78			
JUN 3 '80			
DEC 22 '81			
MAR 16 '82			
APR 27 '82			
JAN 2 1985			
MAY 24 1987			
APR 7 1990			
MAY 11 1991			

DEMCO 38-297